A	B	C	D	E	F	G	H
				73			17
				EP4			70

I	J	K	L	M	N	P	Q
		KT27		MW3			05
				MS4			

0145

RG13

D0409424

Castles in
S · P · A · I · N

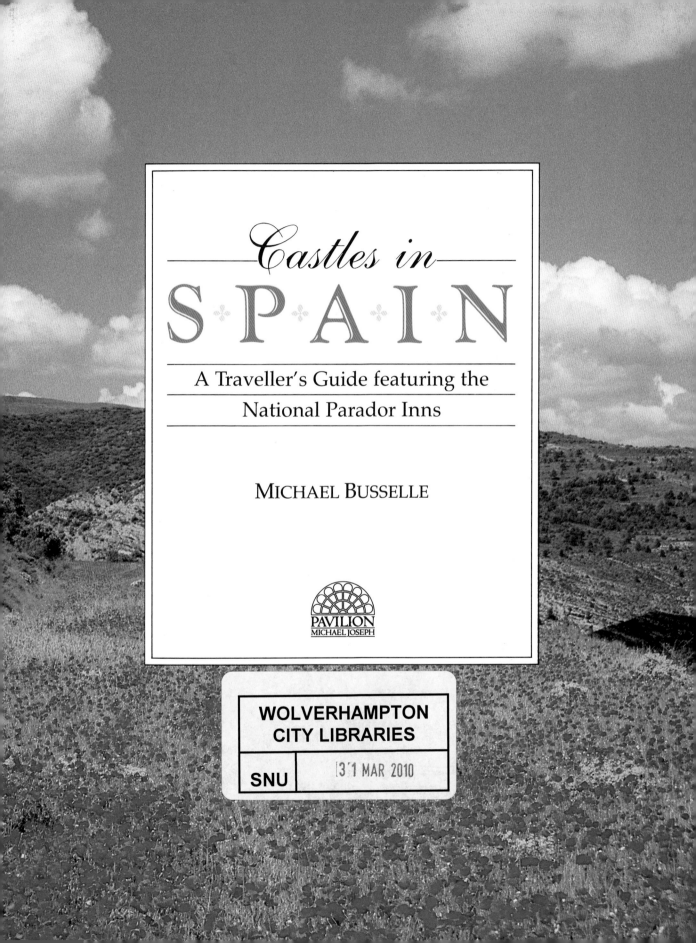

Castles in
S·P·A·I·N

A Traveller's Guide featuring the
National Parador Inns

MICHAEL BUSSELLE

PAVILION
MICHAEL JOSEPH

First published in Great Britain in 1989 by
PAVILION BOOKS LIMITED
196 Shaftesbury Avenue, London WC2H 8JL
in association with Michael Joseph Limited
27 Wrights Lane, Kensington, London W8 5TZ

Designed by Bridgewater Design Limited

British Cataloguing in Publication Data
Busselle, Michael
Castles in Spain: a traveller's guide
featuring the National Parador Inns.
1. Hotels, taverns, etc.——Spain——
Guide-books 2. Spain——Description and
travel——1975——Guide-books
I. Title
647'.944601   TX910.S7

ISBN 1-85145-104-8

Typeset by CST Limited, Hove
Colour reproduction by CLG, Verona
Printed and bound by Graficas Estella, Spain

The Publishers gratefully acknowledge the assistance and
cooperation of Mundi Color with regard to travel
arrangements

**MUNDI COLOR
HOLIDAYS**

O.T.A. Travel Ltd., 276 Vauxhall Bridge Road,
London SW1V 1BE. Tel no. 01-834 3492

Contents

Introduction   7

Northern Spain

1. Santillana del Mar / Gijón / Ribadeo / El Ferrol   14
2. Santiago de Compostela / Cambados / Pontevedra / Bayona / Tuy   26
3. Villalba / Villafranca del Bierzo / León / Cervera de Pisuerga / Fuente Dé 38
4. Fuentarrabía / Argómaniz / Santo Domingo de la Calzada   50
5. Calahorra / Olite / Sos del Rey Católico   60
6. Benavente / Puebla de Sanabria / Verín   68

Central Spain

7. Segovia / Tordesillas / Zamora / Ciudad Rodrigo   78
8. Ávila / Salamanca / Jarandilla de la Vera / Sierra de Gredos   88
9. Sigüenza / Santa María de Huerta / Soria   98
10. Chinchón / Toledo / Manzanares / Almagro   108
11. Oropesa / Guadalupe / Trujillo / Mérida / Zafra   120

Eastern Spain

12. Aiguablava / Vich / Cardona   132
13. Seo de Urgell / Viella / Artiés / Bielsa   142
14. Benicarló / Tortosa / Alcañiz / Teruel   152
15. Alarcón / Albacete / Jávea / El Saler   164

Southern Spain

16. Málaga / Antequera / Córdoba / Carmona   176
17. Ayamonte / Mazagón / Cádiz / Arcos de la Frontera / Torremolinos   188
18. Nerja / Mojácar / Puerto Lumbreras / Cazorla / Úbeda   200
19. Bailén / Jaén / Granada / Sierra Nevada   214

A Note from the Author   226
Index to the Paradors   227
Index   237

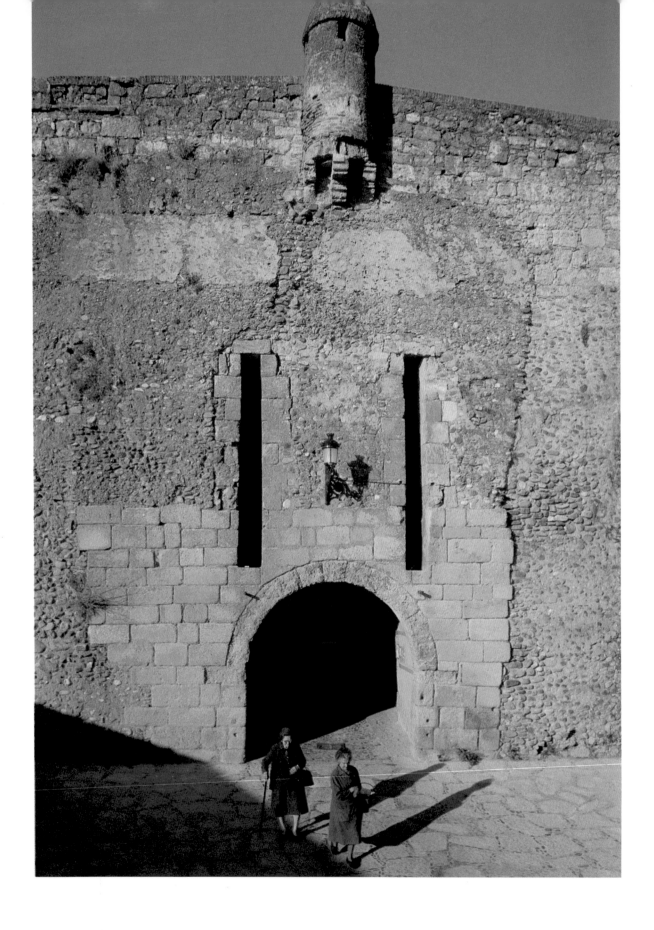

I REMEMBER well my first glimpse of Spain – a good many years ago. It was, I imagine, the same as many millions of other travellers have experienced – from an aircraft window at 30,000 feet while on a flight to one of the Costas. I remember looking down at what seemed to be a featureless beige landscape – almost like a desert. I wondered if anyone lived there.

I rather imagined then that, apart from the occasional city like Madrid, there was really nothing much to Spain until you got to the coast. Happily, I now know better but, amongst many, this impression still prevails.

Although Spain attracts millions of visitors most of them go to the coastal resorts. Occasionally a travel magazine will feature an article entitled 'The Real Spain'. This invariably will mean Seville, Barcelona or Madrid. They are certainly more real than say Torremolinos but they are no more the 'Real Spain' than London is the Real England or New York the Real America.

In researching this book I discovered what almost seems to be a secret. The arid brown landscape which I saw from the plane camouflages hidden green valleys, soaring mountain peaks, vast plains patterned by vines and olive trees, limpid blue lakes and fast-flowing rivers.

The exquisite buildings which Spain possesses are not only to be found in places like Sevilla and Granada but all over the country, often hidden away in unknown towns and villages. It is a country of well-kept secrets and constant surprises.

Adjectives like breathtaking, spectacular and stunning are hard to avoid when describing Spain – I have not used them lightly. The landscape – and buildings – frequently make you catch your breath, exclaim out loud or simply gaze in silent wonder.

THE PARADORS

TO MAKE IT REALLY EASY and enjoyable for the traveller the Spanish government had a very good idea: to provide a string of state-run hotels throughout the country, never more than an easy day's drive apart and located in the most beautiful places. They were to be called *paradores*, the name given to an inn which offers shelter and food to travellers.

This wonderful idea is not something new. Indeed the first of the *paradores* was planned in 1926. The site was selected by King Alfonso XIII – a remote ridge in the Sierra de Gredos to the west of Madrid. He was a keen hunter and this was where he would go to hunt the *capra hispanica*, a rare breed of wild goat.

Today there are 76 *paradores* on the mainland of Spain. The latest to be opened was in 1984 in the Conquistador's town of Trujillo in Extremadura. Many of them are situated in historic buildings like castles, convents and palaces. Others have been specially built in spectacular settings. Some have only a few rooms like the ancient castle tower of Villalba with only six bedrooms. Others can accommodate hundreds of people like the Hotel de los Reyes Católicos in Santiago de Compostela. One thing they all have in common is a constant standard of comfort and service, something which cannot always otherwise be found in the more remote parts of Spain.

Booking ahead is wise. Some are extremely popular, the Parador San Francisco in Granada for example often has a waiting list of many months. The parador in which you are staying will always telephone ahead to make your next reservation.

Many people will probably prefer to make advance bookings for the paradors before they leave home. It can be advisable in the peak seasons and for the most popular paradors. My reservations, flights and car hire were made for me by Mundi Color, a tour operator which specializes in both parador holidays and off-the-beaten-track Spain. They provide both a series of set tours and personally tailored itineraries to suit individual preferences. Most of the paradors featured in this book are, or can be, included in tours arranged by Mundi Color.

As some readers will want to use this book to select individual paradors I have devised a star system in the index to the paradors at the end of the book. It is unavoidably subjective. It is also not like the usual hotel guide based on standards of service, cuisine and comfort. These elements are, in any case, fairly standard throughout the parador chain.

My stars are based on a combination of the ambiance of a particular parador, its setting, its outlook and the interest of the building or its immediate surroundings. In this way an isolated but atmospheric castle like the Parador Marqués de Villena at Alarcón rates the same as, say, a modern building overlooking a stunning beach like the Parador Cristobal Colón at Mazagón.

The *paradores*, like Spain, are very informal. Even in magnificent hotels like the San Marcos in León it is not necessary to wear a jacket and tie for dinner.

Opposite: A fortified gateway at Ciudad Rodrigo.

FRANCE

PYRENEES

El Ferrol
Ribadeo
Gijón
Santillana del Mar
Fuentarrabía
LA CORUÑA
Villalba
ASTURIAS
BILBAO
SAN SEBASTIÁN
Santiago de Compostela
Fuente Dé
Argómaniz
Cambados
Pontevedra
VIGO
Villafranca del Bierzo
LEÓN
Santo Domingo de la Calzada
Olite
Sos del Rey Católico
Artiés
Viella
Bayond
Tuy
Cervera de Pisuergo
Seo de Urgell
Bielsa
Aiguablava
Verín
Puebla de Sanabria
Benavente
BURGOS
Calahorra
ARAGÓN
Cardona
Vich

VALLODOLID
Soria
CATALUÑA
ZARAGOZA
BARCELONA
TARRAGONA
Zamora
Tordesillas
Santa María de Huerta
SALAMANCA
Sigüenza
Alcañiz
NUEVA
SEGOVIA
Tortosa
Ciudad Rodrigo
ÁVILA
LA
Benicarló
Sierra de Gredos
MADRID
TERUEL
Jarandilla de la Vera
Oropesa
Chinchón
CASTILLA
BALEARIC ISLANDS
TOLEDO

PORTUGAL
Trujillo
GUADALUPE
Alarcón
El Saler
LISBOA
Mérida
Manzanares
Jávea
CIUDAD REAL
ALBACETE
Zafra
EXTREMADURA
Almagro
ALICANTE

CÓRDOBA
Bailén
Úbeda
MURCIA
Ayamonte
Carmona
Jaén
Cazorla
Puerto Lumbreras
SEVILLA
ANDALUCÍA
Mazagón
GRANADA
Mojácar
Antequera
Sierra Nevada
Arcos de la Frontera
MÁLAGA
Nerja
MEDITERRANEAN SEA
CÁDIZ
Torremolinos
GIBRALTAR

ATLANTIC OCEAN

N

FOOD AND WINE

SPANISH FOOD is less familiar to most people than, say, French or Italian cuisine. It is also very different. Much of the best Spanish food is simple and straightforward country cooking.

You have only to wander round a country market to see just how good the ingredients are in Spain. Glossy fresh fruit and vegetables with damp soil still clinging to their roots, bunches of fresh mountain herbs and mushrooms from the forests. In the fishing ports the variety of seafood is overwhelming. Fish is extremely popular and wherever you are in the country there will be a standard selection of fish dishes, like *merluza* (flaky white hake), or *rape*, firm meaty monk fish.

Meat is good too: the countryside teems with pigs, goats, cows and sheep, and chickens cluck around every cottage doorway. Game is also abundant: partridge, quail and wild rabbit are commonplace items on the menus. Contrary to popular belief, excellent cheeses

are made in Spain. The delicious Roncales from the Pyrenees, for instance; San Simón, a smoked cheese from Galicia; or Cabrales, a creamy blue-veined cheese from the Picos de Europa are only a few of those you will encounter.

The cuisine is strongly regional in character. In Valencia, for example, there are numerous rice-based dishes like *arroz abanda* or *paella*. In Galicia there are the *empanadas* (pies with a variety of fillings) and *fabadas* (rich bean stews). In Andalucía there are chilled soups like *ajo blanco* and *gazpacho* and in Murcia fish baked in salt. In Cataluña there are fish stews such as *suquet de pescado* and *zarzuela* and in Navarra dishes like *Truchas a la Navarra* (trout with ham), and *cordero al chilindrón* (lamb cooked with peppers and tomatoes). La Mancha has dishes like *migas* (fried breadcrumbs), and *Pisto Manchego* (mixed vegetables), while in Castile there is *cochinillo asado* (roast suckling pig) and *sopa de ajo* (garlic soup enriched with eggs).

The *paradores* are proud of their regional cuisine and

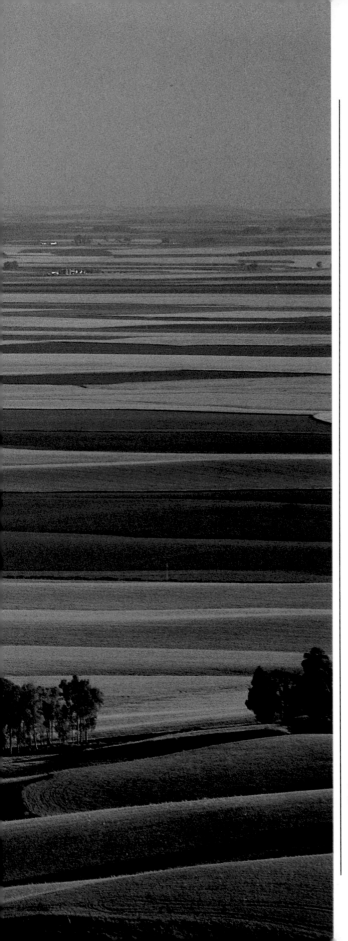

each has a selection of local specialities on the menu along with more familiar dishes. Some of these country dishes are not customarily served with vegetables. If you don't like the idea of, say, an unaccompanied meat dish, it is best to ask specifically for vegetables.

Spanish wine is just as interesting and varied as it is in France and Italy. Wines from Rioja and Penedés are now quite familiar but many others are less well known. Cariñena, Ribeiro, Rueda, Priorato, Ampurdán and Mentrida, for example, are all wine-growing regions which are greatly appreciated in Spain and their wines are well worth looking out for. The wine lists at the *paradores* will usually have local country wines on the list – like Torreperogil and Cebreros, for instance – and these will often be available *a la jarra* (in the carafe). Many *paradores* have a separate wine list with a wider choice, but you will often have to ask for this.

TRAVELLING IN SPAIN

I HAVE PLANNED THE ROUTES to make minimal use of main roads. It's far more enjoyable to travel on country roads. They are usually very quiet and more scenic. On many of the roads I have suggested you will see only the occasional car – you're more likely to be held up by a flock of sheep or an ox-drawn cart. The maps I used were from the Michelin series, and I have indicated the relevant map number at the beginning of each tour.

When you do use main roads you will discover that Spanish lorry drivers are exceptionally courteous and helpful and will do everything possible to help you overtake. They will signal when it's safe and then move over and slow down until you're safely past.

When visiting a large town, or passing through, it can help to plan to do so between say 1.00 pm and 4.00 pm. The siesta is between these hours and most towns are very quiet, shops are closed and there is much less traffic. Don't be deterred when you are approaching a historic town and are confronted by ugly suburbs – an unspoilt medieval quarter invariably lies within.

When using country roads it's best to make sure you have a fairly full petrol tank. Sometimes there are many miles between filling stations. It's also important to know that filling stations will not accept credit cards, although they are widely welcomed elsewhere. Petrol stations also dislike traveller's cheques or Eurocheques – only cash is welcome. I was told once on offering a Eurocheque, 'We are not a bank, señor!'

I will never weary of Spain and hope that this book will encourage you to enjoy regions often ignored by the tourist.

The view from close to the Parador at Carmona. Overleaf: The coastline near San Sebastián.

Northern Spain

SAN SEBASTIÁN

1

2

3

4

5

• VIGO

6

• LEÓN

*T*OUR 1 *Follows the north-western coastline of Spain, passing through the provinces of Cantabria, Asturias, Lugo and La Coruña. It provides an interesting scenic route linking the airport of Bilbao and the car ferry port of Santander to the coastal resorts of Galicia and northern Portugal. Although the road follows the coast quite closely for much of the way, a number of inland detours are included, enabling you to explore fully this fascinating northern region. Linked with tour 3 it forms a complete round trip from the starting points mentioned.*

— TOUR I —
MICHELIN MAP NOS. 42 & 441

El Ferrol   Ribadeo   Gijón

LA CORUÑA   Santillana
                              del Mar

LEÓN •

SANTILLANA DEL MAR
GIJÓN
RIBADEO
EL FERROL

The tour begins in Santillana del Mar, one of Spain's most unashamedly picturesque medieval villages and takes you to some of the most remote, unspoilt beaches in Europe. The countryside is a constant pleasure with green rounded hills, quiet country lanes and small villages. Here the wooden-wheeled oxcart is a far more common sight than the tractor. The *hórreos*, small buildings adjoining most homes in which the winter grain is stored, have distinctive regional characteristics. In Asturias they are square, usually built of wood with ornate wooden balconies. In Galicia however they are long and narrow, made of stone and much more functional in appearance.

SANTILLANA DEL MAR

SANTILLANA DEL MAR is within easy reach of Santander or Bilbao. In spite of its name the town is several kms from the sea – amidst steep, rounded green hills with meadows bordered by dry stone walls. Take the N 611 from Santander towards Torrelavega and turn right on to the C 6316 approximately 1km before the town is reached.

Santillana del Mar is a town of rough stone houses and elegant mansions lining steep cobbled streets and small atmospheric squares. On Sunday morning the bells of a lovely 11th-century collegiate church, at the end of the long, sloping cobbled main street, summon the villagers who walk in procession down the hill.

The town, rightly considered one of the most beautiful in Spain, has been perfectly preserved and it is hard to find a street or a square which does not resemble a picture postcard – though its prettiness is quite unselfconscious. During the day, in summer months, tour coaches arrive and people throng the narrow streets. Alongside the inevitable souvenir and craft shops many of the old houses still have dairies and stables on their ground floors and cows are still led down the main street to graze in surrounding meadows. Some houses offer fresh milk, home-made cakes and biscuits

to visitors. One of the pleasures of staying in the Parador is in sharing the atmosphere of the town in the evening and early morning exclusively with its residents.

Parador Nacional Gil Blas is situated in a graceful manor house facing the Plaza Ramón Pelayo around which are several lovely arcaded buildings. The house was once the home of the Barreda-Bracho family. The name Gil Blas is derived from the French author Le Sage's fictional character whose imaginary exploits took him to the town of Santillana. The atmosphere of the Parador is in harmony with the town itself. The entrance leads into a large hall with hewn stone walls and a floor of pebbles in a mosaic pattern.

The menu has a good selection of the local Cantabrian cuisine. El Cocido Montañes is a stew of white beans, potatoes, meat and chorizo. Fish is an excellent choice in this region and two dishes which were on the menu during my stay were Merluza a la Cantabria, hake cooked with asparagus and prawns, and Hongos de Monte con Langostinos y Jamón, smally spiny lobsters cooked with wild mountain mushrooms and ham. I chose a dry and delicate rose wine from the list, Bodegas Peñascal from Tudela de Duero, near Valladolid.

One of the most famous historical discoveries in Europe is only 2km from the Parador, the Caves of Altamira. Well-preserved 12th-century BC paintings have been found here. Regrettably, fear of deterioration has resulted in access to the caves being restricted and application for a visit from the Museum of Altamira must be made several months in advance of your visit. However it is sometimes possible to take advantage of a cancellation by simply turning up and enquiring.

If you plan to stay at least two nights at Gil Blas you will be able to tour along the coast to the east: continue along the C 6316 towards Comillas for 1km and turn right to Suances. Soon you will be in sight of the sea. At Tagla, a small inlet between two grassy headlands, there is a fine sand beach the colour of ripe corn. Suances is a small resort with several beautiful beaches. Small roads lead from the main (N 6111) road to a number of delightful beaches between Suances and Santander. Playa de Mongro and Liencres are especially fine beaches but there are many others such as Playa de Portio and Somo Cueva. Tracks leading to these beaches thread their way through small farms and meadows – it is a region where it is easy to get away from the crowds. My visit was during the haymaking

The main street of Santillana del Mar.

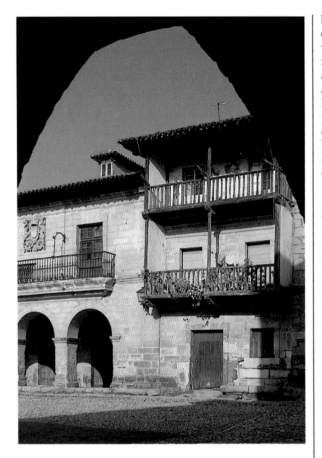

A square in Santillana del Mar.

bream) and *sardinas* (sardines), cooked over the embers of a wood fire – seafood at its best and very popular with the locals at weekend lunches. The landscape is flatter here than to the west of Santander and there are a number of large beaches backed by sand dunes, such as the Playa de Galizano where a river creates a delightful quiet sandy creek. Beyond, at Barreyo, is the pretty Romanesque church of Santa María. The route continues through Isla, Quejo, Ris and Noia, all with beaches, to Santona where there is a busy fishing port, some interesting old houses and a beautiful 12th-century church, Santa María del Puerto.

From Santona the road follows the estuary of the river Asón to rejoin the N 634 where the route continues eastwards to Laredo, another attractive seaside town with a large beach of fine golden sand, sheltered within a deep bay. The well-preserved town of Laredo is quite separate from the resort which has developed around it and contains some lovely old mansions, the 13th-century church of Nuestra Señora de la Asunción and an imposing 16th-century *ayuntamiento* (town hall).

From Laredo the steep, winding, scenic main road, the N 634, continues to Castro Urdiales, an ancient fishing port founded in Roman times with a large 14th-century church, Santa María, strikingly sited high on a rocky promontory overlooking the harbour.

From Castro Urdiales an attractive inland route takes you back to Santillana. As well as avoiding the busy main road it provides a rewarding scenic route through the Cantabrian mountains and reveals a quite different aspect of this region. Approximately 1km towards Bilbao along the N 634 a small road to the south, the S 501, leads to Ortañes and Avellaneda where there is a small *castillo* (castle) containing a regional museum of the countryside known as Encataniones. It is lovely countryside, steep rounded green hills covered with meadows and woodlands. The road continues through Villaverde and crosses the pass of La Escrita into the beautiful valley of Carrenza. The route is a constant delight, quiet rural scenery with wooded hills and plunging valleys. This region is sparsely populated with small villages and isolated farms, surrounded by small market gardens and meadowland. The road continues to Ramales de la Victoria, set in a valley overlooked by a rocky mountain.

The route continues towards Arredondo following the course of the fast-flowing river Asón. The villages dotted throughout this region are a picturesque cluster of ancient houses with wooden balconies brimming with flowers. Beyond Arredondo, which has a dramatic rocky setting, the road climbs up out of the valley with a succession of stunning views. This for me was literally the high point of the return journey. The scenery, almost alpine in character, becomes increasingly spectacular, culminating in the Puerto de Alisas. Here a *mirador* (vantage point) provides sweeping

season and the hillsides were dotted with small wooden donkey carts and entire families were busy scything, raking and stacking the hay. The air was suffused with the sweet summery smell of fresh-cut grass.

Santander is soon reached, an attractive, elegant seaside town with the ambience of the best of the great traditional resorts like Deauville, San Sebastián and Brighton, in its stylish shops, broad tree-lined avenues, promenades, numerous gardens and parks shaded by palm trees and mimosa. It also has a vast crescent of fine sand at the beach of Sardinero.

From here continue the coastal route by taking the N 634 to El Astillero. Beyond, after crossing the river, a road to the left, the S 430, leads to a succession of small coastal towns along the other side of the estuary with views across to Santander. Pedreña is a little fishing village at the mouth of the estuary where there is a harbour and ferry boats which cross to Santander. A cluster of wooden buildings include restaurants offering freshly caught *bonito* (striped tunny), *besugo* (sea

An old farmhouse near Arredondo.

views northwards to the sea. The road now descends to La Cavada and then to Pamanes on the N 634 from where you can return to Torrelavega and Santillana.

GIJÓN

THE NEXT STAGE OF THE TOUR is west to the Parador at Gijón. From Santillana the route continues westwards along the C 6316 towards Comillas. It is a quiet country road winding tortuously round steep green hillsides with frequent glimpses of the sea. At Cobreces there is a sandy beach enclosed by grassy headlands. A few kms beyond is Comillas with a small sandy beach, harbour, castle and plaza surrounded by old buildings. The town is overlooked by an imposing cluster of grandiose buildings including an ecclesiastical university and the 18th-century Seminario Cantábrico. Almost hidden away on the edge of the town is an extraordinary small building by Antonio Gaudí, the Catalonian designer who was responsible for the un-

finished Catedral de la Sagrada Familia in Barcelona. Here he has designed a curious *castillo*-like fantasy known as El Capricho.

Beyond Comillas there is another long sandy beach at Oyambre. A few kms further to the west the road joins the N 634. Continue to San Vincente de la Barquera, most attractively situated on a promontory between two river estuaries – it almost seems to be on an island. Here there is a busy fishing port and arcaded streets lined with many attractive old buildings. There are also the remains of a castle, ramparts and a lovely 13th-century church on a hill above the town overlooking the river.

The road 10km to the west of San Vincente crosses the Ría de Tina Menor. You can make a short detour to the right beyond the bridge by following a small road which runs alongside the *ría* (estuary) towards the village of Pechón. There are some breathtaking views down into the intensely blue water which is enclosed by steep wooded headlands. Returning to the main road the route continues westwards towards Llanes, passing from Cantabria into Asturias. Here the countryside becomes more mountainous with distant views of the Picos de Europa to the south. At Pimiango there are caves with prehistoric paintings. Llanes is an attractive town with fishing boats moored along a quayside lined with old houses. There is also a castle, the remains of ramparts and a 15th-century church. Nearby is a delightful sandy beach, Playa de Toro, with rocky outcrops and grassy headlands.

A little further to the west is another fine beach at San Antolín overlooked by a steep green headland. Nearby is the small Romanesque monastery of San Antolín. The road continues along the coastline to Ribadasella, a largely modern town on the estuary of the Sella. Nearby are the caves of Tío Bustillo where there are cave paintings and stalactites. Beyond Ribadasella the road becomes quite tortuous, winding its way between and around the steep green hills which reach down to the sea. The route continues to Villaviciosa, a town with attractive narrow streets and old houses, and then on to Gijón, the location of the next Parador.

GIJON

GIJÓN is a large modern town which preserves an old quarter down by the harbour. There is an arcaded *plaza mayor* and a 16th-century church down by the sea overlooking the beach. The delightfully old-fashioned beach, San Lorenzo, is a long arc of firm golden sand with a promenade, deckchairs and bathing tents.

Parador Nacional Molino Viejo is a modern building in the centre of the town beside a peaceful wooded park with streams and ponds. The Parador has a quiet rural atmosphere with peacocks strutting in its garden, although in fact it is adjacent to the town's football stadium. *Molino viejo* means 'old mill' which is what previously occupied the site and the waterway which fed the mill has been preserved within the Parador grounds. Regional dishes on the menu during my stay included Pote Asturiano (a stew with ham, *chorizo*, *morcilla* (blood sausage), pigs ears, cabbage, white beans and potatoes flavoured with garlic and paprika); Rodaballo a la Pimienta Verde (turbot cooked with green peppers); and Alcachofas Naturales Rellenas de Bonito (artichokes stuffed with tuna).

From Gijón a small detour to the city of Oviedo can be made along the Autopista A 66. Outwardly it is a modern and not very appealing city but it preserves a number of lovely buildings and an atmospheric old quarter centred around its 14th-century Gothic cathedral. The *plaza mayor* contains an arcaded 18th-century *ayuntamiento*. The jewel of Oviedo is however a small church in the Sierra de Naranjo overlooking the city, built as a palace in the 9th century and converted

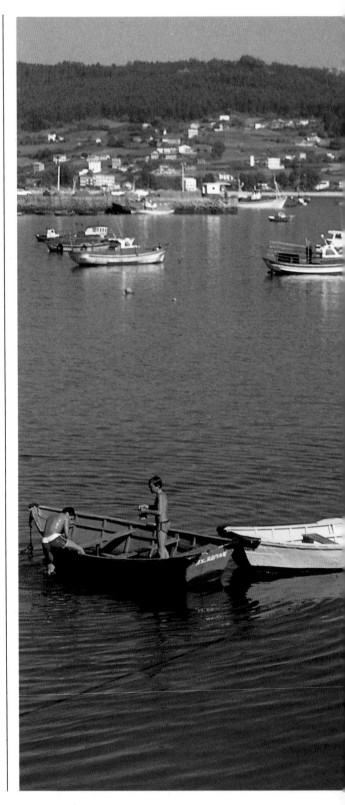

The harbour and Ría of Cedeira.

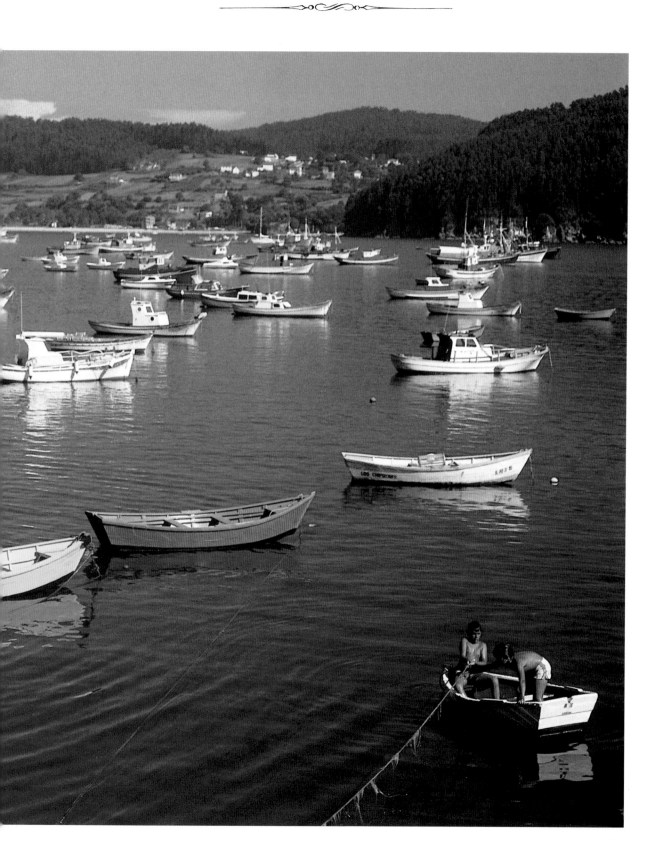

some fifty years later. It is considered by many one of the most beautiful buildings in Spain. Jan Morris describes it as being 'formidable beyond its scale'. It is elegantly proportioned with exquisite detail and its warm mellow stone almost appears to glow from within its green wooded setting.

Returning from Oviedo to Gijón the next stage of the tour is west to Ribadeo. The route continues along the coast road, the N 632 to Avilés, an unattractive industrial town on first sight but with numerous arcaded streets and some fine buildings in the old part centred around the Plaza de España. There is the 14th-century Gothic church of San Francisco, a 17th-century *ayuntamiento* and several palaces with imposing façades. From Avilés the route continues to Soto del Barco on the estuary of the Río Nalón.

From here you can make another small detour along a beautiful wide green valley to Pravia which contains an 18th-century collegiate church and the Palace de los Montes of the same period. Nearby, in the village of Santianes de Pravia, is the oldest church in Asturias. Dating from the 8th century and the residence of the Kings of Asturias, it was restored in 1977 under the personal direction of King Juan Carlos. From here you can follow a small country road back to the coast through steep wooded hillsides via the village of Somado, from which are sweeping views of the coastline and of the estuary of the Río Nalón.

Cudillero, the next town en route, has a busy fishing port, reached by descending a steep cobbled street down to the harbour from where tiers of narrow wooden houses rise up the hillside like a wall. On the outskirts is a rather grand 19th-century palace in the French style containing a collection of paintings and carpets.

In this region you can't fail to notice the *hórreos*, large grain stores adjoining most houses. In Asturias they are square, made of wood and supported on tall stone stilts to protect their contents from hungry rodents. Many are quite large and elaborate with small balconies and windows looking rather like fanciful granny annexes.

The houses of the picturesque fishing town of Luarca are built in a steep semi-circle around a horseshoe-shaped bay, within which is a busy harbour. A small road from the end of the latter climbs round the headland providing a wonderful view of the town.

The route continues approximately 1km inland. The landscape is particularly pleasing with steep green hillocky hills and frequent glimpses of the sea. Beyond Navia a country lane leads through farmland to the small fishing village of Ortiquera. For me, this is the most appealing of all the Asturian fishing towns. Set at the mouth of a narrow rocky inlet in which a small harbour nestles, small whitewashed stone cottages are ranged along the top of the headland. It has a rather wild, remote atmosphere and is completely unspoilt.

The beautiful beach at Tapia de Casariego is in a narrow inlet bordered by wooded headlands with a small stream threading through the fine golden sand. Trees grow almost down to the water's edge, adding an almost tropical atmosphere.

The road continues to the estuary of the Río Eo, known for its trout and salmon fishing. There are lovely views across the broad expanse of water to Ribadeo, opposite which the old town of Castropol is picturesquely situated on a promontory on the east bank. The road skirts around the estuary crossing the river at Vegadeo and continuing along the west bank to Ribadeo. A bridge across the estuary connecting Ribadeo with Figueras was nearing completion at the time of writing.

RIBADEO

RIBADEO is a small town with a fishing harbour beside the river mouth, the 14th-century convent of St Clara and the mainly modern church of Santa María del Campo, containing a particularly beautiful gilded Baroque 18th-century retablo. There is also a rather severe 18th-century *ayuntamiento* and an 18th-century customs building. A small road leads out to the headland at the mouth of the estuary where there are substantial remains of the 18th-century fortress of St Damian.

The Parador Nacional de Ribadeo, a modern building on the edge of the town, is much larger than it appears since the single storey entrance is in fact the top floor of a four-storey building with the bedrooms on the lower floors. It is built on a ledge overlooking the estuary and the small harbour with its cluster of brightly painted fishing boats is immediately below. The bedrooms have large balconies with fine views of the river, Castropol and the hills beyond. The restaurant is an attractive L-shaped room with a marble floor and wide stone-arched windows. Regional fish dishes are well represented on the menu. I had Rodaballo a la Gallega, turbot poached with potatoes, paprika and garlic. Filloas de Mariscos Gratinadas are pancakes stuffed with shellfish in a white wine and cream sauce and grilled. For desert you might try Tarta de Mondonedo, a rich sweet tart filled with a mixture of ground almonds, eggs and sugar, and flavoured with cinnamon. The wine list included a good selection of Galician wines as well as more familiar names from the Rioja and Penedes. I had a bottle of Vino Costeiro Ribeiro; a dry but fruity white wine which is slightly *pétillant*.

EL FERROL

THE NEXT STAGE of the tour is west to the parador at El Ferrol. The route continues along the N 634 towards

Harvesting hay near Ortigueira.

Foz. Before leaving Ribadeo however there is an excellent viewpoint of the estuary and the surrounding countryside from the chapel of A Atalaia on the pine-covered hilltop of Santa Cruz which is clearly signposted along a small road to the left just after leaving the town. A few kms beyond Ribadeo is the fishing village of Rinlo – little more than a cluster of colour-washed stone cottages with grey slate roofs bordering a narrow rocky inlet. About here you will notice the change from the square wooden Asturian *hórreos* to the long narrow stone versions of Galicia.

Here the coastline takes on a flatter and bleaker aspect, with stunted trees and gorse covering the hinterland. The beach of Los Castros is very appealing, a small sheltered inlet of impeccably fine yellow sand bordered by low rocky headlands. At Reinante, just beyond, is another superb sandy beach which extends for several kms, with a small road running parallel to the sea for some distance and bordered by low cliffs, eroded to create a series of curious striated rocky outcrops. One of the finest beaches I have seen anywhere, it is remote and unspoilt but needs to be visited when the tide is low.

Just before reaching Foz a small road to the south leads to the pre-Romanesque church of St Martín de Mondoñedo. At Foz you can make a small detour to the south along the N 634 to the atmospheric old city of Mondoñedo where an imposing twin-towered 13th-century cathedral overlooks the Plaza de España which is surrounded by old houses with galleries and arcades. On the road between Mondoñedo and Foz is Villanova de Lourenza whose huge 18th-century church has a spectacular Baroque façade.

Beyond Burela the countryside becomes more hilly and wooded with increasingly beautiful scenery. Viveiro, situated on the estuary of the Río Androve, with a busy harbour and an important sardine fishing fleet, is a large town with modern buildings but the old centre is still a maze of narrow streets, largely traffic-free, and four of the town gates still survive. The road skirts the Ría de Viveiro with lovely views abounding. After crossing the Ría del Barqueiro a small road leads

to the very pretty small fishing village of Porto de Barqueiro. It has a small harbour surrounded by small whitewashed stone cottages. There are several small waterfront bars and cafés where you can sit and watch the fishing boats bobbing on the tidal currents. A short distance along the main road another small road leads out along the headland, with stunning views, to Porto de Bares at the very mouth of the *ría*, an unspoilt village with a cluster of small fishing boats pulled up on a crescent of pale yellow sand.

Continuing along the coast road Ortigueira is the next large town, which has a long sandy beach backed by sand dunes and pine trees, the Playa de Cazador. At Mera there is a worthwhile detour on to the bleak and windswept headland of Cabo Ortegal. From Pedra a road leads across a wild heath-covered hill with spectacular views of the coastline to the tiny hermitage of San Andrés de Teixido, where an annual pilgrimage is held each year featuring traditional dancing and songs.

The road continues, via the fishing port of Cedeira an attractive town in a beautiful setting on the Ría de Cedeira, to Valdaviño where there is a huge sandy beach and a lagoon. From here it is just 18km to El Ferrol.

El Ferrol, a large, busy town, is Spain's most important naval base and the birthplace of General Franco. The Parador Nacional El Ferrol del Caudillo is on a natural terrace overlooking the naval dockyard and adjacent to a naval building where sailors stand guard and the bugle sounds as the flag is lowered and raised. The Parador is a modern building but with a traditional seafaring atmosphere in its dark wood panelling, polished brass, and maps and charts decorating the walls. The restaurant menu strongly features seafood with an excellent selection of local shellfish, such as *cigalas* (small spiny lobsters), *centolla de la ría* (spider crab), *necoras* (small crab) and *ostras* (oysters). I had Abadejo la Gallega, cod cooked with potatoes, paprika and garlic. There is a good selection of Galician wines on the menu. I chose a bottle of Pazo Ribeiro, an excellent light, dry, fruity white wine with a slight sparkle.

From El Ferrol there are several interesting towns nearby to visit and the Parador makes a good base from which to make a round tour of the Rías Altas. Allow yourself two days, spending one in La Coruña, Pontedeume and Betanzos and the other exploring the Rías Altas.

Pontedeume is a lovely old town on the Ría de Betanzos, with narrow arcaded streets, attractive small squares, interesting shops, the 15th-century fortified

The old port at La Coruña.

The fishing village of Muxía.

Palace of the Counts of Andrade, the 16th-century church of Santiago and a 15th-century *ayuntamiento*. The town has an appealing waterfront atmosphere with the remains of a 14th-century bridge which once had 58 arches.

Betanzos too is a fascinating old hilltop town with extensive town walls and entrance gates, a labyrinth of narrow cobbled streets, tall houses with glazed balconies, small squares and a fine *ayuntamiento*. Among the many churches worth seeing are the 15th-century Santa María del Azogue and the 14th-century San Francisco.

La Coruña, the largest city in Galicia, was the port from which the Spanish Armada sailed against England in 1588 and has been occupied by the Romans and Phoenicians since its original foundation by the Iberians. Today it is a busy modern city but with many old buildings, streets and squares to explore. The Iglesia de Santiago and the collegiate church Santa María date from the 12th century. Perhaps the most photogenic sight of La Coruña is the row of tall glass-balconied houses which border the old harbour. They create

unique and striking setting for the colourful fishing boats moored below. Another unusual sight is the Tower of Hercules, a 2nd-century Roman lighthouse, now incorporated into a more recent structure of vast scale which dominates the headland and is still in use.

The tour of the Rías Altas can be made by taking the C 552 from La Coruña towards Carballo. From here the route is initially along the L C414 to Malpica de Bergantinos, an attractive seaside town with a good sandy beach, then along the C 430 to Ponte Ceso. The road towards Laxe becomes more interesting with steep wooded hills and splendid views of the Ría de Corme y Laxe. Laxe is a small fishing town with an enormous arc of fine white powdery sand. Towards Camarinas it becomes mountainous with rocky outcrops and pine-covered slopes. Camariñas is beautifully sited on the edge of the lovely Ría de Camariñas. The town is known for its lacemaking. Near the pretty riverside village of Ponte do Porto is the attractive small Romanesque church of Santiago de Cereixo and, close by, a small twin-towered palace called the Torres de Cereixo.

Muxía, a small fishing village with a colourful harbour and two lovely white sand beaches, is beautifully situated at the mouth of the Ría de Camarinas with views across the water to Cabo Vilán. From here the road continues through attractive hilly countryside covered with bracken and gorse, and tall pine and eucalyptus trees, to the fishing town of Corcubión. It is the most picturesque of all the fishing towns along this route with its small stone and wooden houses decorated with glazed balconies clustered round a lively and colourful harbour.

From here you can make a detour out to Cabo Finisterre. Its name derives from the medieval belief that it was, literally, the end of the earth. The road out to the cape is however surprisingly beautiful, not at all bleak and rugged as one might imagine. Green wooded hillsides dip into a sea as clear and blue as you will see anywhere in the world and frequent crescents of fine white sand nestle between the rocky headlands. The village of Finisterre is also appealing with the delightful small 12th-century church of Santa María and the diminutive castle of San Carlos. The road continues beyond to the cape where a lighthouse commands an almost 360° panorama over the sea from the very tip of the promontory. Here it is impressively rugged and isolated and it would not be hard to imagine there is no land beyond this point.

From Corcubión the road follows the coastline closely to Muros. Here the landscape is much more open and rocky, with fewer trees. This part of the coastline has a quite striking beauty. There is a remote and wild

A secluded beach near Corcubión.

atmosphere and the coast is scantily populated. The beaches are simply stunning with gleaming white sand and crystal-clear blue water backed by sand dunes and rocks. There is access to the beaches almost all the way along this route. The Playa de Carnota is particularly notable and the village is also famed for possessing the largest *hórreo* in Galicia. In a region especially well endowed with enormous *hórreos* that of Carnota, 100ft long, dwarfs them all. The Playa de Lariño is also magnificent with a long sweeping arc of brilliant white sand. Just beyond, Louro also has a superb beach. Muros is an attractive small town with a harbour looking out across the Ría de Muros y Noja.

The route continues along the side of the Ría to Outes. At this point you can take the road north to Pino do Val from where you can continue back towards La Coruña and El Ferrol along the LC 403 via Santa Comba. It is however a quite long circuit and one which you may not want to rush. An alternative plan would be to drive the much shorter distance via Noia to Santiago de Compostela and stay at the Hotel Reyes Católicos (page 26), where you could join Tour No 2.

*T*OUR 2 *Explores the coastal region of Galicia in the north-west corner of Spain. Begins in the province of La Coruña and then leads south into Pontevedra towards the Portuguese border. A region dominated by the Rías Bajas, the steep and deeply indented river estuaries which penetrate the Atlantic coastline. Hidden between green headlands are beautiful deserted beaches of fine white sand and fishing villages where some of the best seafood in the world is to be found. Behind are green mountains covered with vineyards and threaded by narrow lanes where the oxcart is a more familiar sight than the car.*

— TOUR 2 —
MICHELIN MAP NO. 441
SANTIAGO DE COMPOSTELA
Cambados
Pontevedra
VIGO
Bayona
Tuy

SANTIAGO DE COMPOSTELA
CAMBADOS
PONTEVEDRA
BAYONA – TUY

SANTIAGO DE COMPOSTELA

THE ITINERARY BEGINS in Santiago de Compostela, where the nearest airport is located. The nearest alternative parador is at El Ferrol, 95km (page 23).

The Hotel de los Reyes Católicos is now part of the parador network and is much more than a magnificent hotel – it is a unique experience. The building is a royal hospital founded in 1499 by the Catholic Monarchs, Fernando and Isabel, to give lodging and care to the pilgrims visiting the city. Occupying the north side of the Plaza España, also known as the Plaza Obradoiro, a vast paved square which is surrounded by majestic buildings, the hotel has a long imposing façade with a superb Plateresque portal. Inside are four graceful patios, all quite different. Numerous corridors and grand staircases link the rooms. The bedrooms are contained in several wings which extend from the central patios – it's quite easy to get lost. Beautiful antiques are scattered throughout. The restaurant is in a huge cavernous room with a high ceiling supported on massive stone arches.

From the regional specialities on the menu I chose Pimientos de Padrón, tiny sweet green peppers the size of quail's eggs, which are just sprinkled with salt and fried quickly in oil – absolutely delicious. Empanada de Bonito is tuna fish pie. Vieras de Santiago are scallops cooked in white wine with onions, mushrooms and tomato and flavoured with garlic and parsley. Polpo a Feira are small pieces of tenderised octopus cooked with garlic, paprika and olive oil. This dish is traditionally served on a wooden platter. For desert Tarta de Santiago is a tart filled with a mixture of eggs, sugar and almonds and flavoured with cinnamon.

Santiago is a city which exists because of a legend. It is believed that St James's body, after having been beheaded by Herod, was taken by his disciples to Padrón in northern Spain – a miraculous journey of only seven days. The body was lost and forgotten until in 813 a

shepherd was guided to its hiding place by a star. The Saint appeared on horseback in a battle against the Moors. He was reputed to have killed over 50,000 Moors single-handed and soon became the Patron Saint of the Reconquest.

The news spread quickly and soon miracles began to happen. King Alfonso III founded a monastery on the site of the tomb and pilgrims began to arrive from all over Europe. They established a route known as the Camino de Santiago, the way of St James. Cathedrals, churches and towns sprang up along the route, which crossed France and northern Spain, to provide shelter and comfort to the pilgrims on their long journey.

During the Middle Ages Santiago became one of the most important shrines in the Christian world, along with Rome and Jerusalem. At its peak it is claimed that up to one million pilgrims made the journey each year. In 1589, when Francis Drake attacked La Coruña, the remains were removed from the cathedral for safekeeping. They were then mislaid for another 300 years until their rediscovery in 1879. The relics were authenticated by the Pope and are now, once more, the object of pilgrimages.

One of the pleasures of staying at Los Reyes Católicos is that in the early morning and evening, when the tourists have gone, you can stroll out into the empty square and appreciate it in virtual solitude. The magnificent façade of the cathedral overwhelms you with its presence. It is a truly magical sight in the evening sunlight.

The present building was begun in 1078 after the Moors destroyed the original basilica. The cathedral was extended and modified during many centuries. The glorious Baroque façade was not completed until 1750. Inside, the Pórtico de Gloria, the original west front which now shelters behind the 'new' façade, is a masterpiece of Romanesque sculpture. In its centre is St James set on a column carved with the Tree of Jesse. Here the pilgrims have for centuries placed their fingers into holes worn as smooth as marble into the granite.

There are many other buildings of interest, and the numerous atmospheric streets and squares are built on different levels, creating a theatrical effect. The Parador will provide a guide and a map to the city.

A short excursion from the Parador can be made south-east along the N 525 to Pazo de Oca. Here in a

The cathedral of Santiago de Compostela at sunset.

The Plaza de Leña in Pontevedra.

small village overlooking a wide green is a *pazo*, or Galician manor house known as Pequeño Versailles, or little Versailles. It is a large stern building constructed from massive blocks of granite. Inside are enchanting formal gardens with long rectangular pools and fountains. There is a peaceful and almost unwordly atmosphere. Nearby at Carboeiro, hidden in a deep wooded valley, are the evocative ruins of the 10th-century monastery of San Lorenzo.

CAMBADOS

FROM SANTIAGO the next stage of the journey is southwest to the Parador at Cambados. The direct journey is only 54km but I have described a route which first explores the Ría de Arosa. Initially the route is southwest along the C 543 to Noya, an important port in Roman times, with the 15th-century church of San Martín and the 14th-century Santa María Nova. The latter has a fine Gothic rose window and a fascinating

cemetery with many 13th-century tombs. The road follows the coastline closely to Portosín and Caamano. Nearby is the Playa Río Sierra, a magnificent curve of white sand backed by an enormous sand dune and bordered by a heath-covered headland. Further to the south, near the small fishing village of Corrubedo, is another vast crescent of white sand. The sea here is a translucent shade of turquoise blue, as idyllic as any island in the Indian ocean.

The road continues over the headland to Ribeira, a busy fishing port. From here the road leads east alongside the ría to Puebla de Caraminal, with its 17th-century Baroque church, 15th-century church of Puebla del Deán and 15th-century remains of three pazos. A road leads up to the *mirador* of Culota from where there are sweeping views across the *ría* and to the islands of Arosa and Salvora and the promontory of La Toja. To the north-east you can see the long sandy beaches of Ladeira and Río Sieira. Further east are the fishing villages of Boiros and Rianjo. At the latter are a

The harbour at Combarro.

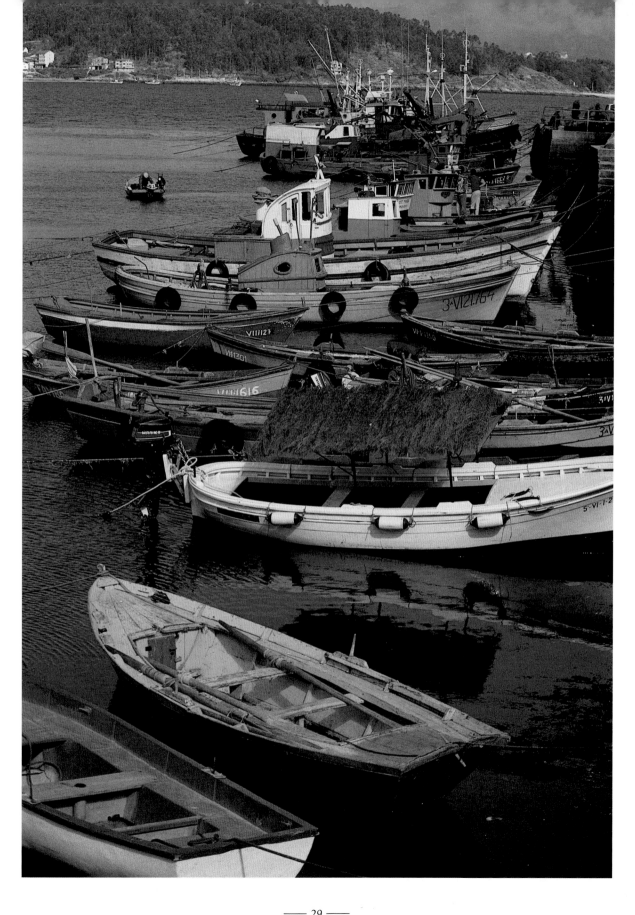

number of old mansions and the 15th-century church of Santa Columba with a Baroque tower and a 16th-century portal.

The road continues to Padrón, a town dating from Roman times and where St James's body is reputed to have been brought from Palestine by boat. There is an interesting 18th-century *ayuntamiento* and nearby the Palacio de Alonso Peña Montenegro of the same period. The 11th-century church of Santa María a Dina was rebuilt in the 18th century but retains a 12th-century portal and a 16th-century tower. The 17th-century Dominican convent of Carmen contains some fine 18th-century sculptures.

The route continues south-west along the C 550, following the south side of the *ría* to Villagarcía de Arosa, a fishing port and harbour since Roman times with several lovely palaces. The 16th-century Pazo of Rubianes has a fine portal; the early 18th-century Pazo Vista Alegre is Baroque in style; and the Palacio del Rial has a chapel and two small towers.

Further south a road leads across a causeway to the pine-covered Isla de Arosa, known locally for its excellent octopus fishing. Octopus is a very popular dish in Galicia. There are even special *pulperias* where it is served. A few kms beyond is Cambados.

The Parador Nacional El Albariño is situated on the seafront in the town of Cambados. Facing it is a broad palm tree-lined promenade. A modern building constructed from huge blocks of granite in traditional *pazo* style on the site of an original building belonging to the Bazán family, the centre is an attractive courtyard with a fountain. The Parador is named after the local wine, Albariño, a dry fruity white slightly *pétillant* wine made from vines introduced from the Rhineland in the 12th century by Benedictine monks. The restaurant is a large L-shaped room with a lofty wooden-beamed ceiling and decorated with large stone pillars.

Regional dishes on the menu are focused strongly upon seafood. Crema de Cangrejos is a rich creamy bisque made from crayfish. Rodaballo con Almejas is turbo cooked in light creamy sauce with clams. Lenguado al Albariño is fillets of sole cooked in a sauce of dry white wine, cream and mushrooms. The Parador has its own label Albariño wine and Ribeiro Pazo is a local light red wine.

The Parador is only a few minutes' walk from the Plaza Fefiñanes, the centre of Cambados. This wide square is bordered by beautiful buildings – the 17th-century Palacio de Fefiñanes, which dominates one side, with its unusual corner balconies, coats of arms and an ornamental bridge; the Palacio de Montesacro and the Palacio de Figueroa. The 16th-century Roman-

The Plaza Fefiñanes at Cambados.

esque church of Santa Marina de Ozo is now little more than an atmospheric ruin. Close to the sea is the 12th-century tower of San Saturnino.

PONTEVEDRA

THE NEXT STAGE of the tour is south-east to the Parador at Pontevedra: being only 25km away it can be considered as an alternative base to Cambados if preferred.

The route between the two towns follows the coastline around the headland to the island of La Toja, where there is a resort with thermal springs known to the Romans. It is also a centre for excellent shellfish. Beyond is a quiet and undeveloped part of the coastline where fishing and farming are the main activities. Here fields of vegetables and vineyards extend almost down to the water's edge. There are beautiful white sand beaches along this part of the coast, especially the Playa Bascuas and Playa de la Lanzada. Near Lanzada are castle ruins and a small 12th-century church, NS (Nuestra Señora) de la Lanzada. The road continues to Portonovo, a busy fishing town with a lively and colourful harbour. Nearby, at Armenteira, is the 12th-century Cistercian Abbey of Santa María.

Further towards Pontevedra is the curious fishing village of Combarro. Built on a huge rock beside the sea, the streets are simply narrow stone pathways. The old houses all have ancient stone *hórreos*, set along the water's edge. Nearby at Poyo a 16th-century monastery occupied by Mercedarian monks has a fine cloister with a lovely fountain.

The Parador Nacional Casa del Barón is on the western edge of the city, a short distance from its centre in the Pazo de Maceda, which was built on the site of a Roman villa. Although it dates from the 16th century it was periodically reconstructed and its present form is essentially 18th century. It has had a variety of uses, ranging from a school to a masonic lodge and an old people's home. Its quite severe classical façade leads into a hall with a magnificent Baroque stone staircase leading to the bedrooms. An old Galician kitchen has been preserved.

Galician cuisine is well represented on the menu. I chose Merluza a la Gallega, hake cutlets cooked in a casserole with potatoes, onions and paprika. Tortilla de Cigalas is an omelette filled with crayfish. Empañada Gallega is a pie filled with pork, chorizo, onions, peppers and tomatoes. For desert Filoas de Manzana are a local speciality – pancakes filled with apple purée. I had a bottle of Atalaya de Monterrey, a slightly *pétillant* dry white wine from the region.

The provincial capital of Pontevedra, believed to have been founded by the Greeks, is set at the head of the Ría de Pontevedra and has a busy harbour, numerous old houses and mansions, and streets and small squares of considerable atmosphere and character. The Plaza de Leña has an ancient stone calvery and is surrounded by picturesque arcaded houses with glazed balconies. The regional museum is situated here in two 18th-century mansions. The Plaza de la Herrería contains an ornate 18th-century fountain and the Plaza de Tuero has a fine Baroque mansion. The 16th-century church of Santa María la Mayor, built on the site of an earlier Romanesque church, has a beautifully sculptured facade and the interior is also richly decorated. The 18th-century Baroque church of La Peregrina is an unusual building with a curved façade flanked by two tall towers. Adjacent is the church of San Francisco with a 14th-century apse.

BAYONA

THE ROUTE SOUTH to the Parador at Bayona – a direct distance of 54km – follows the C 550 along the southern shore of the Ría de Pontevedra. Beyond Marín, the headquarters of the Naval Academy and a large port, are a sequence of superb beaches, Playa de Lapamán, Portocelo, Mogor Aguete and Loira. A road climbs the Montes de Morrazo to a viewpoint with sweeping views of the Pontevedra and Vigo *rías* and continues to Bueu, where there is a maritime museum, and then round the headland to Cangas and Moaña. The road passes under the Autopista at the point where it crosses the *ría*. There are some very fine views from the bridge of the Ría de Vigo and the city. The C 550 however continues along the *ría* to its head where it joins the N 550. Here the route leads south to Redondela where the C 550 continues around the southern shore of the *ría* to Vigo. You will see dozens of large platforms moored in the *rías*, these are for the culture of mussels.

Vigo is a busy modern city, an important port and the centre of the sardine fishing industry. On the hill above are two 10th-century castles. In the old part of town is an 18th-century collegiate church and in the Plaza Almeida are some old mansions. The road follows the coastline closely beyond the fishing villages of Bouzas and Panjón to Bayona.

The Parador Nacional Conde de Gondomar is situated on an island-like rocky promontory surrounded by fortifications. It has been defended against the Romans, and after them the Visigoths and the Moors held the stronghold. In 1585 Francis Drake and his fleet were successfully repelled and pirates used it as a base for attacks on the merchant ships of the British and Dutch in the 18th century. One of three ships which sailed with Columbus sheltered here on its return, bringing the first news of his discovery. Massive cannons still testify to its torrid past.

The Parador is in an enviable setting. The small peninsula, known as Monte Real, is now a large park which surrounds the building and the battlements create a scenic walk from where you can watch the

Ancient hórreos in the village of Barcia.

local fishing fleet plying the waters below. Beyond are far-reaching views of the Cies islands and the coastline towards Portugal and Vigo.

The Parador is a modern building constructed from massive blocks of granite in the style of a *pazo,* but on a massive scale. Inside there is a cavernous entrance hall and a magnificent stone staircase which leads to the public rooms and the bedrooms which are contained in extensive wings. The numerous lounges and salons are furnished with regional antiques and decorated with tapestries and heraldic banners. It is hard to believe that the building dates only from 1966.

The seafood in the restaurant is superb. I chose Parrillada de Pescado Rías Bajas, a magnificent dish of locally caught fish which included steaks of tuna, halibut, hake and salmon with sea bream, red mullet and prawns. It would have fed four people with ease. Cocochas en Cazuela con Almejas are the succulent slivers of meat from the throat of hake cooked in a sauce with clams. Local wines on the list included Ribiera Pazo and Albariño de Chavas.

In the old part of the town is a Romanesque collegiate church and a number of old mansions. Nearby at Gondomar is the beautiful 18th-century palace of the counts of Gondomar.

TUY

THE FINAL STAGE of this tour is south to the Parador at Tuy, a direct distance of 51km. The C 550 follows the coastline to Oya, where there is a Romanesque monastery, founded in the 12th century by Alfonso VII,

with a lovely 16th-century cloister. A small road climbs up into the mountains with stunning views of the monastery and the coastline. Wild horses are left to roam free among the heathland and eucalyptus trees. The region is famous for the Curros, exciting annual round-ups which take place at the nearby villages of Mougas, La Volga and Torroña in early summer.

The coast road continues to La Guardia, a small fishing town at the mouth of the Río Miño. A picturesque cluster of pastel-coloured houses are grouped around the colourful harbour. There are some good fish restaurants here. Above the town is Monte Santa Tecla from where there are superb views of the river and the Portuguese countryside beyond. Nearby, on the slopes, there is a Celtic settlements, founded *c.* 500 BC. The village contains the remains of nearly 1,000 circular houses of rough stone, and many of the finds have been preserved in a small museum. The route continues along the C 550 following the north bank of the river to Tuy.

The Parador Nacional San Telmo is situated just outside the city to the south. It overlooks the Miño river and there are fine views of Tuy with its ancient cathedral perched above the houses. The Parador is a modern building, constructed of solid blocks of granite and decorated in traditional *pazo* style.

Regional dishes on the menu included Empanada de Bacalao, a shallow pie made with a bread-like pastry and filled with dried salt cod cooked with onions and tomatoes. Fabada is a stew of white beans, cooked in a rich sauce with onions, salt pork, chorizo and pieces of meat and flavoured with paprika and garlic. From the local wines on the list I chose a bottle of Vina Costeira, a dry white wine from Ribadavia.

The city of Tuy was the seat of the kingdom of Galicia during the period of the Visigoths. It was later destroyed by the Moors and has, on several occasions, been taken by the Portuguese. The cathedral was begun in 1120 and not completed until the end of the 13th century. Its exterior resembles a fortress with battlements and towers. The main portal, dating from the 15th century, is approached by a broad flight of stone steps and is richly decorated with numerous sculptures and carvings. There is a fine 13th-century cloister with twin arches and columns with intricately carved capitals. The 14th-century church of Santo Domingo, extended in the 18th century, has an interesting Gothic cloister. The 10th-century Romanesque church of San Bartolomé, has an ancient calvary.

From Tuy an excursion can be made along the lovely valley of the Miño and into the Sierra del Suido. A few kms north of Tuy along the N 550 a road leads east

The Parador at Bayona.

The river Miño seen from the Parador at Tuy.

towards Caldelas, where there is a small spa, to Salva-tierra de Miño, the capital of the wine-growing region of Condado. The road climbs along the side of the valley through vineyards with far-reaching views over the river to Portugal, the scenery becoming increasing-ly impressive as you travel further east. At Filguiera a small road winds up out of the valley through densely wooded hillsides. Near the summit is a quite spectacu-lar viewpoint of the silvery river snaking through the deep valley far below. At La Cañiza the main road, the N 120, is joined.

You can make a short detour eastwards to Ribadavia, a charmingly situated old town on the north bank of the Miño, and the capital of the wine-growing region of Ribeiro. It is threaded by picturesque streets and there is an attractive arcaded square and a castle which belonged to the counts of Ribadavia. The 12th-century church of Santiago has a beautiful portal and a rose window in the main façade. The 13th-century convent

church of Santo Domingo is also finely decorated with beautiful Gothic windows in the apse.

Stone *hórreos* are next to almost every home. Near the turning to Ribadavia a road leads north for approx-imately 1km to the primitive village of Barcia. Built on a rock its small houses of rough grey stone are outnum-bered by ancient, picturesque *hórreos*.

A few kms beyond La Cañiza, a quiet country road leads north-west towards Ponte Caldelas. The road climbs high into the mountains with splendid views of the wild landscape dotted with Galician farmhouses and villages, then descends into a rocky valley filled with heather, broom and eucalyptus trees, to Ponte Caldelas. A road leads west to Sotomayor where there is an impressive square turreted castle of grey granite on a hillside overlooking a wide green valley. The road now joins the N 550 and Tuy is about 35km to the south

The nearest alternative Parador to Tuy is at Verín, 178km (page 72).

A farm near Pineiro in the Sierra del Suido.

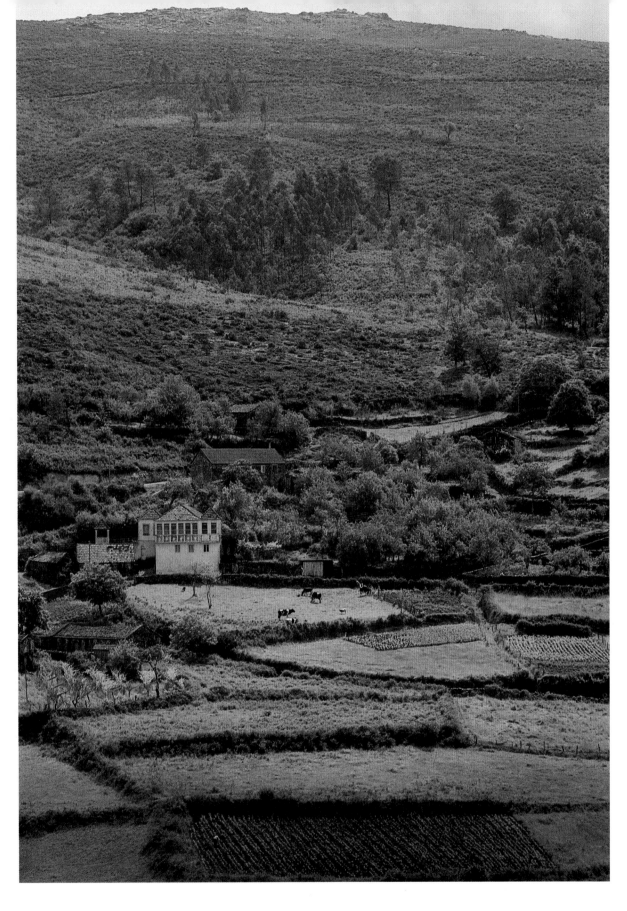

TOUR 3 Explores the inland region of the north of Spain and runs more or less parallel to the coast. Provides an interesting route for those returning from Northern Portugal or Galicia towards the French border, the car ferry port of Santander or the airport of Bilbao. It also makes a complete circuit when combined with Tour No 1 (page 14). The route crosses the provinces of Lugo, León, Palencia and Cantabria with a broad spectrum of landscape and architecture. The itinerary includes two unique hotels (one among the most beautiful in Europe) mountain ranges of outstanding beauty and villages barely changed since the Middle Ages. It follows part of the Camino de Santiago, or the Way of St James, the name given to the pilgrim route to Santiago de Compostela.

—TOUR 3—
MICHELIN MAP NO. 441

Villalba

Fuente Dé
LEÓN

Villafranca
del Bierzo

Cervera de
Pisuergo

VILLALBA
VILLAFRANCA DEL BIERZO
LEÓN – CERVERA DE
PISUERGA – FUENTE DÉ

VILLALBA

THE TOUR STARTS in the small town of Villalba in Galicia. It can be reached by taking, first, the N 6 from La Coruña and then the N 634 from Baamonde. The nearest airport is at Santiago de Compostela.

Parador Nacional Condes de Villalba is quite special. Situated close to the small church square, the building – an octagonal tower – is all that remains of the fortress of Los Andrade. Little is known of its history or when it was built. What makes the Parador particularly unusual is that it has just six bedrooms, two on each of three floors and served by a lift. The ground-floor houses a restaurant and the first floor contains the lounge and reception, entered across a drawbridge. It is an enchanting place to stay and the atmosphere is intimate and friendly. If you ask for the key you can go onto the roof and walk round the ramparts (it takes about 45 seconds) and look over the rooftops to the rolling green countryside beyond.

The menu contains a good selection of Galician dishes. Empanada de Raxo is Galician pork pie and Huevos con Zorza is fried eggs with a local sausage made from pork. I had Pollo con Piñones, a delicious combination of pieces of chicken, pine nuts, tomatoes, peppers and onions. The town is famous for its Queso de San Simón, a firm creamy cheese lightly smoked and slightly aeriated. It is made in a pear shape with a golden rind. A sweet to try is Roscón de Villalba, an almond-flavoured cake.

VILLAFRANCA DEL BIERZO

TRAVELLING SOUTH-EAST to the Parador at Villafranca del Bierzo, if you take the C 641 from Villalba to Rábade you will pass through some of the quiet rural country-

side which typifies this region and will also avoid the main road, the N 6. This however is joined at the village of Rábade where the route continues to Lugo, an atmospheric old city, encircled by imposing and extremely well-preserved 2nd-century Roman walls. They are nearly 1½ miles in circumference, 50ft high and 15ft thick. The walls are punctuated by over 50 towers and numerous gateways.

The old part of the town, centred around the lovely 18th-century cathedral of Santa María, is a warren of narrow streets, many pedestrianised, small squares, numerous fascinating shops, restaurants and small bars. The interior of the cathedral is beautiful with magnificent carved choir stalls and a spectacular retablo with gilded statues, ornate columns and an enormous silver sunrise-like ornament like a monumental Victorian Christmas-tree decoration. Close by is the 16th-century church of San Francisco with its beautiful cloister and housing the provincial museum. In an adjacent small square is the tiny 14th-century chapel of Santo Domingo.

From Lugo the route continues along the N 6 south east towards Villafranca del Bierzo. At first the road runs straight through fairly flat countryside, but from Baralia there are steep wooded hillsides and deep green valleys with lovely views from the Puerto de Árbol of big, rounded rolling hills patterned by woods and fields of wheat and vegetables. At Becereá there are the remains of the 12th-century monastery of Santa María. A short distance beyond at Doncas the ruins of a castle can be seen down in the valley.

The road climbs steadily upwards to the Puerto de Piedrafita. From here a small detour can be made along the Camino de Santiago to the delightful small pre-Romanesque church of Cebrero. Nearby are a number of *pallazos*, small thatched huts built of rough grey stone, which date back over 2000 years. One has been made into a small museum with ancient furniture and artefacts used to create an evocative interior.

About 20km further along the N 6, at the small village of Ambasmestas, a fascinating excursion can be made into the Sierra de Ancares. The road, signposted to Balboa, climbs alongside a sheltered green valley in which you can see the ruins of the castle of Balboa on a knoll above the village.

The scenery becomes incredibly impressive as the road ascends to the pass of El Portello. The top of the steep slopes are covered with broom and gorse, a blaze

The Templar castle in Ponferrada.

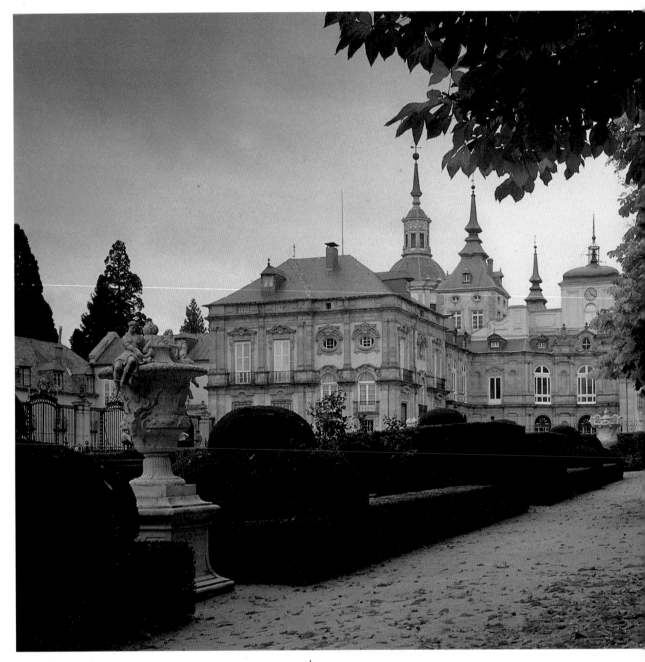

You can continue northwards to Sepúlveda through remote, hilly countryside planted with sunflowers, wheat and vegetables, with only the occasional small farmhouse to be seen between the small villages. Sepúlveda is in a dramatic setting. Its old houses are tiered up the slope of a steep hillside which overlooks a deep rocky gorge. The town's history dates back to Roman times and it contains many historic buildings as well as remains of its medieval walls and castle.

The route returns for about 12km to a junction with the C 112. Nearby is the impressive 12th-century Arab fortress at Condado de Castilnovo. Continuing westwards to Cantelejo, with a 17th-century church, the route then follows the C 603 south to Turégano where, inside the crenellated walls of a hilltop castle overlooking the town, is a 13th-century Romanesque church.

The tour continues to the west along the SG 222, joining the main road, the N 601, at Navalmanzano.

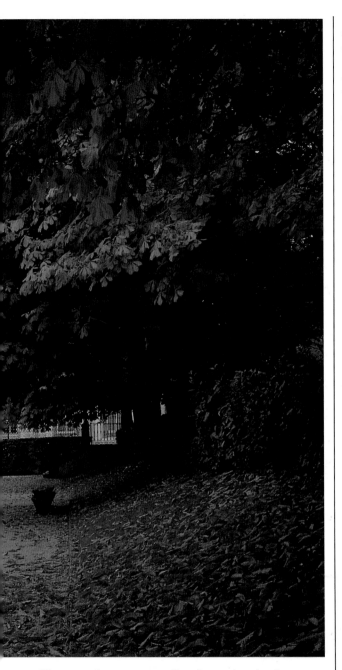

The route is now across flat, featureless landscape relieved only by pine trees and fields of sunflowers. About 23km to the north along the N 601 is Cuellar with a 15th-century castle, many ancient houses and several Mudéjar churches. If you have time, visit the castle of Peñafiel, about 30km further to the north-west. Over 200m long, it is one of the largest and most imposing in the region. The walls of the castle are punctuated by twelve elegant circular towers.

From Cuéllar the route follows the SG 342 to Navas de Oro where a road to the west leads to Coca. Here is one of the most attractive castles in Spain, built in the 15th century in brick by the Moors it has a moat and four octagonal towers. It is a rare and beautiful example of a fortress in the Mudéjar style.

The SG 351 continues westwards to Arévalo, a fascinating small town with a wealth of ancient buildings, a 14th-century castle, two 14th-century bridges and several arcaded squares. Madrigal de las Altes Torres, 26km to the west along the C 605, was the birthplace of Isabella the Catholic and her home until her marriage to Ferdinand of Aragón. The town is encircled by walls, relieved by lofty square towers. There is a well preserved gate with an archway and tower. The 15th-century palace in which Isabella was born now houses the Convent of Madres Augustinas de NS de Gracia. There is also a hospital with a Renaissance façade and the 12th-century Mudéjar church of San Nicolás de Bari.

The tour continues northwards along the C 610 for 26km to Medina del Campo, overlooked by the impressive 15th-century castle of La Mota. This lively, attractive town has many fine buildings including the Casa de Dueñas with a lovely patio, and the 16th-century collegiate church of San Antolín. The N 6 continues north towards Tordesillas, passing the wine town of Rueda with the richly decorated Baroque church of Santa María.

Tordesillas, an old town with narrow streets and an arcaded *plaza mayor*, is set high on a hill above the Río Duero. The most beautiful of its ancient buildings is the Real Monasterio de Santa Clara, a convent in a palace built for Alfonso XI in 1340. This fine example of Mudéjar architecture has an exquisite small patio framed by decorated arches. The Salón Dorado, the golden room, is richly gilded with an intricately decorated ceiling and containing 16th-century frescoes and paintings and a beautiful 13th-century altar.

The Parador Nacional de Tordesillas, a modern building in a pine forest about 1km south of the town (south of the N 620 in the direction of Salamanca) is a single-storey building of mellow brickwork with spacious rooms and a peaceful shady atmosphere. The menu includes a selection of dishes such as Tortilla de Patatas y Ajetes, omelette with potatoes and baby garlic cloves, and Mollejas en Salsa Casera, lamb's sweetbreads with a creamy sauce. Merluza al Ajillo is cutlet of hake cooked in oil with garlic. To finish the meal Santa Clara con Crocantes is a type of cake with ice cream. The wine list includes Verdejo Pálido from Rueda and also wines from Toro and Ribera del Duero.

San Idelfonso La Granja.

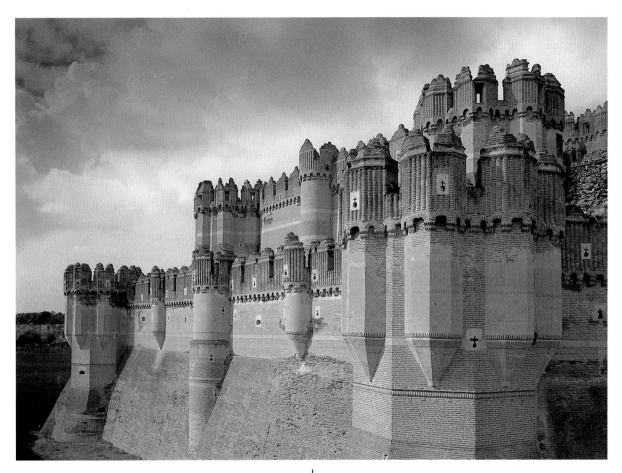

ZAMORA

THE NEXT STAGE OF THE TOUR is west to the Parador at Zamora, a distance of only 65km. I have outlined a circuitous route which first leads 30km north-east to Vallodolid. This large, busy city however would need a full day to do it justice. The main sights include the Cathedral which was completed in the early 18th century, contains a superb 16th-century retablo and fine choir stalls among its many treasures. Numerous churches include the 15th-century Santa María la Antigua and the 15th-century Las Angustias. The Colegio San Gregorio, a lovely building with Plateresque, Gothic and Mudéjar influences in its magnificently decorated façade and a beautiful Plateresque gallery now houses the National Museum of Sculpture. En route to Valladolid you will pass the town of Simancas whose picturesque château-like castle houses the National Archive, containing over 30 million documents.

The medieval town of Sepúlveda.

The Castillo de Coca.

12km to the north of Valladolid is the small town of Fuensaldaña whose well-preserved 15th-century castillo has a square keep and round towers at each corner. A small road, VA 514 follows a small valley to the village of Torrelobatón, dominated by a well-preserved, 15th-century castle. At Mota del Marqués, 16km further east is the lovely hall church of San Martín with a Plateresque portal; the Mudéjar chapel of NS de Castellaños, a Renaissance palace and the remains of a castle.

It is worth making a small detour to the north to visit the ancient, fortified hilltop town of Ureñua, still encircled by crenellated walls with old gateways and towers remaining. Close by, near Villa García de Campos, is the Monasterio de la Espina a lovely old building in a peaceful secluded valley. The villages in this region, formed of adobe houses coated with an ochre-coloured clay, look like old sepia photographs.

Continuing eastwards to Tiedra, where there is a

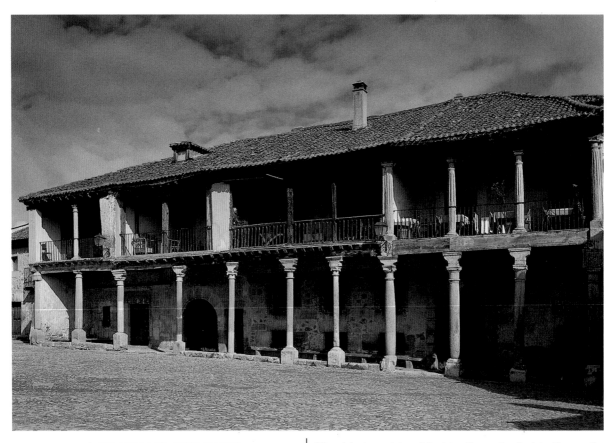

The Plaza Mayor of Pedraza de la Sierra.

ruined castle, then south-east along the C 519 through endless wheatfields to Toro, you pass another ruined castle at Villalonso. Toro, a small, ancient town, is famed for its wines. It has an imposing 13th-century church, the Collegiata Santa María la Mayor, set beside a shady square with views down to the Río Duero far below. Other interesting buildings include an 18th-century *ayuntamiento*, the 13th-century Mudéjar church of El Salvador and a 15th-century palace, now the Convent of Mercedarias Descalzas. The route continues 33km westwards along the N 122 to Zamora.

Zamora, built on a rocky hill, lies on the right bank of the Río Duero and is an historic city, at one time home both to the Romans and the Moors. In the church of Santiago de los Caballeros is the altar at which El Cid is said to have been knighted. The most distinctive of the city's buildings is the Byzantine cathedral which has a cupola tiled in a fish-scale pattern and beautiful doorways, particularly the Puerta del Obispo, decorated with particularly fine sculptures. The interior's treasures include a 15th-century retablo and a collection of

Flemish tapestries. Next to the cathedral is the castle surrounded by gardens with far-reaching views from the battlements.

The Portillo de la Traición, the traitor's gate, commemorates the murder of Sancho II asleep in his tent during a seige of the city in 1072. Other buildings of note include the Romanesque churches of Santa Magdalena and San Cipriano, the 12th-century church of Santa María de la Horta and the 17th-century *ayuntamiento*.

The Parador Nacional Condes de Alba y Aliste, set in a 15th-century palace on a quiet square in the city centre, has been sensitively converted, preserving a magnificent staircase and beautiful cloisters surrounding a courtyard. The decor includes suits of armour, tapestries and banners along with comfortable, traditionally styled furniture and antiques.

The menu includes Dos y Pingada, pieces of pork fillet cooked with eggs; Truchas a la Sanabresa, fresh fried trout; La Sanantonada, a rich dish of stewed white beans; and Chuleta de Cerdo Ahumada, smoked pork chop. The wine list includes some from neighbouring Toro. Sangre de Toro, literally bull's blood, is a full-bodied, highly alcoholic red wine quite different to that of the same name from Penedés in Cataluña.

A detour can be made to the Visigothic church of San Pedro de la Nave by taking the N 122 to the north-west and then forking right after 12km on to a small road to Campanillo. It is an attractive drive through remote countryside of wheatfields and oak trees. The small church, which has fine carved stone capitals, is thought to have been built in about 680. It was moved to its present position in 1932 before its original site was flooded to create the Embalse de Elsa.

Another small detour can be made to the south-east to Arcenillas where the Gothic church contains a collection of beautiful panels painted by Fernando Gallego in 1490. There is also a 13th-century Christ and a collection of religious dolls.

CIUDAD RODRIGO

FROM ZAMORA the next stage of the tour is south-west to the Parador at Ciudad Rodrigo, a direct journey of 151km. I have outlined a route which allows you to explore the countryside bordering Portugal and the valley of the Río Duero. Leaving the city to the south on the N 630, after crossing the river a road to the right, the C 527, leads towards Fermoselle. The first part of this journey is flat with rocky outcrops, stubby oak trees and small, isolated fields of grain. There is little sign of life between the occasional tiny villages.

Around Fermoselle the landscape changes, becoming more hilly and rugged with extensive areas of vineyards. It is a most attractive old town built on a rocky hill, with a castle and a 13th-century church with exceptional groin vaults and a tower. Under the medieval village houses and tangle of narrow cobbled streets there is a maze of ancient wine cellars. I was told by a villager, who insisted on giving me a guided tour, that they were over 800 years old.

The road continues southwards towards Salamanca descending in a series of steep curves into a ravine-like rocky valley, terraced with vineyards, olive groves and almond trees. The Río Tormes flows through it – a delightful spot for a picnic. It is remote, peaceful countryside and on the other side of the valley the ground is strewn with huge boulders. Beyond this is a region of open heathland which gives way to fields of grain and vineyards.

At the road junction the route turns right towards Villariño and Aldeadávila de la Ribera. The road continues southwards across flat heathland to Saucelle, a small, attractive village. About 3km further there is a dramatic viewpoint of the deep, plunging valley through which the Río Duero flows. The landscape here is of immense proportions. At the junction with the C 517 the route leads eastwards towards Lumbrales, with remains of Roman walls. 10km to the south is the ancient walled town of San Felices de los Gallegos, with the impressive remains of a castle surrounded by extensive walls. There is an unusual Romanesque church incorporating a gateway. About 40km to the north-east is Yecla de Yeltes, where there are the remains of an Iberian castle, the 16th-century church of San Sebastián and the Hermitage of NS del Castillo. From San Felices it is only 40km to Ciudad Rodrigo.

Ciudad Rodrigo is an enchanting old walled town set beside the Río Agueda with a splendid 14th-century castle perched high above it. The fortifications are well preserved: massive walls encircling the town are punctuated by impressive gateways and towers. Lining the streets and small squares are a wealth of mellow medieval buildings, many with seigneurial crests. The 13th-century Cathedral of Santa María has magnificent portals (the west in particular is exquisitely decorated), an early 16th-century Gothic cloister and finely carved choir stalls from the end of the 15th century. The 16th-century *ayuntamiento* is also a lovely building as is the Capilla del Cerralbo and the Casa de los Castros. Don't

A medieval mansion in Ciudad Rodrigo.

miss seeing the old post office, which still fulfils its purpose. The original desks and benches, ornate wrought iron grills and decorative panels and ceilings have all been preserved. A lively country market takes place in the square by the Capilla del Cerralbo on Tuesdays where baskets of fruit and vegetables are sold with dark and damp soil still clinging to their roots.

The Parador Nacional Enrique II is situated in the castle and a more enticing place to stay is hard to imagine. It is only a short walk from the *plaza mayor* (main square) which is full of character. I walked down in the evening for a drink before dinner and the sound of animated conversation and laughter reached me long before I arrived – like a distant party in full swing. There is a small garden on the steep hillside in front of the castle which provides lovely views down to the river. The bedrooms of the castle are linked by a series of tunnel-like corridors creating a cosy but fortress-like atmosphere. The restaurant is particularly attractive with a high-beamed ceiling and windows looking out over the river. The menu includes Magras de Cerdo en Cazuela, fillet of pork cooked in a rich tomato sauce and Perdiz Estofada Jardinera, braised partridge stuffed with vegetables. Roscas, delicious almond biscuits, are made in Saucelle.

An excursion to the south-west into the Sierra de la Peña de Francia can be made from Ciudad Rodrigo by leaving the city on the C 515 towards Béjar. Initially the route is quite flat along a quiet country road with a view of distant mountains. At El Maillo the route turns right towards La Alberca. After a few kms a small road detours to the right and climbs up towards the monastery of NS de la Peña de Francia, winding through wooded slopes thickly covered with cork oaks, fir trees and carpeted with bracken, rosemary and thyme. The lovely old blackened stone building could scarcely have a more dramatic setting. It is built on the very summit of a pinnacle of rock which rises more than 6000ft above sea level. It commands astonishing views over a full 360° and a *mirador* with direction signs enables you to identify distant features such as Bejar and the Embalse de Gabriel y Galán.

You can continue on a small circuit through the mountains, firstly to San Martín de Castañar, a small, captivating village with a web of narrow streets and alleys, lined with small rough-stone houses patterned by exposed timbers. They cascade with flowers which hang from wooden balconies and stone arcades. During my visit the villagers were busy with the cherry harvest. Huge brimming baskets of shiny red fruit from the trees on the hillsides around the village were being carried in on mules.

The village of San Martín de Castañar in the Sierra de Peña de Francia.

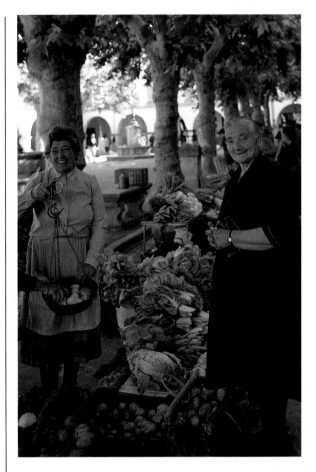

The weekly market in Ciudad Rodrigo.

There are beautiful views all around as the road continues through Sequeros to Miranda del Castañar, which has a castle and Romanesque church. A particularly pretty village with very steep cobbled alleys leading off from the main street, it is entered through a fortified gateway. The countryside is lush and green with orchards, fig and chestnut trees and small market gardens covering the hillsides.

The route continues through Cepedo, Sotoserrano and Madroñal to La Alberca. The road is a scenic delight, winding round the hillsides like a lateral helter-skelter and providing constantly changing views. La Alberca, a slightly larger but picturesque old town, is the capital of the region with an arcaded *plaza mayor* and a 17th-century church. Traditional plays, in which regional costumes and jewellery were worn, take place here in the square in mid-August.

If you do not want to return to Ciudad Rodrigo the nearest alternative Parador to La Alberca is at Jarandilla de la Vera (page 94).

*T*OUR 8 *Explores the provinces of Ávila, Salamanca and Cáceres in the western region of Castile-León and the northern part of Extremadura, including some exciting mountain scenery in the Sierra de Gredos, the atmospheric cities of Salamanca and Ávila and numerous small unspoilt villages. There are also some memorable castles in this region. The paradors featured include one unusual modern building with a superb outlook, two 15th-century palaces and a remote mountain lodge. The itinerary creates a round trip based on Madrid and the first parador at Ávila is about 120km from Madrid airport.*

— TOUR 8 —
MICHELIN MAP NOS. 447 & 441

SALAMANCA

ÁVILA

Sierra de Gredos

Jarandilla de la Vera

ÁVILA
SALAMANCA
JARANDILLA DE LA VERA
SIERRA DE GREDOS

ÁVILA

FROM MADRID the route is initially along the N 6 to the north-west of the city. At Las Rozas it forks left on to the C 505 to San Lorenzo de El Escorial, set in a peaceful wooded valley. This is the location of a vast monastery built during the reign of King Phillip II to mark his defeat of the French in 1557. The building, completed in 1584, is in the form of a large rectangle with towers at each corner. There are 12 cloisters, over 80 staircases, 16 chapels and 16 courtyards. The exterior is severe but its massive façade is extremely impressive.

The Patio de los Reyes (courtyard of the Kings) is entered through the main portal and decorated by huge statues of the Old Testament kings. The interior is a virtual maze of rooms, ante-chambers, corridors and staircases. The Royal Palace contains a wealth of tapestries, paintings and frescoes which decorate the walls from floor to ceiling and depict every aspect of medieval life. The library too is an extraordinary room: extravagantly decorated, it contains the most important collection of books in Spain. There is also an exquisite 16th-century Florentine planetarium. Most of the rooms can only be visited with a guided tour and it would be easy to spend a whole day here. The visitor's ticket also provides access to two Royal lodges nearby, Casita del Príncipe and the Casita del Arriba. 14km to the north of El Escorial is the Valle de los Caídos where there is a memorial to those who died in the Civil War.

From San Lorenzo the road climbs up out of the valley and over a winding pass through barren hillsides. Beyond, the road descends again through a rocky pine-clad valley to Las Navas del Marqués with its 15th-century Gothic church and a 16th-century fortified palace with a beautiful Renaissance courtyard.

The road continues through an open heath-covered landscape with views of distant mountains towards Ávila, a remarkable town set on a hill overlooking the Río Adaja. It is ringed by massive crenellated walls, the most complete and well preserved in Spain. They are 2.5km in circumference, over 10ft thick and 40ft high. Every 30m there is a tower, with 88 altogether. The town is entered through 9 fortified gateways, some of which are extremely beautiful.

The 12th-century cathedral was originally Romanesque in design but was continued in Gothic and Renaissance styles. It is still unfinished: the west façade has an incomplete tower. The interior walls are built from an unusual stone with red and white striations. The 12th-century churches of San Pedro and San Vincente, built of a mellow golden stone, are also of great interest. The 15th-century Dominican monastery of Santo Tomás has three cloisters of which the King's cloister is especially beautiful.

Ávila is the birthplace of Santa Teresa and there is a museum dedicated to her life and works in the Convento de las Madres. The Convento de Santa Teresa incorporates the house in which she was born. La Encarcina is the convent where the saint spent 27 years as a nun and a collection of relics are also kept here. Her cell has been converted into a chapel. The old town of Ávila also possesses many ancient palaces and mansions.

The Parador Nacional Raimundo de Borgoña is situated in part of the town walls just inside the Puerto de Carmen and only a few minutes' walk from the main square. There is a lively country market here on Fridays. The Parador is named after Count Raymond of Burgundy who regained the city from the Moors. The public rooms occupy a 15th-century palace known as the Piedras Altas, the high stones. Inside, an imposing marble staircase leads to the bedrooms which are housed in a modern extension built in traditional style. The Parador has a peaceful, secluded garden shaded by pine trees where you can climb up on to the ramparts and walk along the battlements.

Regional dishes on the menu include: Judías del Barco de Ávila, large white beans cooked in a rich paprika-flavoured sauce with *chorizo* and salt pork; and Pucherete Teresiano, a chunky soup with mixed vegetables and pieces of meat. A delicious and unusual local sweet is Yemas de Santa Teresa, candied egg yolks, golden yellow and intensely sweet that melt deliciously in the mouth. An interesting wine from the region is Cebreros: very strong with a distinctive flavour, it comes from a small village in the hills to the south.

One of the fortified gateways of Ávila.

Landscape near Solosancho.

An interesting excursion can be made into the wild, remote countryside of the Sierra de la Paramera to the south-west of Ávila. The route is initially along the N 110 towards Piedrahita. At Muñogalindo a road leads south through fields of grain bordered by dry stone walls to Solosancho. This region is known as the Wilderness of Ulaca, the site of an Iron age settlement. Solosancho is an ancient village of curious stone houses thatched with dried brushwood. In the centre is the 15th-century castle of Viciosa. Beyond the village an unsurfaced road climbs higher into the mountains where massive boulders are scattered on the hillsides which are carpeted with bushes of yellow broom and heather.

From Solosancho a small road, the C 502, turns back towards Ávila. Shortly a road to the right leads to Mironcillo. From here a rough road leads into a rugged and dramatic landscape to the 15th-century Castillo de Aunque-os-pese set above the village of Sotalvo and belonging to the Medinaceli family. The castle is in an impressive setting, built on a massive border from which its walls appear to be moulded. From here a quiet scenic road leads back via the village of Río Frio to Ávila.

SALAMANCA

THE NEXT STAGE OF THE TOUR is north-west to the Parador at Salamanca. The first part of the route follows the N 501 towards Peñaranda de Bracamonte. After about 1km a road leads to the village of Cardenosa. Nearby is a 4th-century BC Iron Age settlement. Continuing along the N 501 a road to the right leads to San Juan de la Encinilla. Nearby, in the village of Narros de Saldueña is a remarkable Mudéjar fortress complete with its portcullis.

At Peñaranda de Bracamonte are two large plazas surrounded by stone arcades, a large hall church and a Carmelite convent with a good cloister. From here the SA 114 leads south-west to Alba de Tormes, where Santa Theresa died and an important place of pilgrimage. The convent of Carmelitas Descalzas was founded by her in 1571 and contains the saint's relics in a casket beneath the altar. Other churches include San Juan (12th-century), mixture of Romanesque and Mudéjar, and the 12th-century churches of Santiago and San

Miguel also blend Mudéjar and Romanesque styles. A 16th-century tower remains from a palace which belonged to the Duke of Alba. From here the C 510 leads north-west to Salamanca.

The Parador Nacional de Salamanca, just outside the city on a knoll beside the Río Tormes, is aggressively modern in its design, tiered in blocks of white stone like a cubist's impression of a mountain. It commands magnificent views of the city which the bedrooms also enjoy from large balconies. It's worth waking early to see the sunrise over the city and at dusk it is equally memorable.

Among the Castilian dishes on the menu I chose Chuletas de Ternera a la Castellana, veal cutlets braised in sherry and served with asparagus and green beans. Tortilla Española is a potato omelette and has become a staple Spanish dish. It is not just an omelette, however – more like a rich golden brown cake of eggs and potatoes. Sometimes onions, peppers and other vegetables are added but the classic version is just eggs and potatoes cooked in olive oil. Pecho de Ternera con Guisantes is a veal stew with peas flavoured with thyme, parsley and saffron.

Salamanca is a quite magical city, endowed with many of the finest examples of the Plateresque style of architecture. The buildings are of a mellow golden stone which, when seen in the evening light, almost appears to glow.

The Plaza Mayor is arguably the most magnificent square in Spain. Built in the early 17th century it is surrounded by tall arcaded buildings with richly decorated Baroque façades. It is very much the hub of Salamanca and a wonderful place to experience the vibrant life of the city. To sit at a café table with *churros* and a coffee in the morning is to take breakfast in real style.

Nearby are the twin cathedrals. The new in Gothic style dates from the 17th century and the old, linked by a passage, was built in the 12th century. The façade of the early-16th-century University is perhaps the most famous example of Plateresque art. The Casa de las Conchas is also a famous landmark, a mansion decorated with sculpted shells, beautiful windows and coats of arms. The convent of San Esteban has a superb 16th-century Plateresque façade. The massive Roman bridge is also an impressive sight, spanning the Río Tormes on 26 arches and is over 400m long. There is so much more to see that a guide book is necessary to explore it fully.

JARANDILLA DE LA VERA

THE NEXT STAGE OF THE JOURNEY is south to the Parador at Jarandilla de la Vera. The route is south along the

The Plaza Mayor of Salamanca.

N 630 towards Béjar across open heath and pasture land. Béjar is a large busy town set high in a mountain valley at the foot of the Sierra de Candelario. There are remains of Moorish walls and the 16th-century Alcázar del Duque de Osuna with a Renaissance patio. A road leads high into the mountains to the curious village of Candelario in a lovely setting below a mountain peak. Its steep cobbled streets are lined by houses with overhanging balconies and unusual double stable-like doors. Curved tiles are used to cover the walls of the houses, giving them a strange ridged appearance. The older ladies of the village still wear their hair in an elaborately coiffured traditional style.

South from Béjar the road begins to descend along the side of the valley. After about 10km a road to the west detours into a peaceful wooded valley to the pretty hilltop village of Montemayor del Río with its castle and Roman bridge. Beyond Baños de Montemayor, a thermal resort of Roman origins, a road to the west leads to Hervás. Set among meadows and cherry orchards it possesses the churches of Santa María and San Juan Bautista, the latter with a fine Baroque retablo. There is also a well-preserved old Jewish quarter. A short distance further south a road to the west leads to Abadía. Here a Templar's castle was first converted into a Cistercian abbey and then into a palace for the Duke of Alba. It contains an exceptionally lovely two-storey Mudéjar cloister with horseshoe arches. The palace was designed in the 16th century by Flemish and Italian artists and once had a beautiful garden and parklands.

A few kms further to the west, overlooking the Embalse de Gabriel y Galán, is the deserted village of Granadilla with a 14th-century castle and a 16th-century church. Once an important town it was abandoned when the valley was flooded and now rests in serene isolation on the banks of a beautiful lake. It was the home of one of the Conquistadores who named two towns in Perú after it.

The road skirts the edge of the lake and then leads south-east to the ruins of Cáparra where an imposing Roman triumphal arch remains. The main road is regained after a few kms where the route continues south-west to the medieval town of Plasencia. Set on the banks of the Río Jerte it dates from Roman times. Parts of its extensive walls and towers remain together with the castle. The cathedral dates from the 13th century although the main structure was not completed until the 16th century. There are also many interesting churches and mansions.

The Parador at Jarandilla de la Vera is 56km to the east of Plasencia. There is however an interesting de-

The mountain village of Candelario.

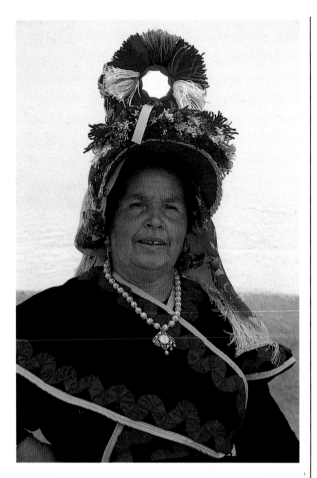

Traditional costume in Montehermoso.

tour further to the west of the city which I will describe now but which would need a separate day's excursion to complete.

The CC 204 leads west to Montehermoso, a small town famous for its curious local costume which is still occasionally worn. The hats, made of plaited straw, are elaborately embroidered and bejewelled, with a distinctly South American appearance. Local shops sell baskets and other gifts in the same style. A road leads south-west to Coria, an ancient city with extensive fortified walls and towers, a 15th-century castle, a Gothic cathedral with Renaissance additions and a fine Plateresque portal, the palace of the Duke of Alba, several interesting mansions, and an impressive Roman bridge spanning the river.

From Coria the C 526 leads south-east, passing the ruined castle of Portezuelo, to join the N 630 beside the Embalse de Alcántara. Continuing south for about 15km a road to the right leads to Garovillas whose spacious arcaded plaza is surrounded by whitewashed

houses and atmospheric old streets. Returning to the main road and heading northwards for 6km a road to the west leads to Monroy where there is a well-preserved castle and a lovely 15th-century Gothic church.

The route leads north-east along the CC 912 to Torrejón de Rubio. About 15km along this road you can make a detour to the left to Serradilla, with two old churches, and Mirabel where there are the ruins of a 12th-century castle, a church and a 16th-century palace.

At Torrejón the route leads north along the C 524 to the castle-like sanctuary of Monfragüe. This beautiful region is a natural park preserved for its wild life. The road runs beside a lake which is overlooked by towering crags. You can see eagles' nests perched on small ledges and watch the huge birds wheeling lazily around the cliff face. From here the road continues northwards to the Puerto de la Serrana and then to Palencia.

The route to Jarandilla continues eastwards along the C 501 with lovely views of the Río Tietar. About 1km beyond Jaraiz de la Vera, the centre of the region's tobacco and paprika cultivation, a road leads up into the mountains to the picturesque village of Garganta de Olla. A few kms further is Cuacos de Yuste, another unspoilt village of ancient arcaded houses.

A road leads into a peaceful wooded hillside to the Hieronomite monastery of Yuste, founded in 1408 and famous because Emperor Carlos V died here in 1558. You can visit the sombre, black-draped room in which he died. Some of his possessions, including his sedan chair – he suffered from gout – his bed and even the sheets in which he died have been preserved. There are two interesting cloisters and a 17th-century refactory decorated with Mudéjar *azulejos*.

The Parador Nacional Carlos V, on the edge of the town of Jarandilla de la Vera, occupies a 14th-century castle which belonged to the Counts of Oropesa and is one of the most evocative and historic buildings in the Parador network. The Emperor Carlos V lived here for two years while preparations were made for him at the monastery of Yuste. Charles de Gaulle also spent the night here.

An impressive inner courtyard is overlooked by a beautiful Renaissance gallery and imposing round towers. The interior is decorated with antique furniture, tapestries, paintings and ancient weapons. High-beamed ceilings, mellow wooden floors and open fireplaces create a medieval ambience combined with modern comfort.

The menu includes a number of regional specialties: Bacalao al Estilo de Yuste, dried salt cod cooked and combined with puréed potato and butter; Caldereta a la Jarandilla, lamb stew flavoured with paprika and garlic; Huevos a la Extremeña, eggs baked in a white sauce with peppers, onions and tomatoes and flavoured with paprika and parsley.

SIERRA DE GREDOS

The Sierra de Gredos near Hoyos de Espino.

THE NEXT STAGE OF THE TOUR is eastwards to the Parador at Navarredonda de Gredos. The route leads along the C 501 through a sequence of small villages similar to Jarandilla with old porticoed houses with wooden balconies and narrow cobbled streets. Candeleda is an attractive little town with timbered houses, balconies and arcades, and a 15th-century Gothic church. Beyond is Arenas de San Pedro, a large, popular summer resort at the foot of the Sierra de Gredos, containing the Castillo de la Triste Condesa (the castle of the sad countess) – a 15th-century castle in which the widow of Don Alvaro de Luna lived after he was beheaded on the orders of Juan II of Castile. There is also an 18th-century palace, a Gothic church and the 18th-century monastery of San Pedro de Alcántara with a fine retablo. Nearby is the village of Ramascastañas where there is an impressive stalactite cavern, the grotto of Romperropas.

From Arenas de San Pedro a small road climbs through impressive scenery to the attractive old village of Guisando set high on the mountainside. A road

continues along the course of a beautiful river, which tumbles down through the pine trees over rocks, and via the dramatically sited village of El Hornillo and El Arenal finally descends into the valley to Mombeltran. Here there is the beautiful 14th-century castle of the Duques of Alberquerque with its imposing façades, courtyards and staircases, strikingly set against a backdrop of the snow-capped peaks of the Sierra de Gredos. The town also has 15th-century Gothic church, a 16th-century Renaissance hospital and several medieval mansions with escutcheons.

The route continues northwards along the C 502 to the picturesque village of Cuevas de Valle where it begins to climb towards the Puerto de Pico. The views from this road are sensational. If, like me, you enjoy driving over mountain passes this is one to remember. At the top you can see the remains of the old Roman road.

The route continues north for about 6km and then the C 500 leads west along a shallow valley to San Martín del

Pimpolar. The countryside here is intensely green with small trees and boulders dotting the meadows and mountainsides.

The Parador Nacional de Gredos – the first ever parador – is over 6000ft above sea level in a peaceful, isolated setting surrounded by snow-covered peaks. Built in 1928 on a site chosen by King Alfonso XIII, it is in the midst of some of the finest hunting and fishing countryside in Spain. It has, not surprisingly, the atmosphere of a hunting lodge with polished pine floors, wooden beams and comfortable leather furniture. A long verandah extends along the rear of the Parador with an outlook of pine forests and snow-covered peaks.

The menu included: Truchas con Almejas con Vino de Cebreros, a delicious dish of mountain trout and clams poached in the white wine of nearby Cebreros; and Codornices a la Casera, quail cooked in the oven with ham, white wine, mushrooms and onions. For the sweet-toothed, Tocino de cielo (literally, 'salt pork from heaven'), a rich egg custard coated with a caramel sauce.

An excursion into the Sierra de Gredos can be made by continuing westwards along the C 500 to Hoyos del Espino, where a medieval bridge spans the Río Tormes. Here a road leads south along a wide green valley deep into the mountains. Broad meadows of springy green turf threaded by brooks reach away to the snow-clad peaks and a fast-flowing river crashes over boulders.

From Hoyos del Espino the road continues to a junction where the AV 932 leads north towards Piedrahita. The road winds high along the side of a steep V-shaped valley through which a river rushes. The slopes are patterned with dry stone walls and as the road climbs higher the views become increasingly impressive. La Herguijela is a tiny village of red-tiled rough-stone houses completely untouched by the 20th century. The landscape here has a stark and savage beauty. Beyond at the Puerto de la Pena Negra the views are immense. The road descends to the lovely small town of Piedrahita with a 15th-century Gothic church, an 18th-century palace where the Duke of Alba was born, the 12th-century church of La Asunción and a Carmelite convent.

The route leads south-west along the N 110 to El Barco de Ávila, on the banks of the Río Tormes. Overlooking the town is the 14th-century castle of Valdecorneja. There is also a 14th-century Gothic church with a massive tower and an interior with many fine features. The return to the Parador can be made by following the C 500 to the east.

The nearest alternative Parador to Gredos is at Oropesa, 90km (page 120). The route back towards Madrid can incorporate an excursion into the eastern region of the Sierra de Gredos. From Gredos the route is initially

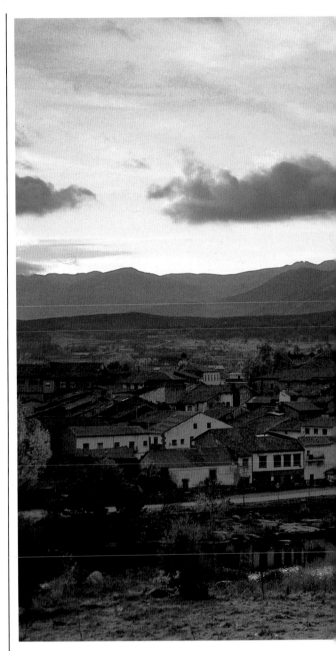

back along the C 502 to the Puerto del Pico. A few km further south a road leads eastwards into pine-clad mountains to the attractive village of San Esteban del Val. The road continues through dramatic mountain scenery to Pedro Bernardo, perched on the very edge of the mountain, from where there are extraordinary views.

The road descends to join the C 501 where the route continues eastwards to Piedralaves, which has a picturesque old quarter with ancient galleried houses and

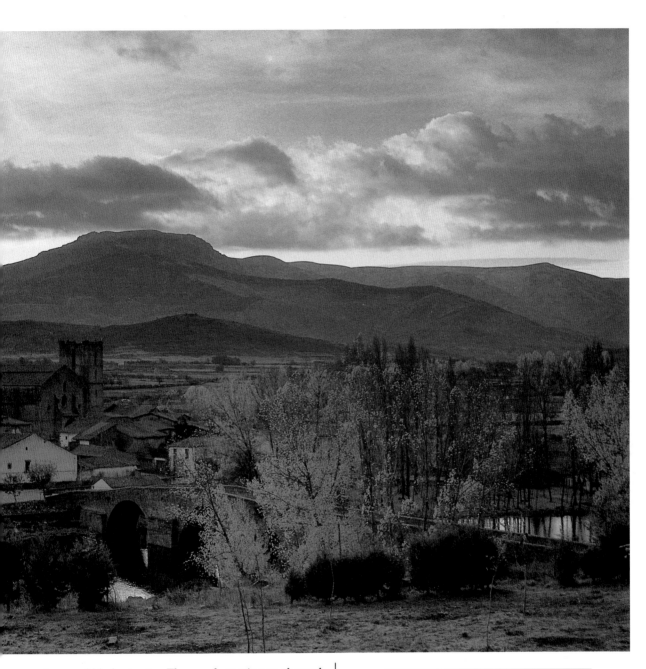

El Barco de Ávila.

steep cobbled streets. The road continues through green meadows to Adrada, with its ruined castle, and San Martín de Valdeiglesias. Nearby are the Toros de Guisando, curious granite sculptures of bulls believed to be of Iberian origin. Here too is the 14th-century monastery of Guisando. A few kms to the north is El Tiemblo where there is a large fortress-like 16th-century church.

Here the AV 501 leads westwards through remote rocky hillsides patterned with vineyards to the wine town of Cebreros. There is a 16th-century Renaissance church, the ruins of a monastery and several medieval mansions in the town – as well as several shops where the unusual local wine can be bought. The road continues north-east to join the C 505 between Ávila and El Escorial.

*T*OUR 9 Explores the region to the north-west of Madrid beginning in the province of Guadalajara and leading north into Soria. It includes one of the most beautiful monasteries in Spain, an atmospheric medieval town, a remarkable hidden valley and numerous villages and castles. Linked with tour No. 5 (page 60) it provides a scenic route between Madrid and the French border. The first Parador at Sigüenza is about 150km from Madrid airport.

SIGÜENZA

FROM MADRID AIRPORT the route leads first along the N 11 eastwards past Alcalá de Henares to Guadalajara, the capital of the province. It continues north-east along the N 11 for about 20km until you reach a road to the right, the C 20. Here you can make a small detour to visit Brihuega, a picturesque old town on a hill beside the Río Tajuna, with a number of interesting old buildings along its typically narrow streets including four Romanesque churches. There is a festival held here in August when the bulls are run through the streets as in Pamplona.

Returning to the main road the tour continues north-east for another 10km and then turns left on to the GU 134 to Jadraque. The road runs along the almost sheer edge of a high ridge which overlooks a vast plain below with superb panoramic views. As the road descends in a series of wide sweeping curves the 15th-century castle of Jadraque comes dramatically into view. It is set on the summit of a steep conical hill on the side of the valley. A rough track leads up to the castle from where you can see for miles across the vast patterned plain.

Returning a short distance back along the road and then taking a right fork on to the C 101 leads to Hita, a picturesque walled village strikingly set at the foot of a lofty hill. Here there is a well-preserved, 12th-century gate, an arcaded plaza and the ruined monastery of Sopetrán. A small road, the GU 144, heads north to the town of Cogolludo set below a ruined castle. On one side of its large arcaded plaza is the magnificent 15th-century Palacio de Medinaceli, built in Renaissance style with a finely decorated façade of mellow golden stone and a Plateresque portal.

From Cogolludo the GU 151 continues northwards towards Hiendelaencina. The countryside here is peaceful with gently sloping hillsides planted with pine forests and covered in green springy turf and heather. Hiendelaencina is a most curious place, a village of small stone houses set in a wide green valley with few trees and divided by numerous dry stone

—TOUR 9—
MICHELIN MAP NO. 442
• VALLODOLID
• Soria
Santa María de Huerta
Sigüenza

SIGÜENZA
SANTA MARÍA
DE HUERTA – SORIA

walls and dotted with the remains of ancient silver mines, now abandoned.

From Hiendelaencina the GU 152 continues northwards through a small secluded rocky valley covered in brush. Wild thyme, sage and rosemary grow beside the road and a small river traces its course over a rocky bed. The village of Naharros is built out of the grey stone boulders scattered on the slopes, as are the numerous dry stone walls bordering the fields. Just beyond, the medieval walled village of Atienza comes into view at the widening of the valley. Its houses are spread down the slopes of a steep rocky hill and a ruined castle looks down over the village rooftops from the summit and the towers of several old churches are visible. A road goes up to and beyond the village and a small track leads up to the castle where there are far-reaching views over endless fields of wheat and sunflowers to distant mountains. There are seven churches dotted throughout the village.

The route follows the C 114 eastwards towards Sigüenza. Just beyond the village of Imon there are extensive salt pans which are still in use with two enormous, ancient stone warehouses to store the salt. At the junction a little further on a brief detour to the left brings you to the village of Riba de Santiuste where there is an impressive castle on a rocky hill beside the small village.

Returning southwards, about 5km before reaching Sigüenza, a small road to the right leads to the partially deserted village of Palazuelos, with well-preserved remains of its walls, the ruins of a castle and a gateway. Although rather derelict it has considerable charm and atmosphere. Continuing south for a few kms a curve in the road suddenly reveals a dramatic view of the old town of Sigüenza. It is set on a hill in the fertile valley of the Río Henares and is surrounded by orchards and fields of grain.

Sigüenza is a quite magical place. Very old and with a rather faded glory it evokes the feeling of a medieval stronghold and is dominated by its castle which, built by the Arabs in the 12th century, looms high above the steep cobbled streets of the town. The 12th-century cathedral is also fortified. Facing on to a beautiful plaza surrounded by stone arcades, it contains the tomb of a young nobleman ornamented by one of the most important Romanesque religious sculptures in Spain, known as the Doncel. The sacristy contains a beauti-

The cathedral of Sigüenza.

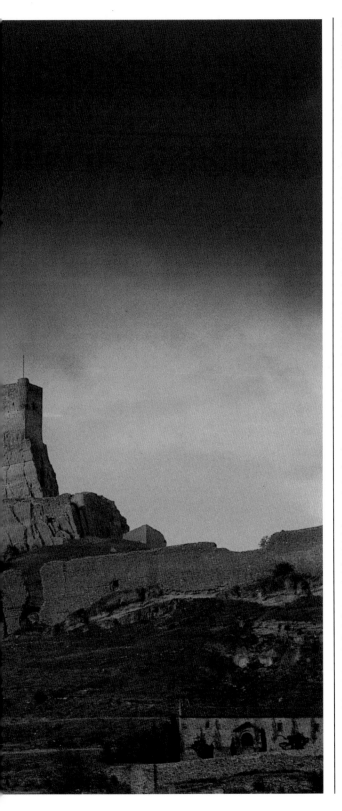

fully decorated ceiling by Covarubias and there are paintings by El Greco and Titian. Many interesting old buildings and the narrow streets provide rewarding hours of exploration. A lively market is held just outside the town walls on Saturdays.

The Parador Nacional Castillo de Sigüenza is situated within the Moorish castle walls and is one of the most magnificent of the historic paradors. It is a few minutes' walk down the hill to the cathedral and the *plaza mayor*. The lounge is an enormous room with a lofty beamed ceiling luxuriously furnished and decorated with tapestries, suits of armour, banners and seignorial crests. The restaurant, situated in the tower of Doña Blanca, is dominated by huge stone arches.

The menu has a good selection of Castilian dishes, including excellent roast meats like suckling pig and lamb; Chuletas de Ternera a la Madrileña, pork chops coated with chopped onion garlic and herbs and roasted; and Cocido Castellano, a stew with chick peas, potatoes, cabbage, salt pork and chorizo. Navercillos appear on the menu in the autumn when in season and are the wild orange-brown fungi found in the pine forests. Cooked with garlic and serrano ham they have a unique flavour and texture. Along with the more familiar Riojas and Valdepeñas wines, look out for those from Ribera del Duero, a wine-growing region to the north around the town of Aranda de Duero. Of these the most renowned is the fine red wine of the Vega Sicilia vineyards.

SANTA MARÍA DE HUERTA

THE NEXT STAGE of the tour is north-east to Santa María de Huerta, a direct journey of only 64km. Leaving Sigüenza on a small road to the north-east leads to the small village of Guijosa where there are the remains of a castle. A fascinating house has been carved out of a huge rock in the nearby village of Alcolea de Pinar, next to the main road, the N 11. It took Luis Bueno 20 years to carve a series of tunnels and chambers to form a small home with a fireplace and even windows.

The route leads along the N 11 north for 17km to the town of Medinaceli. This is reached by a small road leading off about 1km to the west. Set on the summit of a high hill, commanding sweeping views over the plain below, it is an ancient Iberian settlement which subsequently became both a Roman and Arab stronghold. It has an impressive 2nd-century Roman arch, the 16th-century church of Santa María and the Monasterió of Beatario San Ramón. An imposing arcaded plaza is overlooked by an 18th-century Ducal palace. However, the town is now almost completely

The hilltop village of Atienza.

deserted and has a strange, ghost-town atmosphere.

Continuing north-east from Medinaceli along the N 11, the route follows the valley of the Río Jalón to Arcos de Jalón, which has the remains of a castle. It is a richly fertile region with crops of all varieties including orchards. The river flows dark and thick like red mud. Santa María de Huerta is unremarkable but for the impressive Benedictine monastery in its midst. Founded in the 12th century by Alfonso VII, among the features that make it one of the most beautiful in Spain are enormous rose windows, a magnificent Gothic cloister and an 18th-century Baroque retablo. There are also fine Plateresque choir stalls, frescoes illustrating the battle of Navas de Tolosa and a huge vaulted Gothic refactory. The guided tour which is offered provides a fascinating hour or so.

The Parador Nacional de Santa María de Huerta, situated just off the N 11 about 1km east of the town, is a spacious, comfortable and modern, motel-style building. The restaurant, in common with all paradors, offers regional food as well as the more familiar

The fortified gateway of Hita.

Spanish dishes: Potaje de Garbanzos y Espinacas, a substantial soup of chick peas, spinach, salt cod, tomatoes, onions and eggs; and Perdiz Escabechada, partridge cooked in a sauce of olive oil, onions, herbs, wine and wine vinegar, left to marinade for several days and served at room temperature. The wine list includes those from the region of Cariñena, 50km to the east, as well as Ribera del Duero and Riojas.

A further enjoyable excursion can be made into the countryside to the east. Leaving Santa María the route leads to the east for about 25km through a rocky valley which becomes progressively deeper and narrower. The spa town of Alhama de Aragón is situated between two cliffs in the deepest part of the valley, the road passing through a tunnel. A few kms further east is the old town of Ateca which possesses two imposing Mudéjar towers. 14km further to the east is the old town of Calatayud, a castle set among, and blending with, clay-coloured hills within which are troglodyte dwellings – some still populated. The town contains many old buildings including a ruined castle the 17th-century church of Santo Sepulcro and the 16th-century church of Santa María. There are several Mudéjar towers and an old Judería. The Convent of Santo Domingo is just outside the town.

Returning westwards to Ateca an attractive scenic road, the Z 461, leads south to Nuevelos, passing along the side of the Embalse de Tranquera. Although the hills are dry and clay-like the valley is rich and fertile with orange and almond trees mingling with fields of vegetables and grain. From Nuevelos the road continues to the beautiful Cistercian Monasterio de Piedra, founded in the 12th century and now converted into a luxury hotel. The monastery is built on the side of a deep wooded valley into which water cascades from all directions. It varies from a gentle trickle between mossy banks to a raging torrent, bouncing over boulders creating dramatic waterfalls.

A series of footpaths lead down into the valley, into numerous hidden corners and along the shores of lakes and rivers. At one point a pathway is tunnelled vertically into the hillside behind the largest of the waterfalls which is 40m in depth. Halfway down it opens into a huge cavern behind a massive wall of water – a memorable experience.

The route returns to the N 11 at Alhama de Aragón following a small scenic road to the left, the Z 410 just after crossing the head of the Embalse de la Tranquera. The road passes a picturesque village, Godojos, with a ruined castle and a church with a Mudéjar tower. At Alhama de Aragón the route leads west along the N 11 towards Santa María.

SORIA

THE NEXT STAGE of the tour is north to the Parador at Soria, a direct journey of 104km. Leaving the parador at Santa María de Huerta, the route is first for a few kms along the N 11 to the east. Then turn north on to the C 116 to Monteagudo de las Vicarias. Here there are impressive town walls with gateways, a 15th-century castle and a 16th-century church with a Gothic portal.

This road continues north through remote countryside to Moron de Almazán where there is a lovely 15th-century church with a Plateresque tower overlooking a small square surrounded by medieval mansions. After continuing north for 14km the road joins the N 11 at

The cloister at Santa María de Huerta.

In the valley of the Monasterio de Piedra.

Almazán, an attractive old town beside the Río Duero. A bridge crosses the broad river with tall poplar trees lining its banks. It has the 12th-century church of San Miguel, the 18th-century Ermita de Jesús, the Puerta del Mercado and the medieval Palace of Altamira set on the banks of the river.

Just to the south of the bridge a small road, the C 116 leads west to Berlanga de Duero. Here there is a most impressive 15th-century castle set on a stony ridge with vast encircling walls. Narrow cobbled streets radiating from a picturesque *plaza mayor* are lined with many old houses decorated with wooden arcades. A detour of 12km to the south-east leads to the Ermita de San Baudelio, an 11th-century Mozarabic chapel.

From Berlanga the road continues west to Gormaz where there is another vast, impressive castle with extensive walls encircling the steep hill on which it is built. A road winds up the hill towards it and there are magnificent views over the plain below with a patchwork pattern of fields reaching away to the horizon. The road leads west through vast pine forests to El Burgo de Osma, an atmospheric old town with arcaded streets and a magnificent 13th-century cathedral that is considered one of the finest in Spain.

A short detour 14km to the west along the N 122 leads to San Esteban de Gormaz beside the Río Duero, with an ancient bridge and two attractive 12th-century churches with exterior galleries, San Miguel and del Rivero.

From El Burgo de Osma the route continues northwards along the SO 920 towards San Leonardo de Yague, an attractive scenic route along the valley of the Río Ucero, with rocky, pine-clad hillsides and poplar trees lining the river banks. The town of Ucero is picturesquely sited with an impressive castle mounted above it. Beyond the town a small road leads off to the left into the Canyón de Río Lobos, a small, secluded valley bordered by high cliffs and pinnacles of rock which soar above you. A small river runs between grassy banks and pinewoods – a perfect place to take a picnic lunch.

Returning to the main road it climbs northwards up a steep winding pass out of the valley with magnificent views. At San Leonardo de Yague, where there is a 16th-century castle, the route turns right on to the N 234 towards Soria, an agreeably quiet road passing through hills covered in pine forests. At Abejar you can turn to the north on to the SO 840 to Molinos de Duero, town of warm-coloured stone houses set beside the river.

The road continues through vast pine forests to Vinuesa, an attractive old town set on a hillside with narrow cobbled streets and ancient houses. Along this road I stopped to watch an elderly couple collecting Nacillos the large brown fungi which grow wild under the pine trees. They showed me a huge basket which they had collected that morning and were taking to market on the following day.

From Vinuesa a small road, the SO 830, turns to the left to head deeper into the pine forest towards La Laguna Negra de Urbión. Bracken and green springy turf cover the ground under the pines and the peace is undisturbed. You need to follow the road to the very end and from here a rough footpath leads off over rocky ground towards the lake. Nearby a river tumbles over small boulders and is almost hidden by the trees which line its banks. When you reach the lakeside you have to clamber over huge rocks before it is revealed. On the opposite side a monumental cliff towers above the glasslike water and a cascade tumbles down its face. It is rimmed by enormous rocks and boulders, between which pines and small trees grow – a tempting place to linger and there are beautiful walks into the surrounding woods – and would be worth considering as a separate excursion from the Parlor at Sovia. From here you must retrace the road to Vinuesa and follow the SO 821 until it joins the N 234 18km west of Soria.

Soria, situated on the right bank of the Río Duero between two hills, is an ancient city regained from the Moors by Alfonso of Aragón and later ceded to Castile. Its ancient buildings are of a reddish stone giving it the quality of an old sepia photograph. One of the most beautiful buildings is the 12th-century church of Santo Domingo whose exquisite Plateresque façade is decorated with fine sculptures. The co-Cathedral of San Pedro is situated on the edge of the town close to the river and has a fine Plateresque portal as well as a 12th-century Plateresque cloister. Nearby, on the banks of the river, is San Juan de Duero, an old monastery of the Order of the Templars, which has preserved a most unusual cloister with horseshoe arches. Among many other interesting buildings in the old part of the city is the Renaissance Palace of the Counts of Gomara, an enormous building with an imposing and ornately decorated façade.

The Parador Antonio Machado, a stylish modern building set on the very brink of the hill overlooking the river, just outside the city, occupies the site of the ruined castle and is now a park with sweeping views over the ancient rooftops, the mountains beyond and the silvery Duero far below. The Parador is named

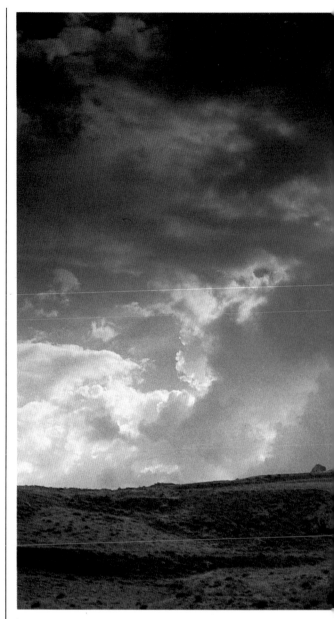

after a renowned Spanish poet who made Soria both his home and his inspiration. The restaurant has large picture windows providing an impressive panorama. The furnishing and decor are a departure from many of the more modern paradors since elegant contemporary furniture is used, together with polished pine floors and pastel-coloured walls which are decorated with modern prints and paintings.

The menu contains Castilian dishes as well as some from neighbouring Rioja and Navarra: Judías del Burgo de Osma, green beans cooked in a casserole with garlic and serrano ham; and Trucha Escabechada, fried trout

The Castillo of Gormaz.

marinaded in olive oil, white wine and wine vinegar and flavoured with herbs and garlic, and served at room temperature. The wine list includes a selection from Navarra and Ribera de Duero as well as those from the Rioja.

From Soria it is only a short distance to visit Numancia, an ancient settlement of the Iberians and the site of a heroically defended siege against the invading Romans. In 134 BC they could hold out no longer and, rather than surrender, destroyed their city and committed mass suicide. It is situated on a hilltop 7km to the north of Soria along the N 111 near the village of Garray. Today there is little left to see other than stones which trace the course of streets and the foundations of dwellings. The site however commands extensive views all around and evokes a heroic sense of history.

The nearest alternative paradors to Soria are at Calahorra, 116km (page 60) and Santo Domingo de la Calzada, 151km (page 58).

*T*OUR 10 *Encompasses one region which is associated with Cervantes, the plain of La Mancha. Comprising five provinces rich in Spanish history – Cuenca, Ciudad-Real, Guadalajara, Toledo and Albacete, traditionally known as New Castile and now forming the Autonomous Community of Castile-La Mancha – it also includes the southern environs of the city of Madrid and the beautiful medieval city of Toledo.*

Miguel de Cervantes has probably done more to promote tourism in inland Spain than any other person and through his legendary character, Don Quixote, has helped to impart a romantic, almost unworldly atmosphere to a region of Spain that is, on the surface, the least well-endowed scenically.

The countryside of La Mancha (from the Arabic *manxa* = 'parched earth') is an extraordinarily flat and expansive tableland, starkly contrasting with the hills and plateaux that rise above the plain – almost, it seems, in defiance – and which, by sheer comparison, are as grand and lofty as any mountain range.

The land itself is called *secano* (unirrigated), but ironically it is a richly fertile region. Vast cornfields alternate with the largest areas of vineyards in the country (from whose grapes come the famous Valdepeñas wine) and they combine with the regimental silver-green rows of olive trees to create the uniquely patterned nature of the La Mancha landscape.

The soil is predominantly a rich terracotta brown with occasional patchworks of chalky white, but through the spring and summer months the Meseta is transformed: entire fields of poppies of a colour and intensity which would otherwise only exist in a paintbox; acres of purple-flowering saffron; or small areas smothered in flowers of every colour and hue that nature has to offer.

The tour starts in the village of Chinchón, less than an hour's drive south of Madrid, then west to the city of Toledo. From here the route strikes south to the adjacent towns of Manzanares and Almagro in the heart of La Mancha.

CHINCHÓN

THE TOWN OF CHINCHÓN can be reached by leaving Madrid on the N 3 and then turning right on to the M 302. The latter part of this road provides an attractive scenic drive as it climbs out of the wide, flat valley of the Río Jarama into the rocky hills among which Chinchón is situated.

The Parador Nacional de Chinchón was once an

— TOUR 10 —
MICHELIN MAP NO. 444

CHINCHÓN
TOLEDO
MANZANARES
ALMAGRO

Augustinian convent. The original convent was founded by the lords of Chinchón in the 15th century in a different part of the town and the present site has been occupied since the 17th century. Since then, however, the building, constructed of the slim, ochre-coloured bricks typical of the region, has been used as the town's courthouse and jail. It adjoins a lovely old church, Santa María del Rosario, the entrance of which is next to the Parador.

This elegant building has a large patio and extensive gardens at the rear. Leafy green trees create a cool and shady retreat. Here, on the garden benches, you can relax and contemplate. Nearby is a large swimming pool within a separate walled patio, shaded by a tiled rood.

The interior contains numerous corridors linking a series of staircases and ante-rooms, all beautifully furnished with antiques and decorated with paintings, tapestries, painted ceilings and frescoes. The atmosphere is peaceful and luxurious.

The superb restaurant is lined with painted alcoves on one side and long, garden windows on the other. The menu includes many regional dishes: Sopa de Almendros, a light, creamy soup, delicately flavoured with almond, garlic and lemon, and garnished with lightly toasted, flaked almonds; Lechazo al Horno con Patatas Panaderíos, roast baby lamb served with potatoes; and Merluza a la Cazuela con Almejas, casserole of hake with clams.

Two puddings which are specialities of the Parador are Pastel de Monje, monk's cake, a rich creamy concoction, and Yemas de Chinchón, candied egg yolks. The wine list includes red, white and *rosé* wines from Chinchón and the neighbouring village of Colmenar as well as a selection of Riojas, Penedés and Manchegan wines.

The Parador could hardly be more conveniently situated, tucked away behind one corner of one of the prettiest and most unusual *plazas mayores* (main squares) in the region. It is a circular 'square', surrounded by three-storeyed houses with arcades and wooden balconies supported on ancient timber beams. The square is overlooked by the 16th-century parish church of NS de la Asunción set on a hill above the square. A tree-shaded square next to the church is a popular gathering place for the villagers in the cool of the evening. Here they can enjoy a delightful bird's-eye view of the village rooftops and the square below.

The square has been a venue for bullfights since 1502 and one is still held each year on 25 July. Theatrical performances are also mounted in the square during

Holy Week and a lively market takes place every Saturday. Other buildings of interest in the town are the Monastery of the Mothers of St Clare, the Hermitage of San Antonio, and Chinchón Castle which is on the edge of the town. The 15th-century castle is in the Gothic style – four-sided with circular keeps. Although parts of the ramparts have crumbled away, the large stone bridge and drawbridge remain and the building still has a formidable presence.

Chinchón is also famed for its anisette liqueur which is popular all over Spain.

THE ENVIRONS

CHINCHÓN IS NEAR ENOUGH to Madrid for it to be a convenient base for visiting the capital, for those who prefer not to stay in the city centre. Of course, like any major city Madrid has an enormous variety of interests to offer the visitor and a separate guidebook to the city will be essential if you are to explore it fully, or even if you only have time for a brief visit.

Before starting the journey to Toledo, which is the next parador on the route, a detour of some 50km to the north-east is well worth while in order to visit the town of Alcalá de Henares. From Chinchón you take

The Plaza Mayor of Chinchón.

the M 330 towards Madrid and after about 10km turn right on to the C 330 through Morata de Torres to Arganda, which is known for its wines. Here you cross the National Highway 3 and continue along the C 300 to Alcalá de Henares.

There is however an interesting detour which you can make en route – to the ruined 13th-century Castillo de Casaola. At the point where you should turn right for Morata de Torres, turn left, instead. After about 1km you will see an unsurfaced road to the left leading off into the countryside through vineyards and small farms. Crossing a bridge over the river Tajuna, turn right and soon you will see the ruined castle perched up high on a large rock. Although in ruins, its precarious setting and the sweeping views from its precipitous walls make it a memorable place.

Alcalá de Henares is a lively town with a unique character. It has been the seat of a number of Spanish kings as well as the home of a great university, Universitas Complutensis. It was also the birthplace of Miguel de Cervantes Saavedra (1547–1616). His

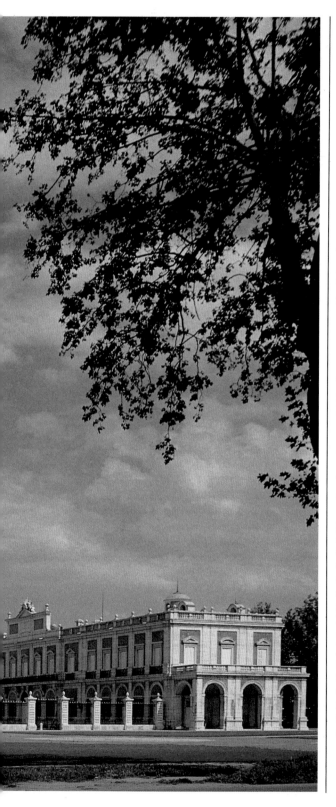

memory is marked by a square shaded by plane trees, Plaza Cervantes, and also by the Casa Cervantes, a reconstruction of a 16th-century house on the site of his original home.

The most important building however is the Colegio de San Idelfonso, the university building first founded in 1498 by Cardinal Cisneros and completed in 1508. The Plateresque façade (so called because its ornate style of decoration resembles the intricate, embossed work of silversmiths) was built in 1543 and is considered one of the most beautiful in Spain. Among the many other lovely old buildings are the church of San Idelfonso and the Archbishop's Palace. There is also a Hostería Nacional del Estudiante, a restaurant run by the National Tourist Board which is situated in a Castilian hall, once part of the former Colegio de San Jerónimo. In addition to the excellent regional food (you can try the wines of Arganda here), there is an enchanting patio named the Three Languages Patio, because Latin, Hebrew and Greek were once taught in the college.

The route I have suggested from Chinchón to Toledo will take you to a number of other places of interest. 5km to the south of Chinchón along the M 330 is the wine-growing village of Colmenar de Oreja. During my 1986 visit the *plaza mayor* with its arcades and balconies was undergoing extensive restoration. There is also the 15th-century church of Santa María la Mayor.

From Colmenar de Oreja continue a short distance to the south the TO 315 to Noblejas and turn right along the N 400 to Ocaña with its arcaded *plaza mayor*, several interesting churches and the palace of the Dukes of Frías. From here it is only 16km to the north along the N 4 to the town of Aranjuez.

This town is something of a surprise: it is lush and green with broad avenues and gardens shaded by huge trees. Like an oasis in the summer-bleached plain south of Madrid, the town is known for its asparagus and strawberries. It is also famed for its imposing, pink and orange stone royal palace (built in 1727 by Philip V as a summer residence), flanked by pavilions with arcades facing a green, tree-shaded open space. The Parterre, a beautiful formal garden, is to be found to the east of the palace. Two other lovely gardens are the Jardín de la Isla, set on an island in the middle of the river Tajo, and the Jardín del Príncipe, containing many magnificent trees and situated to the north-east of the town. The Casita del Labrador, or the workman's house is a small, classical mansion built by Charles IV with an extravagantly furnished and decorated interior, set within a pretty park.

The Royal Palace at Aranjuez.

Leaving Aranjuez on the N 4 to the north for about 10km and then turning right on to the TO 421 will take you first to the village of Esquivias, where the marriage of Cervantes is recorded in the church register of Santa María, and then to Illescas. The town was a royal residence in the 15th-century and its 13th-century parish church has a 14th-century Mudéjar bell tower. Mudéjar is a blend of Moorish and Gothic architectural styles. The Hospital Santuario de la Virgen de la Caridad contains five paintings by El Greco as well as a wealth of fine sculptures, altar pieces and altar paintings.

From Illescas, before continuing south along the N 401 to Toledo, take a brief detour to the north-west along the N 403 to visit the Castillo de Barcience, a well-preserved castle set on a quiet pine-covered hillside.

TOLEDO

THE NATIONAL PARADOR Conde de Orgaz, situated on a hill overlooking the city of Toledo, is spacious and modern, built in the style and out of materials typical of the region. A small road winds around the edge of the ravine (which encloses the Río Tagus) and the city,

and climbs to the Parador from which there are breathtaking views. The old town is almost encircled by a loop in the river and gives the impression of being on an island, or appears like an impregnable fortress surrounded by a moat.

The Parador takes full advantage of its commanding situation and has been designed to give the majority of the bedrooms memorable views from their balconies. An enormous terrace provides the perfect setting to relax with a drink in the evening and watch the lowering sun turn the ancient buildings below to gold. The building has a rocky garden in front with a small path which winds down to join the road below. The city is only about 3km away so that it is quite possible to walk into the centre without needing to be too energetic.

Among the many Castilian specialities which the menu features is Mojo de Habas Verdes, fresh broad beans cooked in a casserole with onions, tomatoes and eggs. Jabalí Estofado is a stew of wild board simmered in a wine rich sauce. Magras de Cerdo con Pisto is loin

The Plaza Mayor at Tembleque.

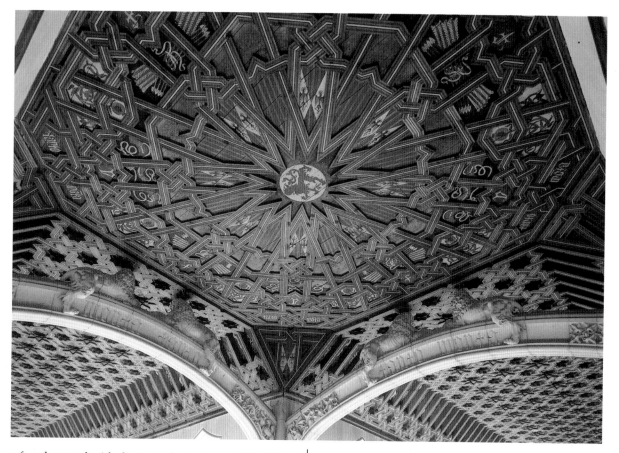

The Mudéjar ceiling in the cloister of San Juan de los Reyes at Toledo.

of pork served with the typical mixed vegetable dish of the region, similar to ratatouille. Castile is known for its abundant wild partridge and this is an excellent place to try some, Perdiz a la Toledana being the local version. A sweet which is a particularly nice ending to a rich meal is Cuajada con Miel, milk curds with the local honey.

The wine list includes *jarras* (jugs), of the local wine, and other wines to look out for in the area include Yepes, from the countryside surrounding the nearby village of Villasequilla de Yepes and also some excellent wines from Escalona, a village some 50km to the north.

Toledo is a beautiful and historic city – and, unusual for Spain, the old part has been kept quite separate from its modern suburbs, largely because it is virtually self-contained on its 'island'. Indeed from a distance there is little sign of any modern building to mar the vista of its medieval heritage. It is however very popular: its wealth of architectural and art treasures and its proximity to Madrid, 70km away, mean that it is nearly always crowded. For this reason you should book the Parador Conde de Orgaz a day or so in advance.

You could easily fill several days exploring Toledo

fully and as with Madrid, a separate guidebook is essential. Wandering through its steep narrow streets is a pleasure in itself, as indeed is lingering during the afternoon siesta, or in the evening, at the café tables around the Plaza de Zocodover. However, if time is short there are several features you should make a point of seeing. The Cathedral is the finest example of the Gothic style in Spain after Burgos and its towering spire dwarfs the web of narrow streets which surround it. Built between 1227 and 1493, its interior is virtually a museum both of Spanish history and of Spanish architectural styles.

The church of Santo Tomé, built in the 14th century by the Count of Orgaz, contains a superb example of El Greco's work, *The Burial of the Conde de Orgaz*, and has a Mudéjar tower. Nearby is San Juan de los Reyes: completed in the 17th century it was a Franciscan convent first founded in the 15th century. The cloister has an intricately decorated Mudejar ceiling in the upper part.

The Alcázar is a vast building which dominates the Toledo skyline in distant views. It has had a sad history of burnings and batterings, culminating in almost total destruction during the Civil War, after which it was rebuilt.

It is also rewarding to drive along the winding road which follows the course of the Río Tagus to see the city walls with their numerous gates and bridges. Don't miss a glimpse of the Toledo railway station a short distance along the road to Ocaña – a fanciful blend of Art Deco and Mudéjar.

THE ENVIRONS

A SMALL DETOUR of 10km to the south-west along the C 401 will bring you to the Castillo of Guadamur, the kind of Spanish castle of which dreams are made – well-preserved, turreted building of ochre-coloured stone set in the midst of peaceful pinewoods.

Leaving Toledo on the N 400 towards Ocaña, take the right fork after a short distance on to the C 400 and soon after fork right again on to the N 401 to Orgaz where another enchanting castle is set nonchalantly among the small white houses of the village. It seems to have become just as much a part of the village life as the local grocer's shop and bar.

From here continue south for 10kms along the N 401 to Los Yebenes. From the plain the road climbs a steep hill giving sweeping views over the patterned landscape through which you have passed. Above the town of Los Yebenes the hill crest is dotted with the pretty, toylike windmills Don Quixote himself tilted against and which are such a delightful feature of the region.

In Los Yebenes take the TO 231/232 to Consuegra. A dramatic stony hill towers above the town upon which a row of ten gleaming white windmills are lined up along its ridge together with an imposing *castillo*. A small road allows you to drive up to this remote, romantic spot from where there are breathtaking views over the surrounding landscape. Here the horizon is as distant as if it were the sea. The town of Consuegra is the centre of the production of saffron. First introduced by the Moors, it is now a valuable crop.

From Consuegra you can join the C 400 for 7km to Madridejos. A detour to the north is recommended along the N 4 to Tembleque, a delightful 'white' town of small single-storey houses and narrow streets with an exquisite *plaza mayor* surrounded by buildings with stone arcades and slender timber balconies, decorated with crests. There is also a pretty, balconied gateway into the square and an interesting 16th-century Gothic church.

Windmills on the hill above Consuegra.

A meadow near Manzanares in the spring.

After returning to Madridejos take the N 4 south for 17 km to Puerto Lápice, where a local inn is reputed to be the very hostelry in which Don Quixote was dubbed a Knight by the innkeeper. From here take the N 420 to Alcázar de San Juan, an important wine centre. The town is named after a Moorish castle, or *alcázar*, later taken over by the Order of St John. Only the restored tower remains. Continuing along the N 429 for 10 km will bring you to the atmospheric town of Campo de Críptana, a maze of steep narrow streets lined with dazzlingly white houses scattered up the slope of a rocky hill. At the top, and almost part of the village, a cluster of windmills completes the scene which so charmingly epitomises La Mancha. The mills, many rebuilt, still work for their living and new vanes were being installed while I was there, in readiness for the imminent harvest from the vast fields of grain which stretch away to the horizon. There are wonderful views from here and it is the gathering place for the villagers' evening stroll.

For devotees of Cervantes, a detour to the nearby village of El Toboso will enable them to visit the house of Dulcinea, the damsel of whom Don Quixote dreamed. It is furnished in keeping with period and region, and contains a large collection of Cervantes' work, including over thirty different language publications of *Don Quixote de la Mancha*. Continue along the N 420 to Moto del Cuervo, where yet more mills decorate the hilltop, and from here along the same road to *Belmonte*.

The *castillo* of Belmonte is the most imposing in the region: much of its vast perimeter battlements remain and still partially surround the town. The heavily fortified castle was built in the 15th century and restored in the 19th century. Its now empty interior can be visited, and some beautiful Mudéjar ceilings may be seen, together with far-reaching views of the countryside from its walls. The collegiate church contains interesting altarpieces and 15th-century choir stalls.

Returning to Moto del Cuervo, continue back along the N 420 to Pedro Muñoz and then along the CR 122 to the town of Tomelloso. This is the heartland of the wine industry: vast areas of vines dominate the landscape, the endless rows of green vines contrast vividly with the red-brown soil. Tomelloso itself has been described by the Spanish writer, Victor de la Serna, as being built over a reservoir of wine. In the nearby town of Argamasilla de Alba you can visit the Cueva de Medrano, the small lodging house in which it is claimed Cervantes spent his time writing the first chapters of *Don Quixote*.

Make a detour along the valley of the Río Guardiana to the Lagunas de Ruidera. Here the landscape differs from the familiar fertile red soil patterned with vines and olive trees, for it is wild and rocky, with hillsides covered in shrubs and stunted trees. Lavender and rosemary scent the air; hawks trace lazy circles in the sky, rabbits run across your path and partridges flutter from every bush. At the point where the river runs free of the dam, the Embalse de Peñarroya, there is the 12th-century ruined castle of Peñarroya set high up above the lake and containing a small chapel in which an image of the Virgin of Peñarroya is still worshipped.

From Ruidera los Villares the road runs alongside the lakes of Ruidera. Contained in a rocky basin they descend in a series of shallow steps, emptying into each other by pouring over the edge like a tilted saucer, or in a network of tumbling streams across the separating terrain. Some of the lakes have been developed as summer resorts, with villas, small hotels and restaurants by the waterside together with small beaches. The road continues up to the source of the lakes, where it is quiet and remote, the turquoise water fringed with reed beds and the rocky hillsides dotted with gorse and pine trees.

From the head of the lakes, continue to the town of Ossa de Montiel where you can take the AB 640 to Villa Hermosa and then the C 415 to Villanueva de los Infantes, a spacious town with an elegant *plaza mayor* surrounded by classical arcades and façades of white stone. There are many lovely old buildings including the palace of Los Baillo, the convent of Los Dominicas de la Encarnación and the house of El Duque de San Fernando. Now take the C 415 towards Valdepeñas and after about 20km turn right on to the CR 644 to San Carlos del Valle. Here, in a quiet and outwardly nondescript small town, there is a surprisingly large and beautiful *plaza mayor*, lined with brick-built houses decorated by wooden balconies and overlooked by an imposing church. Continue north along the same road to Solana, where there is also an attractive *plaza mayor*, and then take the N 430 to Manzanares.

MANZANARES

THE PARADOR NACIONAL DE MANZANARES is a large modern hotel on the N 4, the Madrid/Bailen road, just to the south of the town and about 2km away from the centre. Essentially a stopping place for travellers, its proximity to Almagro makes it a useful alternative to the Parador there if the latter is fully booked. Its com-

fortable, spacious rooms are air-conditioned and there is a garden and a swimming pool.

The menu contains many regional dishes such as El Pisto Manchego, a dish of mixed vegetables cooked in olive oil and flavoured with garlic. Las Migas are coarse breadcrumbs sautéed in olive oil and garlic and often mixed with small pieces of ham, salt pork and sausage. They are sometimes included in the breakfast buffet and make a wonderful accompaniment to fried or scrambled eggs. Caldereta de Cordero a la Manchega is a casserole of neck of lamb with a wine-rich, glutinous sauce and El Guiso de Bodas is a hearty peasant-style chicken soup.

For those with a sweet tooth, try Leche Fritas, literally fried milk but in fact slices of a rich, stiff custard coated in batter, fried to a golden brown and then sprinkled with sugar – very naughty. The wine list includes Yuntero excellent red and white wines from the neighbouring town of Damiel which is also well-known for its wine.

Manzanares is an important wine centre whose wines, along with those of Valdepeñas, are allowed to be sold under its own name. The bustling town contains a delightful *plaza mayor* and a 14th-century church with an imposing Renaissance façade.

The town of Valdepeñas lies just 30km to the south and its name has become a genetic term for the wines of La Mancha. There are numerous *bodegas* (bars) and wine cellars to which visitors are welcomed. Throughout the region you will see large clay, aladdin-shaped pots, often used to decorate the entrance to farms and villas. These are the traditional vessels in which the wines of La Mancha were fermented. Today the wine is made on a much grander scale and in huge quantities but, rather charmingly I think, the enormous modern concrete containers holding 15,000 litres and more are still made in the same traditional shape.

ALMAGRO

ALMAGRO IS JUST OVER 30km to the south-west of Manzanares and, as a base for exploring the region, the Parador in Almagro is much to be preferred to the one at Manzanares. The Parador Nacional de Almagro is situated in the ancient convent of San Francisco, built in 1596. It is a vast pale-orange-bricked building with a maze of corridors and staircases which link together no less than sixteen courtyards and patios. The spacious, atmospheric interior includes a *bodega* (bar) furnished in rural style with flagstone floors and solid wooden tables and benches. Beautiful antique furniture decorate the public rooms. In one a lady from the town demonstrates the local craft of lace-making, which she also sells. There is also a swimming pool. The Parador is only a few minutes' walk from the *plaza mayor*.

The Plaza Mayor of Almagro.

A good selection of regional dishes and wines on the menu includes the local speciality Berenjenas de Almagro, egg plants in a spicy sauce. On the occasion I tried them they were served in a casserole with ham and shrimps. Puelos y Quebrantos is scrambled eggs served with *chorizo* (sausage) and brains, and another dish with which to start the meal is Judías Verdes Almagrenas, green beans cooked in a sauce. Mojete de Conejo Manchega is pieces of rabbit sautéed with garlic and white wine.

To finish you might try Tocinello de Cielo, a rich custard somewhere between a mousse and a flan. If you don't have a sweet tooth you could end with Queso Manchego, the cheese for which the region is famous. There is a good selection of local wines including Vino Albalí, red, white and *rosé* wines from Valdepeñas and an excellent full-bodied, deep-red wine, Vega Fría.

The *plaza mayor* of Almagro is quite outstanding, even for a region noted for its lovely squares. It is very large and long with a central paved area, and surrounded by houses with arcades, the upper floors of which have literally hundreds of small windows with uniform green frames. It almost seems unreal but for the local people who go about their business or stroll around it in the evening as if it were nothing special at all.

The town was the centre of the Order of Calatrava and there are numerous mansions and palaces with beautiful doorways decorated with crests. The 17th-century church of San Augustín beside the square contains paintings by Zurbaran. The Corral de Comedias is the town's most important sight, after the square, and is delightful. It is a tiny open-air theatre with decorated wooden balconies. Classical plays are still performed there in August on the feast of St Bartholomew.

THE ENVIRONS

THE REGIONAL TOWN OF Ciudad Real, less than 40km away along the C 415, was founded in the 13th century and retains some of its ancient buildings. The Puerta de Toledo, the town gate, is one of the most important examples of the region's Mudéjar architecture and the cathedral of Santa María del Prado, built in 1531, is also

The Castillo of Belmonte.

worth a visit. So too is the church of San Pedro and the church of Santiago, the town's oldest building.

The town of Damiel, about 30km along the N 420 to the east has a 14th-century church, Santa María with a lovely Renaissance façade. The 16th-century church of San Pedro possesses a beautiful baroque retable, and the town has an attractive arcaded *plaza mayor*.

On the way to Damiel at the village of Carrión de Calatrava there is a small detour to the north to the ruined castle of Vieja Calatrava in an atmospheric setting beside the Río Guadiana and the nearby hermitage of La Encarnación. It is set amidst delightful and peaceful fields and vineyards. As I drove by I saw at least half a dozen pairs of Bee Eaters flitting from tree to tree with their iridescent turquoise and gold plumage flashing in the sunlight.

From Damiel a small road to the north leads to the Parque Nacional de las Tablas de Damiel, protected area of lakes, brooks and marshy terrain fringed with reeds, created by the confluence of the Ríos Guadiana and Ciguela. Signposted walks through this region allow you to observe a fascinating variety of plants and birdlife.

After returning to Almagro you can take the C 417 to Calzada de Calatrava where a few kms to the south-

west is the ruined castle of Calatrava la Nueva, a vast construction with its imposing towers and walls intact, seemingly in defiance of neglect and the passage of time. By taking the C 410 southwards you will come to the village of Viso del Marqués, where the magnificent Renaissance palace was built in the 16th century by the Marqués de Santa Cruz.

From here it is only 6km to the Madrid/Bailén road. If you are continuing south to Andalucía a brief detour to the north is worth while to visit the sanctuary of NS de las Virtudes. It has a small, very pretty 16th-century chapel containing a beautiful gilded retable and small exquisite painted domed ceiling. Adjoining it is one of the oldest bullrings in Spain. Built in the 17th century it is square. Bullfights are still occasionally held there.

If you are continuing south it is less than two hours' drive to the paradors of Bailén or Úbeda (the tours for this region are described on pages 200–225). The parador of Córdoba is less than a further two hours' drive to the west (the tour for this region is described on pages 176–187).

*OUR 11   Begins in the pro-
vince of Toledo and leads south-
west into Extremadura to the provinces of Cáceres and Badajoz, providing a
scenic route between Madrid and the western region of Andalucía and the Costa del
Sol. Combined with tour No 10 (page 108)
it can also be used to create a round trip.
Extremadura is perhaps one of the least
visited regions of Spain. It is certainly one
of the most sparsely populated areas. The
tour includes several historic towns, a
magnificent monastery and numerous
spectacular castles. The countryside is richly
varied and there are a wealth of beautiful
buildings. The paradors featured include
two magnificent 15th-century castles, two
convents and a medieval pilgrims' hospital.*

—TOUR II—
MICHELIN MAP NO. 447
Oropesa
Trujillo   GUADALUPE
Mérida
Zafra

OROPESA
GUADALUPE
TRUJILLO
MÉRIDA–ZAFRA

OROPESA

THE ITINERARY BEGINS AT the Parador of Oropesa,
about 150km from Madrid. The route, from the capital,
is initially along the N 5 to Navalcarnero and Magueda.
Here there is a 15th-century castle with round towers
at each corner and Mudéjar archway. A detour can be
made 12km north to Escalona; an old town whose
magnificent 11th century fortress has extensive battlements and towers and is set on a hillside overlooking
the Río Alberche. Some of the town walls and gateways survive and there are numerous arcaded houses
lining the ancient streets and square. The 16th-century
Convento de Immaculada Concepción has an especially fine Plateresque portal.

The N 5 continues westwards to the large, busy
town of Talavera de la Reina, set at the confluence of
the Ríos Tajo and Alberche. Famous for its ceramics,
there is a museum, Ruíz de Luna, with an important
collection of work and numerous churches and mansions in the old part of town. The 15th-century church
of Santa María is in Gothic style and the churches of
San Miguel and San Pedro are of Mudéjar design.

The Parador Virrey Toledo, is situated 33km further
to the west on the edge of the town of Oropesa. This
imposing 12th-century castle, which can be seen on its
hilltop long before you arrive, has been the source of
many battles – both feudal and with the Moors – because of its important strategic position. It was extensively rebuilt in the early 15th century by Don Garcia
Álvarez de Toledo to whom it was given by King
Enrique III.

It is a massive building surrounded by impregnable
walls. The entrance to the castle is through a tunnel-
like gateway into a large courtyard overlooked by a
gallery, balconies and towers. Outside the castle a
small square and a promenade are a popular place for

the villagers to gather in the evening.
There are sweeping views over the
plain towards the distant Sierra de
Gredos – a wonderful sight at sunset.
The interior is full of medieval atmosphere with tiled floors, high
wooden-beamed ceilings, large stone
fireplaces and antique furniture.

Regional specialities on the menu
included: Perdiz a la Oropesana, partridge stuffed with pâté and braised
in a red wine sauce; and Salteado de
Ternera Lagarterana, veal stew with
mixed vegetables. A delicious sweet is
Suspiros de Monja (literally 'nun's
sighs'), light fluffy puffs of whisked
egg-white, poached in a creamy
cinnamon-flavoured egg custard. The house wine is
from the vineyards which surround the castle.

Some of the old town walls have survived and the
streets are lined with old houses and mansions. There
are two 16th-century Renaissance churches, one with a
fine Plateresque portal. A few kms to the east of
Oropesa is the town of Lagartera, famous for its unusual embroidery, a local craft which dates back to the
16th century.

GUADALUPE

THE NEXT STAGE of the tour is south along the TO 701 to
the Parador at Guadalupe a distance of 90km. This
quiet country road at first runs through open countryside with gentle hillsides planted with wheatfields and
dotted with oak trees. A few kms before reaching
Puente de Arzobispo there is a small chapel, the Ermita
NS de Bienvenida, which dates from the 16th century.
Puente de Arzobispo is known for its ceramics, in fact
rivalling Talavera de La Reina. Numerous shops line
the main road. The town is named after the 14th century bridge over the Río Tajo, built by Archbishop don
Pedro Tenorio.

Beyond Puente del Arzobispo the landscape becomes
more hilly with views of the distant Sierra de
Guadalupe. At Navalmoralejo there are the ruins of the
Roman town of Vascos. The road climbs steadily into
the mountains, which are covered in dense pine forests
and carpeted with yellow broom and rock rose, to the
Puerto de San Vicente. This marks the division between Castile and Extremadura and the scenery becomes stark and dramatic. You can see for miles over
the mountainsides with no sign of farms, houses, or
even other roads.

The Parador Nacional Zurbarán, in the centre of the
medieval mountain village of Guadalupe, is adjacent to
the huge monastery which dominates the surrounding
countryside. The Parador occupies the old hospital of

San Juan Bautista founded in the 15th century to care for the pilgrims who came to pay homage to the Virgin of Guadalupe. It is named after the famous Spanish artist Zurbarán (1598–1664). An important collection of his work is kept in the monastery's vestry.

The public rooms are ranged around a lovely patio with Mudéjar arches. Moorish-style gardens, shaded by orange and lemon trees, surround a pool and a Mudéjar fountain. The bedrooms have balconies which overlook the garden and the monastery beyond. The interior has a wealth of wooden beams, stone arches, terracotta-tiled floors and comfortable traditonal furniture.

Local cuisine on the menu included: Bacalao Moncal, dried salts cod cooked in a casserole with spinach and potatoes and flavoured with garlic; and Cabrito Asado a la Serrana, kid cooked in the oven with garlic. A deliciously rich pudding is Puding de castañas, a thick creamy custard-like purée of chestnuts. Local wine included those from neighbouring Cañamero and Mentrida. I had a bottle of Castillo de Escalona, an excellent full-bodied red.

The village of Guadalupe is criss-crossed by a web of fascinating old streets, lined by ancient houses decorated with balconies and arcades supported on

The Castillo and Parador of Oropesa.

massive weathered wooden beams. The monastery was originally a small hermitage consecrated to NS de Guadalupe. When the Moors invaded in 1711 the figure of the Virgin, reputed to have been carved by St Luke, was buried. It was not discovered again until the 13th century when a shepherd found it by chance. In spite of being buried for 600 years it was perfectly preserved. A spate of miracles soon made the Virgin, and Guadalupe, a principal place for pilgrimages.

The monastery is a monumental building containing an extraordinary collection of treasures. There is a magnificent Mudéjar cloister with horseshoe arches, a well and a beautiful Plateresque staircase. As well as paintings by Zurbarán there are many other works by great Spanish painters decorating the rooms as well as a museum of miniatures and embroideries. The monastery was endowed with many gifts of treasure from noblemen, explorers and the Conquistadores. Hernán Cortés spent his last days here before departing for his conquest of Mexico. Permission for Columbus' voyage by the Catholic Monarchs was first granted in Guadalupe and he named an island to honour it.

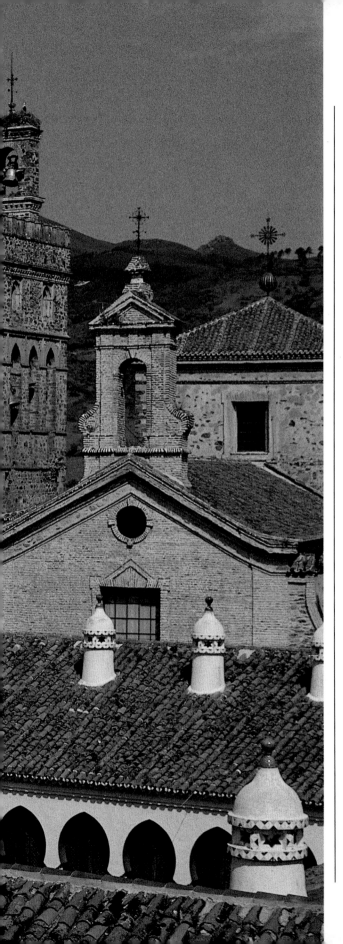

Nearby is the 15th-century hermitage of El Humilladero, the 16th-century palace of Granja de Valdefuentes and the 17th-century palace of Granja de Mirabel, built for the Catholic kings.

An interesting round trip can be made from the Parador into the countryside to the south. From Guadalupe the route leads south-west through attractive mountain scenery to the wine town of Cañamero. A few kms further a small road leads south-east across flat, open countryside to Valdecaballeros on the banks of the Embalse de García de Sola. The road skirts the lake which is fringed by pine trees and surrounded by rugged mountains. At Herrera del Duque there is a 16th-century Gothic church, a ruined Renaissance convent and the remains of a hilltop castle. The route leads north-east across a flat open landscape to Castilblanco and then to the edge of the Embalse de Cijara, designated as a National reserve. The road returns towards Guadalupe joining the C 401 just below the Puerto de San Vicente.

TRUJILLO

THE NEXT STAGE of the tour is west to the Parador at Trujillo, a distance of abut 80km. Returning to Cañamero the route continues along the C 401 to Logrosán, with a 14th-century church, a 15th-century hermitage and the ruins of a castle. The road continues along a broad green valley covered by wheatfields and meadows and shaded by oak trees. At Zorita the C 524 leads north-west to Trujillo.

The Parador Nacional de Trujillo, located in the 16th-century convent of Santa Clara, overlooks a small square and is only a few minutes' walk from the *plaza mayor*. In front is a small courtyard with a well. By the door is a small revolving cubby hole where the nuns would place their home-made sweets to be sold .to passers-by. Although most of the bedrooms are situated in a modern extension at the rear, the nuns cells in the original building have also been converted into bedrooms. The public rooms open on to a charming cloister with an ancient stone well set in the centre of the patio. There is also a patio in the modern wing with a small swimming pool in its centre.

The restaurant is in the refectory, a long room with a high arched ceiling decorated by a large mural of blue azulejos on one wall. Among the regional specialities represented on the menu was: Caldereta de Cordero, small pieces of lamb on the bone, casseroled with onions, peppers and ham in a wine rich sauce and flavoured with garlic; Patatas y Judías a la Extremena, potatoes and green beans cooked in a casserole with

The Monastery of Guadalupe with the parador in the foreground.

onions, tomatoes and peppers and flavoured with garlic and parsley; and Ternera a la Extremena, veal cutlets cooked in a sauce with onions, garlic, peppers and *chorizo*. The regional wines on the list included those from nearby Montánchez and Almendralejo.

Trujillo is set on a rocky hill overlooking a wild heathland, rimmed by distant mountains. Parts of the fortified walls have survived and above the town is a massive Arab fortress with towers and gateways. The hub of the town is the *plaza mayor*, a delightful, irregular square surrounded by old mansions and arcades. In one corner is a statue honouring Francisco Pizarro, the conqueror of Perú. Many other Conquistadores also came from the town and its surroundings. The Gothic church of Santa María was built on the site of a mosque and contains a beautiful painted retablo by Francisco Gallego.

Overlooking the *plaza mayor* is the Palacio de Marqués de la Conquista, built by Hernando Pizarro, the son-in-law of the Conquistador. It has a lovely Plateresque façade and is richly decorated with coats of arms, statues and window grilles. The Palacio de los Orellana-Pizarro also has a beautiful Plateresque façade and a patio in the same style. Numerous other

A street in Guadalupe.

Trujillo seen from outside the city walls.

fine buildings are dotted throughout the town, making it a pleasure to explore. A walk along the battlements in the evening is one of the best ways of capturing the atmosphere of the place. From here you can look down onto the ancient rooftops and into the huge untidy storks' nests which adorn every building.

The provincial capital of Cáceres is only 47km to the west of Trujillo. This too is an exceptionally beautiful city and merits an extended visit. Within surrounding walls are a wealth of exquisite building, towering above the narrow streets like medieval skyscrapers of golden stone. The entrance into the old city is by the Plaza del General Mola, a lively square buzzing with the chatter of the students of the University of Extremadura, who tend to dominate the city. The Parador, or the tourist office in the square in Cáceres, will provide a map and a guide to the buildings.

MÉRIDA

FROM TRUJILLO the next stage of the tour is south-west to the Parador at Mérida, a direct journey of 90km. The route is along the CC 800 to Montánchez. This old hilltop town is famed for its hams and sausages made

The Castillo of Medellín.

from the velvety brown pigs which forage beneath the oak trees. Montánchez is also known for its wines from the vineyards which cover the surrounding hillsides. There are the remains of a large Moorish fortress above the town. The road continues south-west along the CC 801 to join the N 630 where the route continues south to Mérida.

The Parador Nacional Vía de la Plata is situated in a 15th-century convent which faces on to a quiet square. It is a short walk from the centre of the town. The Baroque building contains elements of much older origin Among its many uses in the past it has been a jail and is believed to occupy the site of a Roman temple. There is a small, pretty patio with columns decorated with Moorish inscriptions. The beautiful lounge was once the convent chapel.

The menu includes a variety of Extremaduran dishes: Cordero Asado a la Pobre, lamb baked with potatoes and garlic, and Gaspacho Extrameño, a soup made by combining olive oil, egg yolks, garlic, bread-crumbs, wine vinegar and water to make a thick creamy liquid and served chilled. A delicious pudding is Tarta del Convento, flaky pastry layered with cream, quince jelly and chocolate. Local wines are from

Montánchez, Cilleros and Ceclavin. I had a bottle of Fuente Vieja, a dry fruity rose from Villafranca de los Barros.

Mérida is set beside the Río Guadiana and was once the capital of the Roman province of Lusitania. Today it is largely a modern town but possesses the most extensive Roman remains in Spain. There is a superb Roman bridge, over 2,500ft long spanning the Guadiana with 60 arches. Nearby, beside the Plaza de España, is a massive Moorish alcázar built on the site of a Roman castle. There are also the remains of two aqueducts and the Circus Maximus which could contain 25,000 spectators.

The pride of Mérida is however, the Roman theatre. Dating from C. 20 BC it is one of the best preserved Roman buildings anywhere in the world. It is extremely impressive with a colonnaded stage and a façade containing more than 30 marble columns with Corinthian capitals. The terraced auditorium can seat over 5,000 spectators, even the entrance passages are all intact. Nearby is the amphitheatre which could seat

15,000 people. It is quite remarkable complex and still used today for theatre and concert performances.

ZAFRA

THE NEXT STAGE of the tour is south to the Parador at Zafra, a direct journey of only 60km so I have outlined a roundabout route which explores some of the places of interest between. From Mérida the route is first along the N 5 north-east towards Miajadas. After 24km the N 430 and then the C 520 lead south-east to Medellín set beside the broad Río Guadiana. This town was the birthplace of Hernán Cortés, the conqueror of Mexico, and there is a statue of him in the main square. The town is dominated by an impressive castle on the high-domed hill. Nearby is a 17th-century Gothic church where the Conquistador was baptised. There are a number of old mansions in the town and a stone bench marks the site of Cortés' birthplace.

The road continues to Don Benito, where there are two 16th-century churches, several old mansions and an arcaded *ayuntamiento*. The route leads south-west from here to Alange where there is another Moorish castle set on a hill and very well-preserved Roman baths contained in two round chambers with high-domed roofs. The C 423 continues south-west to Almendrelajo through countryside patterned with vineyards and olive groves. The town, an important wine centre, has a 16th-century Renaissance church and the 18th-century Palacio del Marques de Monsalud, which houses an important collection of Roman antiquities.

The route leads south-west along the C 423 through gentle vine-covered hillsides to Villalba de los Barros, where there is a Mudéjar castle and a 16th-century church. Beyond, at Santa Marta, a quiet country road leads south through vine-covered hills to Salvatierra de los Barros. Here too there are the imposing remains of a 13th-century castle. Returning to the main road, passing the hilltop castle of Feria, another small road continues north-east to Fuente del Maestre whose 15th-century Gothic church has a fine Mudéjar tower and an imposing granite portal. Nearby is the 13th-century monastery of San Pedro with a Baroque chapel and a Mudéjar gallery. The road continues to Villafranca de los Barros, where the 16th-century church of Santa María del Valle has a fine Gothic portal.

A goatherd near Mérida.

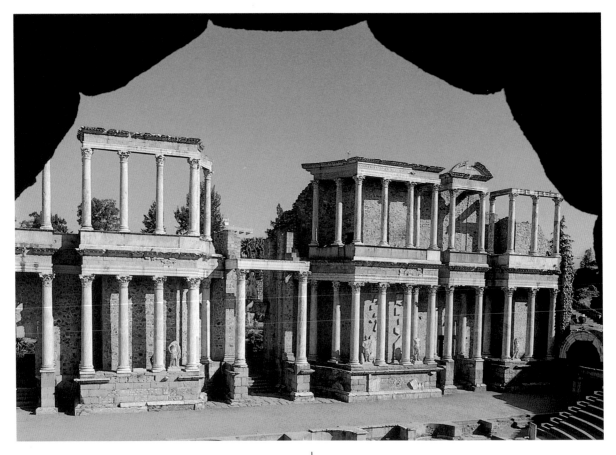

The Roman Theatre at Mérida.

The BA 613 leads east through peaceful rural scenery to Ribera del Fresno, where there are a number of old mansions. Further on, the town of Hornachos is dramatically situated below a steep rocky mountain overlooking a wide fertile valley. There are the ruins of an Arab castle and a Gothic church with Mudéjar additions. A small road leads south-west from here to Zafra.

The Parador Nacional Hernán Cortés is located in the 15th-century fortified palace where Hernán Cortés lived before he departed for Mexico. It is square with round towers at each corner and semi-circular towers between. At the rear is the keep which overlooks a garden and swimming pool. In the centre is a magnificent two-storey Renaissance patio with galleries supported by Ionic and Doric columns, constructed in white marble and, reputedly, designed by Juan de Herrera, the architect of the Escorial. It is quite stunning. There is also a lovely chapel with an octagonal Gothic cupola. The *sala dorada* (golden room), situated in the main tower has a beautiful painted ceiling.

Regional dishes on the menu include: Menestra de Alcegas a la Extremeña, a dish of sautéed potatoes, greens and onions; and Berenjenas a la Extremeña, eggplants coated in flour and then fried in olive oil. Local wines on the list included Viña de los Barros and Castell de Zafra, a full-bodied red.

The Parador is only a few minutes' walk to the main square of Zafra, the Plaza Grande. Adjoining is the Plaza Chica, an enchanting small square surrounded by arcaded whitewashed houses with balconies brimming with flowers. Zafra is known as Sevilla la Chica, little Seville, for the resemblance of its character to the Andalucian towns further to the south. The 14th-century collegiate church of NS de la Candelaria has a retablo decorated with nine paintings by Zurbarán. The convent of Santa Clara, founded in the 15th century by Don Gómez Suárez de Figueroa, contains the tomb of Don Lorenzo Suárez de Figueroa who built the castle. The 16th-century hospital of Santiago has a fine Gothic portal and lovely patio.

An interesting excursion can be made into the countryside to the south of Zafra. The N 435 and the C 4311 lead south-west of the town to Burguillos de Cerro where a Knight Templar's castle is set on a hill

The Plaza Chica at Zafra. Overleaf: Aiguablava.

above the village. There is also a church with an 18th-century Baroque tower. 20km further is Jerez de los Caballeros. The name stems from the Knights Templars who took the town from the Moors in 1229. They were later defeated by Ferdinand IV's army who had them beheaded in a tower now called Torre Sangrienta, the bleeding tower. Parts of the town walls and the fortress remain, together with two of the gates. The most remarkable building in the town is the massive 17th-century church of San Bartolomé which soars above the narrow streets surrounding it. Its ornate Baroque façade and lofty towers are studded with polychrome azulejos and glazed decorations. It is a quite remarkable sight.

Adjacent to the castle is the 16th-century Baroque church of Santa María, founded in the 7th century and the oldest in Extremadura. In the town centre is the 16th-century Baroque church of San Miguel with a massive and ornately decorated tower. The church of Santa Catalina also has a fine Baroque tower.

The N 435 leads south-west to Fregenal de la Sierra. Above the town is an impressive 13th-century castle and there are two churches and several old mansions. The route continues south-east along the C 434 to Segura de León, a quite delightful old town built on a hill and threaded by impossibly steep narrow streets. It has a well-preserved 13th-century castle and a fine Gothic church.

The route leads north-east from here along the C 437 to Fuente de Cantos, famous as the birthplace of Francisco de Zurbarán. It has a 16th-century church, NS de la Granada, with a Baroque retablo, and the convent of NS del Carmen which has a fine Baroque altar. There is also an 18th-century hermitage, NS de la Hermosa, with a 13th-century image of the Virgin.

A small road leads due east to Llerena. Here there's an elegant and spacious *plaza mayor* surrounded by classical arcaded buildings overlooked by the imposing church of NS de la Granada. Its tower is reminiscent of the Giralda in Sevilla and its façade is decorated by graceful arcaded galleries.

The Parador at Zafra is about 40km north-west along the N 432. The nearest alternative parador to Llerena is at Córdoba, 155km (page 182).

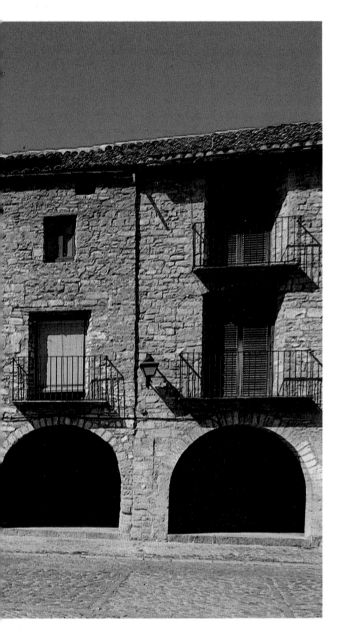

fireplaces create a cosy hunting lodge atmosphere.

The Parador is close to the French border, and the restaurant is very popular with French visitors who make weekend trips into Spain. The menu reflects this French influence: Magret en Salsa de Roquefort, is breast of duck cooked with blue cheese; and Surtido de Pates del Valle are a selection of pâtés from the region. I chose Cabrito a las Hervas del Monte, kid grilled with wild mountain thyme and garlic, followed by Guiso del Pirineo, a selection of mountain cheeses.

Viella is a lively town with access to ski slopes nearby. It makes an excellent centre for exploring the Val de Arán. In the old part of town is the 13th-century church of San Miguel with a large octagonal tower. It contains a carving of Christ called the Cristo del Mig Arán which is considered to be one of the finest examples of early Romanesque art. There are also a number of lovely 17th-century mansions.

The Desfiladero de Collegats.

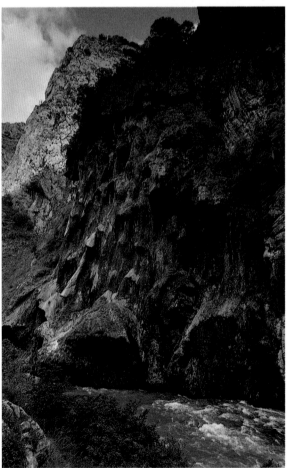

Landrover taxis can be hired in some of the villages.

The road to Viella follows the course of the Río Noguera and passes under the mountains through a 5km-long tunnel. The Parador Nacional Valle de Arán, located close to the road a few kms beyond the tunnel exit, is high on the mountainside overlooking the valley and the town of Viella, 2km further on. It has an exceptionally beautiful setting. The most striking feature of the Parador is a huge, round tower-like room with a conical grey slate roof, housing a two-storey lounge enclosed by an almost circular window commanding 360° views along three valleys. Central open

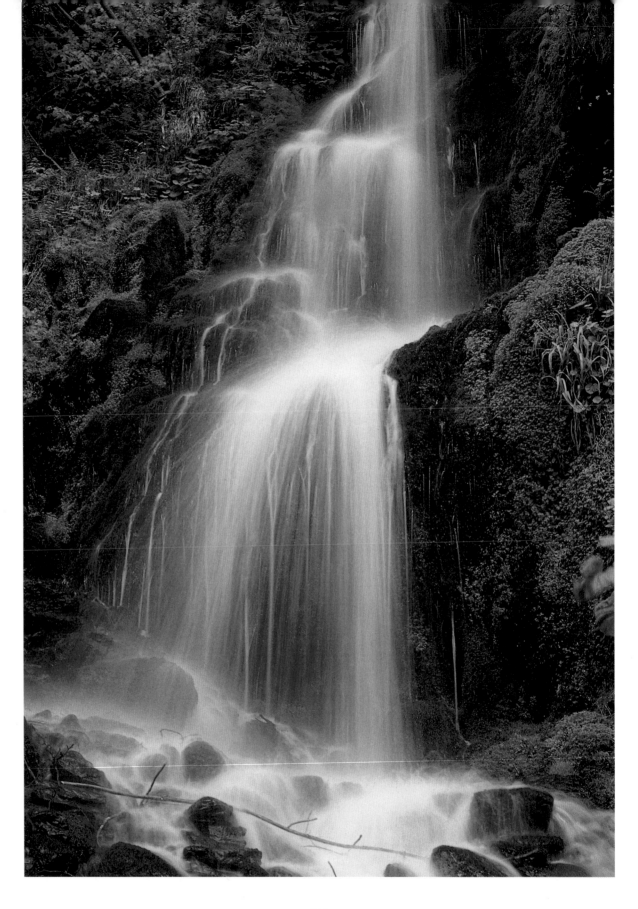

The town is the capital of the region. The Val de Arán has been part of Spain for many centuries but was isolated from the rest of the country until earlier this century when the pass of Bonaigua was built. Consequently the valley has a strong individual character with a language of its own quite different from both Catalán and Castilian Spanish.

ARTIÉS

THE PARADOR NACIONAL DON GASPER DE PORTOLA is situated in the village of Artiés only 9km away along the Val de Arán. Unlike Viella, Artiés is a quiet village in a completely rural setting with few signs of tourism. It is located where the valley of the Río Valarties meets the Val de Arán. The community of grey-stone houses is surrounded by peaceful meadows and overlooked by the imposing Pico Montarto. The cows are led through the village streets to pasture each day to the accompaniment of a carillon of bells. There is a 13th-century church and close to the village are Roman baths fed by hot sulphur springs.

The Parador, named after a famous 18th-century military character who founded the Mission of San Diego during his exploration of California, is on the edge of the village close to the road which passes through the valley. It is a modern building constructed in the local style with a steeply pitched grey-slate roof. The bedrooms have memorable mountain views. The lounge is an attractive two-storied room with a gallery and open stone fireplaces. Adjacent to the parador is an *hostería* which is only open during the winter months and contains a 17th-century chapel and a medieval tower.

The restaurant is in a large L-shaped room with a pine floor, ceiling and furniture which creates an agreeably rustic atmosphere. I had Olla Aranesa as a starter, a substantial soup of mixed vegetables, chick peas, pasta, *chorizo* and salt pork. To follow I had Perdiz a la Salsa de Higos, a deliciously rich dish of partridge served in a sauce of figs. The wine list included a good selection of regional wines including an excellent dry rose from Bodegas Raimat of Lerida.

Since the two paradors of Viella and Artiés are so close to each other you can consider them as alternative bases for the tours which follow.

The Val de Arán is one of the most beautiful mountain valleys and you do not have to travel very far to enjoy it to the full. One of the pleasures of exploring this region is that you are able to drive along small forest roads which penetrate high into the mountain valleys. Most are unsurfaced but quite easy to drive,

In the valley of the Río Torán.

giving you an opportunity to see a remote landscape which could otherwise only be reached by an arduous climb.

From the village of Artiés one of these roads follows the course of the Río Valarties along a valley where the meadow grass is knee-deep and a carpet of wild flowers creates a pointillist dapple of colour. From the head of the valley, walkers can continue to the Pico Montarto and to a ring of lakes called Colomes.

A few kms to the east of Artiés is Salardu, the capital of the upper Aran with a 13th-century church containing the 12th-century Cristo de Salardú. To the south of Salardú a small road leads along the valley of the Río d'Aiguamoix into a small valley of exeptional beauty. The river runs fast over boulders with swirling white water and small cascades. Trees line its banks, enclosing it in a tunnel of foliage and, beyond, there are meadows through which small brooks ripple.

Beyond the village of Tredos, where there is a 12th-century church, a road leads north to the ski slopes of Baqueira Beret. As it climbs to the plain of Beret there are wonderful views along the valley of Arán towards the pass of Bonaigua. You can see the road begin its serpent-like ascent of the mountain. The plain is a peaceful spot in summer with a small river meandering through the moist springy turf. From this point walkers can visit the deserted mountain village of Montgarri which has a Romanesque monastery.

The pass of Bonaigua is a worthy excursion in its own right and can be used to create a longish round trip, enabling you to visit another valley which leads into the National Park of Aigues Mortes. From the summit of the pass the road descends towards Esterri de Aneu, passing the mountain village of Sorp to the left. Just after passing Valencia de Aneau a tiny winding road to the right leads up the mountainside to Son del Pino, a village of ancient stone houses with vast views of the valley.

The road skirts the Embalse de la Torrasa and just beyond a road to the west follows the Río Mauricio to the small mountain resort of Espot, a base from which excursions into the Aigues Tortes can be made. Four-wheel-drive taxis are for hire which makes it possible to drive across the mountains to Caldas de Bohí.

Beyond the town a good road continues much higher up into the mountains to the lake of San Mauricio. The landscape is dominated by the peaks of Los Encantats – evocatively named 'enchanted mountains' whose bare conical peaks of grey, snow capped rock look like a child's drawing of mountains – quite unreal. The countryside here is enchanting with a vigorous river rushing over boulders and winding between grassy banks overhung by trees. It's a wonderful place to take a picnic or go walking.

The route continues along the valley of the fast-flowing white-water Río Noguera Palleresa to Lavorsi and

Rialp. Here the valley opens out and the river calms down a little. At Sort there are the remains of a ruined castle. Beyond, at the pretty riverside village of Gerri, a fine 12th-century Romanesque church is picturesquely sited on the far bank of the river. A few kms past Gerri the road enters a dramatic gorge, the Desfiladero de Collegats, where monumental cliffs tower above, rising sheer from the river bed for hundreds of feet.

At Pobla de Segur the route follows the C 144 west-ward to Pont de Suert. This road too is a continual source of pleasure as it winds through quiet, unspoiled countryside, passing the attractive village of Sarrocca de Bellera which teeters on a rock jutting out from the mountainside. A little further along the valley is Perbes another charming village of small stone houses. The road climbs out of the valley to a more rugged, rocky landscape, covered in a blaze of yellow broom. The road descends again into another peaceful valley. This

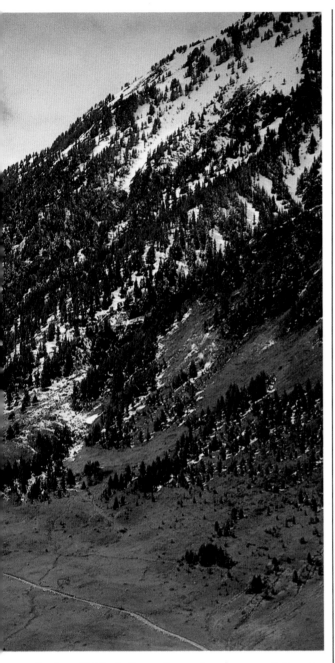

The Puerto de Bonaigua seen from the Puerto de Beret.

The road meets the opening of a valley through which the Río Joeu runs and then continues along this high into the mountains. The slopes are densely wooded and the riverbed is so steep in places that it is almost like a waterfall. Overlooking the valley is the dramatic jagged mountain of Aneto.

The return from this road leads to the village of Es Bordes. A short distance to the south at the village of Arros a road leads into the valley of the Río Varrados. This too is spectacularly beautiful. Turning northwards again the road leads to Bosost where there is a ruined castle and a 12th-century church. Just beyond Les a road to the west leads to Bausen, a primitive hamlet of ancient stone farms and houses high up on the tree-covered mountainside. It has the appearance and atmosphere of a medieval community.

A short distance beyond, a road to the east leads along the valley of the Río Torán. A fork to the left weaves tortuously around the mountainside to Caneján, an attractive village located high above the valley with quite awesome views. The road continues, however, much higher into the mountains beyond the curious old hilltop village of San Joan de Torán. Here, among towering peaks, deep forests, meadows and rushing rivers, is another quite unforgettable place.

BIELSA

THE NEXT STAGE of this tour is to the Parador at Bielsa, a distance of about 200km. The route is initially to the south of Viella along the N 230. Just beyond Villaler it turns to the west along the C 144, passing through a quiet green valley. It then climbs steadily towards the Col de Espina with distant views of the Pyrenean peaks to the north. The wooded mountainsides give way to open heathland and the road continues higher to the Col de Fadas. The route descends into a wide green, fertile valley to Castejon de Sos where the road joins the C 139.

You can make a short detour to the north along the valley of the Río Esera to Benasque in a steep valley at the foot of the Sierra de Maladeta. The town has a 13th-century Romanesque church and the Palacio de los Condes de Ribagorza, as well as some old houses along its narrow streets. It is the centre for climbs to the Pic d'Aneto and the Pic de Posets, the two highest mountains in the Pyrenees.

Continuing south from Castejon de Sos the road passes through the Congosto de Ventamillo, a spectacular gorge where steep jagged cliffs overhang the road. The route continues high along the side of a steep mountain slope and then descends into a rocky

leads to Pobla de Segur from where you can follow the N 230 back to Viella.

The road north of Viella leads to the French border along the valley of the Río Garona, which becomes the Garonne in France. There are some lovely detours to be made from this road. The first of these is a small road from Viella to the village of Gausac whence the road climbs high up along the mountainside running parallel to the valley through a beautiful pine forest.

The Romanesque church of Gerri.

valley. Beyond, it heads westwards along the C 140 and crosses a rugged mountain range over the Collado de Fordada.

The road descends gently into a wide fertile valley, planted with wheatfields and vineyards, to Ainsa, an ancient town set on a low hill beside the Río Ara. Once the capital of the medieval kingdom of Sobrabe, it is surrounded by fortified walls and there are the ruins of a castle, which has a lovely courtyard and a tall tower. There is a broad cobbled *plaza mayor* surrounded by old houses with arcades and balconies and overlooked by 12th-century church. Around the square are a maze of steep narrow streets lined by warm brown stone buildings.

The road to Bielsa continues to the north along the valley of the Río Cinca. At Escalona a road leads to the west along a small green valley. This is a detour not to be missed. As you progress through the valley it begins to narrow. Quite suddenly you realise you have entered a canyon. Sheer jagged cliffs soar upwards for hundreds of feet and a clear, ice-blue river crashes over boulders beside the road. As you penetrate deeper into

the gorge the cliffs become higher and steeper. At one point it feels as if you are entering a funnel with the cliffs converging above you. The canyon continues for more than 10km, then opens out on to a quite remarkable landscape of red rock mountainsides covered in yellow broom. To the north the Río Añisclo cuts its way through the mountains, forming another dramatic gorge towards the Pico de Añisclo. This wild, wonderful region is the National Park of Ordesa and Monte Perdido.

Returning to the main road, the C 138, the route continues along the valley which becomes progressively narrower while the mountains soar majestically above it for thousands of feet. Bielsa is an old town, damaged during the Civil War. It retains a 16th-century *ayuntamiento* and some old arcaded houses.

The Parador Nacional Monte Perdido lies 11km to the west at the head of the Valle de Pineta. A semicircular wall of rock rises up from the valley floor and enfolds the Parador. Looming higher still is the massive snow-capped peak of Monte Perdido. The building is in the style of a hunting lodge built from solid blocks of granite with a grey slate roof. Inside it is warm and welcoming with pine floors and ceilings and decorated with hunters' trophies and oil paintings of animals and flowers. The views from its windows are stunning. A large sun terrace adjoins the restaurant and, a footpath below leads down through a meadow to a small wooden bridge which crosses the river.

The menu included some suitably hunter-like dishes: Receo de Binefar, a hearty soup with beans, potatoes, onions and salt pork; Codornices con Pimientos al Horno, quails baked with green peppers; and Caldereta de Cordero, a rich lamb stew with peppers, onions, mushrooms and tomatoes. I chose a bottle of Lalanne, a soft, fruity red wine from Bodegas Somontano de Sobrabe.

Some breathtaking views of the valley can be had by taking a small road to the north about 7km back towards Bielsa. It climbs high up on to the mountainside to the village of Espierba and beyond. Although very steep, the slopes are covered with green pastures and dotted with small stone cottages and barns.

To the north of Bielsa the road passes through a tunnel under a monumental wall of rock, the Circo de Barrossa, into France. About 1km before the tunnel a small road climbs westward into the mountains to the village of Parzán and far beyond. Although unsurfaced and narrow, it is passable for many miles. Here, isolated shepherds' huts and green meadows are to be found in the highest and most remote places just below the savage rocky peaks. A shepherd showed me where

The village of Torla with Monte Perdido in the background.

the ground had been disturbed by wild boar feeding and pointed out a flock of wild sheep high up on a distant ridge.

A memorable excursion can be made from the Parador to the National Park of Ordesa along the road back to Ainsa and then following the C 138 west to Boltana. The route follows a steep rocky valley beside the Río Ara. Just beyond Broto, attractively set beside the river, a road to the east leads to Torla, an ancient small town with medieval houses and an old church set on a rocky outcrop. The massive range of Monte Perdido creates an imposing backdrop. As the road enters the Valley de Ordesa; a broad river, shaded by trees, flows across the wide valley floor. You are, seemingly, surrounded by sheer mountainsides which rise to a dizzy height with trees clinging obstinately to the slopes. Above, massive peaks of bare rock seem to reach up to the sky. It is a place of magnificent natural beauty.

From Ordesa you can return to the Parador at Bielsa by the same route. The nearest alternative parador is at Sos del Rey Católico, 240km to the west (page 65).

TOUR 14 Begins on the Costa del Azahar, the orange blossom coast of the province of Castellón, where millions of orange and lemon trees pattern the plains; continues northwards into the southern region of the province of Tarragona where the broad Río Ebro finally makes its exit into the Mediterranean. The route then delves eastwards into the province of Teruel to a mountain region of severe and epic beauty, the Maestrazgo. Here small villages are almost completely isolated from the 20th-century way of life. Within the rocky and often barren landscape there are hidden valleys where green meadows and wheatfields are rimmed by dry stone walls and wildflowers grow in vivid profusion. The tour continues south to Teruel, a city with a wealth of Mudéjar architecture.

The four Paradors which are featured include two dramatically sited hilltop castles, one an ancient fortified palace. Another is set beside the blue waters of the Mediterranean and the fourth overlooks the historic city of Teruel.

— TOUR 14 —
MICHELIN MAP NOS. 43 & 445

Alcañiz
Tortosa
Benicarló
TERUEL

BENICARLÓ
TORTOSA
ALCAÑIZ
TERUEL

BENICARLÓ

THE PARADOR NACIONAL COSTA DEL AZAHAR, the starting point of this itinerary, is situated on the edge of Benicarló on the seafront. This town is on the N 340 between Tarragona and Valencia, only a short distance from the Autopista A 7 which connects Alicante with the French border. The nearest airport is at Valencia, 140km away. The nearest alternative Parador is at El Saler, 153km (page 172).

The Parador is a two-storey building in the form of a large open-sided square. The spacious airy bedrooms open on to private sun terraces which face a wide lawn shaded by palm trees. In the centre is an enormous swimming pool. Just beyond is the sea. The restaurant and lounge open on to a broad shaded terrace, furnished with comfortable wicker chairs and tables: a perfect spot in which to enjoy a drink after a few laps of the pool.

The menu includes dishes like Pucherete del Maestrazgo, a comforting country soup of rice, haricot beans, cabbage, onion, salt pork and *chorizo*. A similarly rustic dish is Lentejas Estofados de Manitas de Cerdo, lentils cooked with pig's trotters. Arroz Abanda is a creamy rice dish in which the rice is cooked in a strongly flavoured fish broth seasoned with paprika and saffron and garnished with prawns. It is rather like a *paella* without the pieces of meat and fish. A potent garlic mayonnaise is served with it for you to stir in. Gambas con Salsa Romesco, large prawns served with a typical spicy sauce of the region, is made with peppers, tomatoes, almonds, garlic, olive oil and wine vinegar. I had a bottle of Castillo de Liria, a crisp dry white wine from Valencia. The wine list also included, unusually, Vega Sicilia, the renowned and expensive red wine from the Valladolid region.

Benicarló is an attractive but unexceptional town with a 16th-century Baroque church with an octagonal tower and a dome of blue azuleos and some interesting old streets. It also has a busy and important fishing fleet which plies a region rich in crustacea known as the Triángulo de Langosta, the lobster triangle.

The Parador is set at the northern extremity of a particularly fine long beach of good sand. At the southern curve of the beach is a massive dome of rock, jutting out into the sea like a small peninsula. Upon this the fortified town of Peniscola, creates a most striking sight. Walls encircle a labyrinth of steep cobbled streets and there are imposing tunnel-like gateways through which you enter. The castle was built by the Templars and looks down over the brilliant blue water of the Mediterranean which laps around it. The town is almost like an island with only a small spit of land linking it to the mainland. It was the refuge of Pope Don Pedro de Luna when he fled from Avignon.

The coastal plain is flat but a short distance inland the countryside becomes quite hilly and mountains rise in the distance. The land is very fertile and is heavily cultivated with olive and almond trees, vineyards and fields of vegetables. As you travel south however the agriculture is dominated by vast orange and lemon groves with dense green foliage studded with millions of brilliant orange and yellow fruits.

The main road, N 340, runs parallel to the coast, but some distance inland. Access to the sea is by roads which lead to the coastal towns and adjacent beaches. Most of these are not very attractive, many being extensively and tastelessly developed. Oropesa, just to the north of Castellón de la Plana, is however an interesting and appealing old town set on a hill overlooking the sea and ringed by castle walls. There are also two good beaches here, Playa de Morro de Gos and Playa de la Concha. Oropesa makes a good alternative to Benicarló or Peñíscola for a day on the beach but, in general, it is not a coastline which offers rewarding sightseeing.

Just a little to the south of Oropesa a small road climbs high into the pine-covered mountains to the Desierto de las Palmas. Here you will come across an 18th-century monastery and will be able to enjoy beautiful views of the plain of Castellón, as well as of the shimmering blue sea beyond.

TORTOSA

The fishing port of Vinaròs.

THE NEXT STAGE OF THE TOUR is to the Parador at Tortosa. An interesting and scenic route can be made by, first, taking the N 340 north to Vinaròs, a busy fishing town with a lively and colourful harbour. I spent some time watching the boats bobbing around in the harbour, waiting for a place by the quayside to unload their catch. The skippers wheeled and manoeuvred their large, brightly painted boats around with the casual abandon of dodgem cars at a fairground. Most of the boats had lines draped from the rigging from which filleted anchovies were hung to dry in the sun like strange miniature washing. A frenetic fish auction takes place in the market house on the dockside.

From Vinaròs the route continues westwards along the N 232, signposted to Zaragoza. Initially the road is quite straight across flat, open country planted largely with almond and olive trees. The village of Traiguera has an atmospheric old quarter and is also known for its pottery. The landscape soon takes on a more rugged and mountainous character. San Mateo, a few kms to the south along the C 238, is an important town of the lower Maestrazgo with many old buildings and known for its wine. There is a fine *ayuntamiento,* an arcaded *plaza mayor* and a 13th-century parish church. A short distance further along the N 232 a road to the south leads to the old town of Cati. Set amidst wild rocky countryside patterned with ancient dry stone walls, its narrow streets contain many medieval houses, some with seignorial crests, and there is an arcaded *lonja,* or market house.

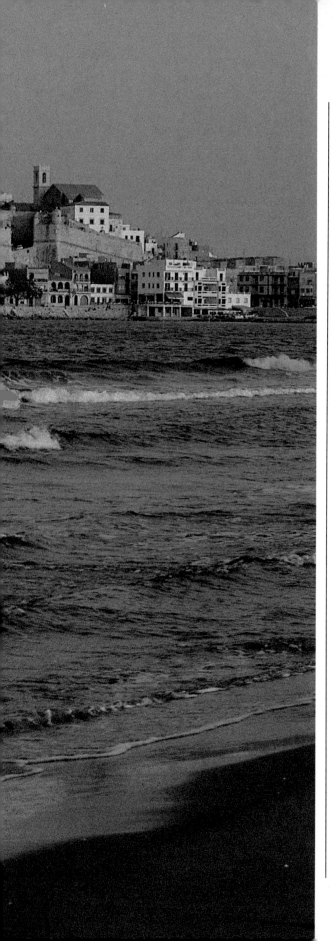

Continuing to the west along the N 232, the road follows the course of a dry riverbed bordered by steep sandy banks. Fig trees line the road and the dusty hillsides are covered with broom and gorse bushes. It is a severe and inhospitable landscape, sparsely populated. The road climbs progressively towards the Puerto de Querol in a series of sweeping hairpin bends. This pass is sometimes closed in the winter because of snow. Here the countryside becomes thickly wooded with oak and pine trees covering the steep mountainsides. From the summit of the pass the road crosses a plateau where wheatfields are planted in small terraces bordered by dry stone walls.

Soon you approach Morella. The first glimpse is almost startling. The old houses are tightly packed on terraces around the steep sides of a large domed hill. Above there is a circular wall of rock, crowned by castle walls and towers. The town retains a strong medieval atmosphere with ancient stone houses decorated with wooden balconies. Its steep narrow streets and alleys are entered through fortified gateways. There is a beautiful Gothic church, Santa María la Mayor and outside the town are the remains of a 15th century aqueduct.

From Morella the route continues northwards on the N 232 along a scenic road which climbs through steep mountainsides to the Puerto de Torre Miro, an open moorland landscape with few trees. Beyond, Monroyo, strikingly set below a dramatic rocky outcrop, overlooks a broad fertile valley planted with vineyards, wheatfields, and almond and olive groves.

The route now heads north-west along the TE 302 through a wide valley bordered by rocky pine-clad mountainsides. A brief detour to the south can be made to the picturesquely sited old town of Penarroya de Tastavines. Some 20kms further is Valderrobres beside the Río Matarrana. An ancient bridge crosses the river and the town is entered through a fortified gateway. Looming high above the village houses is the massive 14th-century castle of the Knights of Calatrava. There is also the lovely Gothic church of Santa María and a fine 16th-century *ayuntamiento*. The town is a fascinating tangle of narrow cobbled streets, alleyways, steps and small squares.

A short distance beyond Valderrobres a road leads off into a quiet fertile valley to the small village of Beceite, surrounded by small market gardens and vineyards and overlooked by the imposingly rugged mountain range of the Puertos de Beseit.

At Horta de San Juan there is a porticoed plaza said to be the inspiration for one of Picasso's first cubist paintings. There are many old buildings including an

Peñíscola.

ayuntamiento, the convent of Sant Salvador d'Horta and the church of Sant Joan Baptista. The scenery here is most impressive with plunging vine-cloaked valleys and the soaring mountain peaks of the Salto de Sutorras. This is the region of the Terra Alta, known for its strongly alcoholic wines.

Beyond Horta de San Juan the road joins the N 230 which leads south along the valley of the Río Ebro to Tortosa, an ancient city whose history dates back to Iberian and Roman times. The 14th-century cathedral was not completed until the beginning of the 18th century. Other buildings of interest include the 14th-century Episcopal Palace, with a lovely courtyard and gallery, and a *lonja,* a covered market hall, from the same period. The town is built along the river bank and a sculptured memorial has been created from the one remaining pile of the bridge which was destroyed during the Civil War.

Above the town on a hilltop crowned by extensive walls is the remains of the citadel of La Zuda. Within is the Parador Nacional Castillo de la Zuda, the site of an

Vineyards of the Terra Alta near Horta de San Joan.

Iberian settlement, then a Roman acropolis and finally a Moorish fortress. Remains of columns from Roman times are scattered within the grounds and there is a swimming pool which is very welcome during the summer months. There are superb views from the castle walls of the old city rooftops, the Río Ebro and the mountains beyond.

The Parador building is a modern construction using traditional methods with huge blocks of granite. The bedrooms have large wooden balconies with fine views. The restaurant has a high-beamed ceiling and retains some of the original large windows and fireplaces. The menu features Catalan cuisine including some specialities from the nearby Ebro Delta: Ancas de Rana Fritas, fried frogs legs; and Angulas en Suc, baby eels cooked in a garlicky sauce, brought to the table in a small earthenware crock and eaten with a wooden fork. There is an excellent selection of regional wines on the list including some from the Priorato region south of Tarragona. I had a bottle of Gandesa Sec Blanco, a strong dry white wine from the Terra Alta.

A fascinating excursion can be made easily from the Parador to the Ebro Delta, an almost tree-less marshy region as flat as the sea which surrounds it. From Tortosa the C 235 leads to a junction with the N 340. One

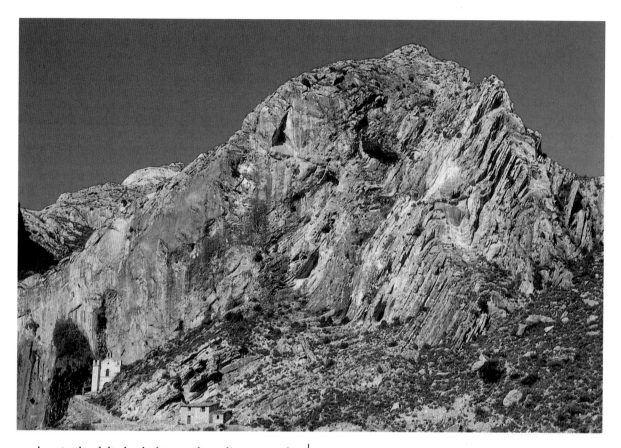

Castellote.

road on to the delta leads from a short distance to the north of this junction and follows the northern bank of the river through the villages of Jesus Y María and La Cava to Ríomar. From here it is possible to cross the Ebro on one of the typical barges to the Island of Buda.

A little to the south along the N 340 another road leads on to the Delta following the southern bank of the river. Extensive rice fields are criss-crossed by narrow paths which lead to small island-like farmhouses. It is said that it is possible to experience mirages in this region equal to those in a desert. The road continues to the edge of the delta where there is an enormously long beach, the Playa de los Eucaliptus, whence another road returns to the fishing town of San Carlos de la Rápita. Here there is a busy harbour and fish market and a long sandy beach just outside the town. The return to Tortosa can be made by returning north along the N 340 to the same junction with the C 235.

ALCAÑIZ

THE NEXT STAGE OF THE TOUR is to the Parador at Alcañiz. A very attractive route along the valley of the Ebro can be followed by taking the T 301 northwards along the east bank of the river from Tortosa. It is a very fertile valley planted with small market gardens and huge orchards of apricot, peach, orange and lemon trees. The road soon climbs out of the valley along a rocky pine-clad mountainside. There are dramatic views of the valley and the Río Ebro far below from this small, quiet road.

Further north the road descends again and continues along the, now, broad open valley of the Ebro. Just beyond Rasquera a small road leads down to the river bank where you can cross the river by driving your car on to a small chain-operated ferry. It is simply a large platform supported on two hulls. It is a pleasant spot for a picnic lunch. The ferry crosses to the village of Miravet, set below a large rock from which a massive castle looks down over the river.

The alternative to the ferry is to continue for another 10km to the north and to cross the river at the twin towns of Mora la Nova and Mora de Ebre. A road follows the river south again to Miravete whence a quiet country road leads west to El Pinell de Brai, strikingly

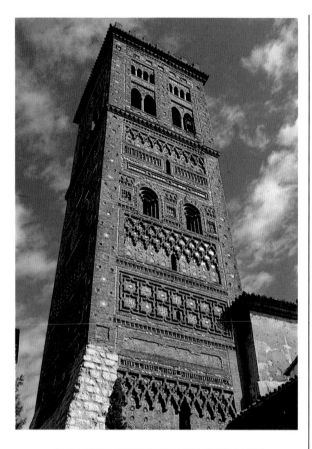

The Mudéjar tower of San Martín in Teruel.

set on a jagged ridge of rock with many of the old houses rising sheer from its edge. Just outside the village is a wine co-operative with a striking modern mural of *azulejos*.

Beyond is a junction with the main road, the N 230. This leads northwards to Gandesa passing through a quite spectacular rocky defile called the Serra de Cavalls. Gandesa is an important wine town set among the extensive vineyards of the Terra Alta. It has a 13th-century Gothic church, an arcaded square and many old buildings.

At Gandesa the route continues to the west along the N 420, passing through Calaceite, an old town with a fine *ayuntamiento,* an arcaded plaza and a Baroque church. Nearby are the remains of an ancient Iberian settlement. This road provides an attractive scenic route along a high ridge with wonderful views of mountains and valleys covered in a sea of vines.

About 40km beyond is Alcañiz, a small town beside the Río Guadalupe with a most attractive *plaza mayor* overlooked by the massive early-18th-century Baroque

church of Santa María la Mayor. Adjacent is a beautiful 16th-century *ayuntamiento* and a 14th-century galleried *lonja.*

On a hilltop above the town is the Castillo de los Calatravas, a 12th-century fortified palace visible for miles around. The location of the Parador Nacional La Concordia, it looks down over the old rooftops of the town to the river tumbling over a weir and the patterned plain reaching away beyond. In the distance the hazy blue ridges of the Maestrazgo can be seen.

The castle is a magnificent building, its imposing façade flanked by two huge square towers. There are Gothic wall paintings in the castle keep and a small cloister nearby contains the tombs of the Knights of Calatrava. There is also a partially destroyed alabaster tomb built for Juan de Lanuza, the Viceroy of Aragón, in the 16th century.

The Parador interior is satisfyingly atmospheric with a huge stone staircase, terracotta-tiled floors and walls decorated with heraldic flags and tiled murals. The restaurant occupies a long room with a high wooden ceiling and an impressive open-stone fireplace. It is illuminated by rows of huge wrought-iron candelabra and casement windows which provide superb views.

The menu offers dishes from the regional cuisine of Aragón, such as Pechugas de Pollo a la Aragonesa, chicken breasts cooked with red peppers, onion, tomatoes, ham and garlic; and Arroz Arogones, rabbit cooked with rice. I tried Muslos de Pollo Turolense, chicken legs cooked in a deliciously rich sauce of white wine, garlic, ham and almonds. The deserts included Dulces Tipicos de Alcañiz, pastries which included wickedly sweet honey turnovers and meringues made with ground almonds. The wine list included a good selection of regional wines. I had a bottle of Don Ramon, a good full-bodied red wine from Cariñena.

Alcañiz is an excellent base from which to make excursions into the Maestrazgo. A day's round trip can be made by taking the N 429 south across an open landscape planted with wheatfields to Calanda, a town known for its ceramics and its attractive arcaded plaza. From here a small road, the T 832, strikes off towards the mountains. It skirts the shores of the Embalse de Calanda towards Mas de la Mata. Here the landscape becomes more hilly with woods and meadows mingling with the wheatfields. The road then climbs into more rugged and mountainous countryside. It enters a narrow green valley, dominated by a massive striated mountain of red rock, and then passes through a tunnel to the village of Castellote, dramatically situated with the old houses strung out below a jagged rocky ridge. Above the town, and almost appearing to be moulded from the cliff, are the remains of a castle.

The road then climbs around the edge of a beautiful lake, the Embalse de Santolea. Its vivid turquoise water is enclosed by bare red rock cliffs. The Maestrazgo is a landscape of boldly contrasting colours. There are rocks and soil of a deep reddish brown, wheatfields the colour of white gold, bright green vineyards and the deep dense green of the pine trees which cloak the mountainsides. There are few signs of human life between the small scattered villages. I drove for several hours along this road without seeing another car.

A few kms beyond the picturesque small village of Olocau del Rey the route turns back to the north-east towards La Mata de Morella. However, a brief detour can be made further south at this point to the enchanting village of Mirambel, encircled by walls with entrance gates, one of which is incorporated into a small tower-like house. There is a beautiful old church, and numerous elegant mansions lining its ancient cobbled streets. It is quiet and unspoilt.

Beyond La Mata de Morella the road leads through the broad fertile valley of the Río Cantavieja to Forcal. An appealing old town beside the Río Caldes and overlooked by jagged mountains, it has an attractive arcaded plaza, a lovely church and many old houses linked by narrow streets and alleys. A small road now leads north along the shallow rocky valley of the Río Bergantes to Ortells and Zorita del Maestrazgo. The latter is an ancient crumbling village of small houses stacked up above each other like a house of playing cards. Their rough stone walls are decorated with small wooden balconies. Above sits a lovely old church with a tower and dome of blue *azulejos*.

A few kms beyond Zorita is the sanctuary of the Virgin La Balma set into a crevice in a massive wall of rock. The road continues through a dramatic canyon with startling views at every turn. At the end of the canyon is the village of Aiguaviva in a broad green valley planted with vineyards and wheatfields. The road returns to Mas de la Mata from where the same route can be followed back to Alcañiz.

TERUEL

THE FINAL STAGE OF THIS TOUR is south-west to the Parador at Teruel. The route I have suggested leads through more of the magnificent Maestrazgo countryside. The first leg of the journey is along the N 420 to Las Mata de los Olmos. A few kms beyond, the TE 821 turns southwards to the picturesque village of Ejulve.

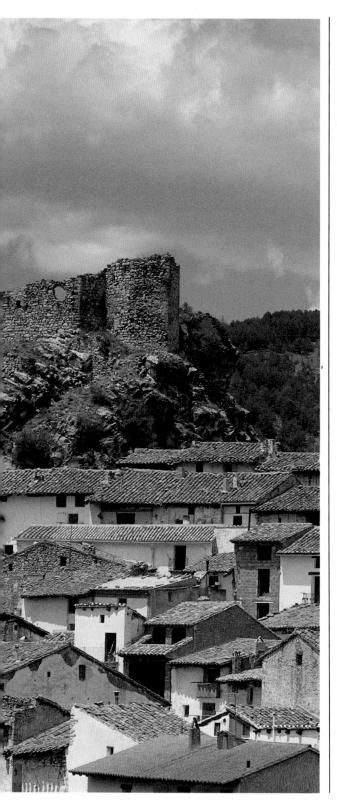

A few kms further south the road enters a steep rocky valley and begins to climb towards the Puerto de Villarluengo. There is a spectacular towering peak of ridged rock, called the Órganos de Montoro, which dominates this valley. A short distance beyond, a small road to the right leads through a huge chasm in the rocks to the village of Ritarque in a peaceful, hidden, green valley through which a small river cascades over boulders and overlooked by two massive mountain peaks. Nearby is the Hostal de las Truchas, an isolated riverside hotel which would make a wonderful base from which to explore this region more fully. The countryside here is simply magnificent – wild, rocky and uninhabited – one of the most beautiful places I have seen anywhere.

The beautiful town of Villarluengo is just on the other side of the pass in a magnificent setting high on a terraced hillside overlooking a rocky valley. It contains a warren of narrow streets with ancient houses and a lovely 18th-century church. Like most villages in this region, it is completely untouched by tourism. Further along this road is another strikingly situated village, Cañada de Benatanduz. The road continues to the Puerto de Cuerto Pelado where the scenery has an almost Alpine quality with springy green turf strewn with wild flowers and dotted with pine trees, gorse and yellow broom.

At this point there is a junction with another road, the TE 800, leading westwards to Teruel, the capital of the province and the seat of a bishop. The city was founded by the Iberians and destroyed by the Romans in 218. After the conquest of the Moors in 1171 they were allowed to remain until the last mosque was closed early in the 16th century. Because of this the city became the focal point of Mudéjar art, a blend of Moorish and Christian architectural styles.

Among the many fine examples of this style to be seen in the city are the Cathedral and the 12th-century churches of San Salvador and San Martín, both with enormous, intricately decorated towers. The city is also famous for its tragic lovers, Isabel de Segura and Juan Diego Martínez de Marcilla, who, in the 13th century, were prevented from marrying by family prejudices and who died of grief. They have been the subject of much poetry and prose and their remains are preserved in the church of San Pedro. There is also a 16th-century aqueduct, a 16th-century Episcopal palace and the remains of the medieval city walls.

The Parador Nacional de Teruel, 2km to the north of the city on the road to Zaragoza, the N 234, is set on a quiet wooded hillside overlooking the city whose Mudéjar towers can be seen rising above the houses. It

Linares de Mora.

is a modern building constructed of stone in traditional style. The ground floor has tall French windows framed by pointed stone arches. There is a grand octagonal entrance hall with marble columns and a large stone staircase. Adjoining the bar and restaurant is a spacious conservatory furnished with cane chairs and tables. Marble floors, high ceilings and simple white decor create a cool, peaceful, elegant atmosphere.

Local dishes on the menu included: Sopa de Teruel en Pelico, garlic soup thickened with bread and enriched with egg; and Crema Fría de Pepino y Mariscos, a delicately flavoured chilled soup of shellfish and cucumber. I had Cazuela de Trigueros y Almejas Marinera, a delicious combination of slender fronds of wild asparagus cooked in a casserole with clams. The house wine is from the vineyards of Cariñena.

Teruel is a good base from which to make an enjoyable excursion into the Maestrazgo, taking the N 234 south-east to La Puebla de Valverde. From here the C 232 leads to Mora de Rubielos, an attractive old town with a massive 13th-century castle dwarfing the small community over which it presides. Adjacent is a 15th-century Gothic church. The road continues through rocky pine-clad mountainsides to the nearby and confusingly named village of Rubielos de Mora. It is particularly delightful, enclosed within medieval walls with entrance gates and threaded by narrow cobbled streets. There is a lovely 16th-century *ayuntamiento* with a charming arcaded patio and 17th-century church; and a 17th-century convent with a beautiful cloister is now a hotel.

From here the route continues to the north-east along the TE 811 through a deep green valley, climbing steadily along the mountainside and quite suddenly revealing the spectacularly sited village of Linares de Mora. Its small red-roofed houses with crumbling stone walls and wooden balconies seem to jostle for position on the hillside. The ruins of a castle and an old church are poised on a ridge of rock above them. The road continues to climb the mountainside beyond the village to the Puerto de Linares. The views from here are simply astonishing. The tiny village seems almost to be suspended above the valley. The surrounding hillsides are ridged and patterned by dry stone walls and terraced fields.

From the top of the pass the road continues along a high plateau, carpeted by meadows and fields of wheat. In the distance is a rim of hazy pine-clad mountainsides. The curious village of Puertomingalvo is like a ghost town and well worth a small detour. Encircled by walls with entrance gates, there is a castle perched on a rock at one end. Its quiet narrow streets are lined with ancient houses.

The road continues through the village of Mosqueruela to La Iglesuela del Cid, another fascinating old town with a 16th-century church and 16th-century arcaded *ayuntamiento*. The T 800 now leads north-west to Cantavieja. This too is a gem: an old walled town with a beautiful arcaded plaza overlooked by an imposing 17th-century church. The road continues to the Puerto Dé de Cuarto Pelado where the same route is followed from the previous itinerary to Allepuz.

The TE 802 now leads along a lovely valley through the Sierra de Gúdar to Alcala de la Selva. This too is an exceptionally beautiful and unspoilt old town in a picturesque setting overlooking a steep narrow valley, with a castle set on a rock, atmospheric streets, a pretty church and square. From Mora de Rubielos, 20km further south, you can return to Teruel along the outward route.

Another interesting excursion can be made to Albarracín only 40km from the Parador at Teruel and worthy of at least a few hours' exploration. It is reached by taking the N 234 north towards Zaragoza for a few kms and then the TE 901 westwards along the valley of Guadalviar. Albarracín is set at the head of this valley at a point where steep red cliffs form a semicircular wall of rock. The pinkish brown village houses are tiered up the mountainside almost appearing to be sculpted from it. Along one side of the rock a vast castle wall extends like a spine of stone. Inside the village there is a jumble of steep, narrow streets and alleys with steps and small squares. It has retained a strong medieval atmosphere. There is a 13th-century cathedral, El Salvador, and the parish church of Santa María which is of Mozarabic origin, although its present form dates from the 16th century. The Episcopal Palace has an imposing Baroque façade. For the energetic, a path leads up to the castle walls from where there are stunning views.

Beyond Albarracín a road leads into the Sierra de los Montes Universales to Orihuela del Tremedal. Here, among deep pine forests is the birthplace of the Río Tajo and dozens of springs which feed many other of Spain's rivers.

An appealing route back to the Parador can be made by taking the TE 900 from Albarracín to Bezas, a quiet country road which runs along a rocky mountainside covered in pine trees. In some places the mountain has been eroded into weird and wonderful shapes creating a quite surrealist landscape. It would make an ideal place to take a picnic lunch.

The airport at Valencia is about 150km from Teruel. The nearest alternative paradors are Santa María de Huerta, 170km (page 104), El Saler, 170km (page 172) and Alarcón, 220km (page 164). The latter can be used to join Tour No. 15 to complete a round trip back to Valencia.

A medieval gateway in Albarracín.

*T*OUR 15 *Begins in the province of Cuenca and leads south to the province of Albacete and the plains of La Mancha, then turning east to the provinces of Alicante and Valencia and exploring the fishing towns and resorts of the Costa Blanca. The countryside through which it leads ranges from the vast wheatfields and vineyards of the plains to the little-known mountain range of the Sierra de Alcaraz, the Valencian huertas and the marshy flatlands and lagoon of La Albufera. It is a region of impressive castles and hill-top towns as well as white fishing villages and palm-fringed beaches. The four Paradors which link the tour include one of the most beautiful and atmospheric castles in the Parador network and a beach-side modern hotel which has one of the loveliest golf courses in Spain on its doorstep.*

— TOUR 15 —
MICHELIN MAP NO. 445

• Alarcón

• El Saler

ALBACETE

• Jávea

ALARCÓN
ALBECETE
JÁVEA
EL SALER

ALARCÓN

THE STARTING POINT of the tour is the Parador Nacional Marqués de Villena, situated in a small village set on a rocky, island-like, promontory in a loop of a gorge where the Río Júcar emerges from the Embalse de Alarcón. It is a short distance from the main road, the N 111, which links Valencia with Madrid. The nearest airport is at Valencia, about 160km distant. The nearest alternative Paradors are at Teruel (page 161), Chinchón (page 108) and Manzanares (page 117).

The Parador occupies one of the loveliest castles in the region and was built during the early part of the Moorish occupation. The village itself is encircled by extensive walls and guarded by towers and fortified gateways. Indeed the approach to the village is along a narrow ridge between two towers which gives the impression that you are crossing a drawbridge. The castle played an important role in the final overthrow of the Moors. The Parador is named after one of the castle's more notable owners, Juan Pacheco the Marqués de Villena. He was a powerful friend of Henry IV of Castile who gave him the castle along with many other properties throughout Spain.

The restaurant occupies one of the castle's great halls with massive rough stone walls. The local Manchegan cuisine is represented on the menu with dishes such as Morteruelo, a highly spiced dish of chopped pigs' liver fried with breadcrumbs; Tortilla Guisada, an omelette made with potatoes and onions and served in a sauce flavoured with paprika and garlic; and Queso Manchego con Mostillo, the local ewes' milk cheese served with a slice of a delicious jelly-like preserve, similar to *membrillo* but made from grapes instead of quinces. Local wines include those of Valdepeñas, Utiel and Jumilla. I sampled the Castillo de Almansa, which is a good red

wine from the vineyards of Yecla.

The village of Alarcón is a peaceful and unspoiled place with an almost deserted atmosphere. There is an arcaded *ayuntamiento* in the plaza and many ancient houses decorated with escutchions along its quiet cobbled streets. There are several old churches: Santa María has an attractive façade with a portal decorated by sculptures and pillars.

The Parador is a convenient base from which to visit the town of Cuenca about 80km to the north. An attractive and quiet route, which avoids the main road and leads through pleasant rolling farmland, is to take the N 111 east towards Motilla del Palancer and after a few kms turn north on to the CU 721 and then the CU 714 to Olmedilla de Alarcón and Valeria. Here there is a ruined castle and the remains of a Roman town. Beyond Valeria the road joins the N230 a few kms south of Cuenca.

Set on a rocky V-shaped promontory, created by the junction of the gorges of the Río Júcar and the Río Huéscar, it is an attractive old town with a lovely plaza mayor. Here café tables spill on to the street and it's a charming place to relax a while with a drink or meal. Overlooking the plaza is the cathedral, a most imposing building with a monumental facade. It contains many treasures including paintings by El Greco, Flemish tapestries and a magnificent 16th-century screen.

The town is famed for just two buildings, the Casas Colgados, the hanging houses. These houses quite literally hang over the edge of the 600ft cliffs which tower above the Huéscar gorge and are occupied by a restaurant and an art gallery. A flimsy suspension bridge spans the gorge, enabling you to walk out and obtain a dizzy view of the already vertiginous houses. Way below a small road runs alongside the river with lovely views of the hanging houses, and the small rocky valley, to Palomera where there are some attractive riverside spots, perfect for a picnic. In the gorge of the Río Júcar is the prettily situated church of San Miguel in which concerts of religious music take place.

From Cuenca a round trip can be made into the Sierra de Valdecabras, a rocky, pine-clad mountain range. A natural curiosity can be visited along this route called the Ciudad Encantada, the enchanted city. A series of paths lead off into the pine forests to a region where the rocks have been eroded into strange and exotic shapes. One, for example, is like a monumental mushroom 100ft high and others look like the hulls of huge beached galleons. The return from Cuenca to Alarcón can be made more swiftly by taking the N 320 back to Motilla del Palancar.

ALBACETE

The Castillo and Parador of Alarcón.

THE NEXT STAGE of the tour is south to the Parador of Albacete. I have suggested a slightly circuitous route, first visiting the town of Villanueva de la Jara, 17km to the south of Motilla del Palancar on the N 320, with a lovely 16th-century church, an arcaded plaza mayor as well as the remains of medieval walls. The CU 804 then leads westwards across a land as flat as an expanse of water and planted with vineyards, wheatfields and olive trees. San Clemente is a most attractive old town with numerous medieval buildings to admire including an arcaded *plaza mayor* and an elegant porticoed *ayuntamiento*.

About 20km to the south-west, after crossing the N 301, is Villarobledo, a town known for its excellent wine and also a centre for Manchegan cheese and saffron. It too has a fine 18th-century *ayuntamiento* and an interesting church of the same period. Upon returning to the N 301, Albacete is some 70km to the west along a road which runs as straight as a plumb-line across the plains. The red soil is patterned by endless rows of green vines and golden wheatfields.

Albacete is a largely modern town at a busy cross-

roads, founded in the time of the Moors. It is now the main centre for saffron and is also known for the manufacture of knives and daggers, Puñales and Navajas, which have rather evil-looking spring-loaded blades. The only notable old building which remains is the 16th-century cathedral of San Juan Bautista. There are excellent shops, bars and restaurants however.

The Parador Nacional La Mancha is situated a few kms to the south-east of the town along the N 430. It is set like an island amidst the flat and seemingly endless plain which surrounds it. The low modern building makes full use of space. It is in the form of a vast square with additional wings. In the centre is a garden shaded by trees. There is a spacious bar and café popular with the local people, especially at the weekends. An outdoor swimming pool is nearby in the garden. Long cool corridors link the spacious bedrooms and terracotta tiles and mellow wooden furniture and fittings help to create a pleasingly rustic atmosphere enhanced by the use of antique farming equipment as decor.

The restaurant with its high, sloping beamed ceilings also enjoys local popularity. Regional handicrafts decorate the walls. There are two rooms, one offering à la carte meals and the other a lavish buffet of both hot and cold dishes from which you serve yourself. The local speciality here is Gazpacho Manchego. The name is misleading since it is not served cold and it contains meat: it is a rich and substantial soup made from pieces of rabbit, flavoured with garlic, onions and mushrooms and thickened by the addition of pieces of a special local, unleavened bread, like pitta. It is most unusual, delicious and very filling, calling for a very light main course. I, mistakenly, ordered Paletilla de Cabrito al Romero to follow, kid braised in a rich sauce and flavoured with rosemary. I chose a bottle of Estola, a strong, dry white wine from Villarobledo.

Strangely the most enjoyable excursion to make from the Parador is in mountain countryside, although scarcely a molehill is visible from the building. It is to the Sierra de Alcaraz 100km or so to the south-west of Albacete. You can continue beyond the Parador along the small road which leads from the main road. This joins the N 301 where the route leads south for a few kms before branching to the right along a small country road to Pozohondo.

From here a road leads west to Peñas de San Pedro, where there are the remains of a hilltop castle. The route now turns south again along the C 3211 to Ayna. At first the countryside is as flat as only La Mancha can be, but as you travel further south it becomes more undulating with the promise of distant hills and mountains. At Villarejo a small road leads eastwards to the small town of Lietor, on the edge of a steep rocky hillside and overlooking a luscious green valley through which a small river runs. Beyond Lietor the road joins another, the C 3211, which leads north towards Ayna through a rugged, dramatic landscape. Initially it runs high along the side of a deep valley bordered by pine-covered mountainsides and then descends to follow the Río Mundo through a steep narrow canyon.

Ayna is in a spectacular setting high on the mountainside with dizzy views down into the plunging rocky valley. The road continues to climb high above the village with increasingly awesome panoramas. On

The cathedral of Cuenca.

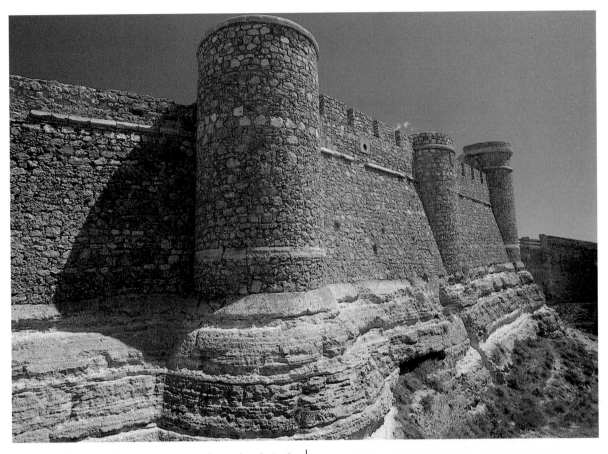

The Castillo of Chinchilla de Monte Aragón.

reaching the summit the road passes through relatively flat countryside, planted with olive and almond trees, towards Bogarra.

Quite suddenly the landscape opens out and a broad deep valley is revealed far below – a startling sight. The reddish soil is planted with thousands of olive and almond trees creating a vivid pattern. The road descends into the valley and follows it to Bogarra, attractively set at its head. The road follows a series of small valleys through gently sloping mountainsides. It is hard to believe that you are only an hour or so away from the unrelieved flatness of the La Mancha plains.

Beyond Paterna de Madera the road joins the C 415 where the route continues north-west to Alcaraz. It is a historic town, originally an Iberian settlement with a wealth of ancient buildings, built from the pinkish brown stone characteristic of the region and dominated by the remains of a Moorish fortress. It retains a strong medieval atmosphere within its narrow-stepped streets and alleyways. There is an attractive arcaded *plaza mayor* overlooked by a fine 16th-century *ayuntamiento* and the beautiful 15th-century church of La Trinidad. Other interesting buildings include two *lonjas*, a 16th-century clock tower, the 16th-century church of San

Miguel and the remains of a medieval aqueduct. From Alcaraz the return to Albacete can be made by following the N 322 to the north-east, a distance of about 80km.

JÁVEA

THE NEXT STAGE of the tour is to the Parador at Jávea. The route is eastwards towards the coast following the N 340 towards Almansa. Chinchilla de Monte Aragón is a delightful old town set on an isolated ridge overlooking the plains. A web of steep narrow streets radiate from the *plaza mayor* where there is an 18th century *ayuntamiento* and the 15th-century church of Santa María del Salvador with a beautiful façade and tower. Nearby is the 14th-century monastery of Santo Domingo. A massive castle crowns the top of the hill which can be reached by a rough track. There are superb views from here of the vast La Mancha plain.

Almansa is dominated by a very picturesque castle set on a steep conical outcrop of rock. The town, largely modern in appearance, also possesses a fine Gothic church, Santa María a la Asunción, and a 16th-century convent. Beyond Almansa the route continues along the N 330 to Villena, where there is another impressive castle and the 15th-century Gothic church of Santiago. From here the route turns eastwards along the A 210, through a landscape which becomes progressively more mountainous, to Biar. Its small houses are grouped below a castle mounted precariously on a pine-covered rocky bluff. Just beyond is the hilltop town of Castella, with the remains of a castle.

The road continues to a junction with the N 340 where the route proceeds northwards for a few kms towards Alcoy. Just before reaching the town a small road, the C 3313, leads west into the mountains to Benasau. The mountainsides here are covered in pines and layered by small terraces planted with peach, apricot, almond and olive trees. Beyond Benasau the road climbs steadily along the side of a steep valley with the landscape becoming impressively rugged. A few kms past Confrides a small road leads to the village of Abdet from where there are magnificent views of the mountain landscape.

The road continues to Guadalest, a curious village built on an enormous pinnacle of rock high on the side of a valley. A small church teeters on the very edge of the cliff. The village, little more than a single street and a few houses, is entered through a tunnel in the rock. It is a very popular excursion from places like Benidorm so it is best to plan your visit early or late in the day when the tour coaches have departed.

The road now descends from the mountains through Callosa de Ensarriá and Altea la Vieja to join the N 332 coast road. Here the route is north to Calpe, an attractive scenic drive, following the coast closely along rocky red-brown mountainsides which slope down into a deep blue sea. The hillsides here are heavily developed and peppered with villas and apartment blocks. Calpe is distinguished by a towering pinnacle of rock, the Peñon de Ifach, which juts out into the sea. Below this is the harbour where brightly painted fishing boats lie alongside yachts and motor boats.

A small road follows the coastline from Calpe to the resort of Moraira, from where it crosses the headland to Jávea. The town overlooks a glorious wide sandy bay from a hill about 1km inland. There are the remains of old city walls and many ancient towers dot the mountainsides around it. Narrow streets within the old town indicate its Moorish past and there is a fine Gothic church.

The Parador Nacional Costa Blanca is at the northern extremity of the long curve of sand, one of the finest on

The Sierra de Alcaraz near Ayna.

the Costa Blanca. To the north is the Cabo de San Antonio and to the south the Cabo San Martín and Cabo de la Nao. The Parador is a modern building in the Spanish Mediterranean style with the bedrooms opening on to large sun balconies with sweeping views of the bay. They are thoughtfully provided with canvas sun awnings. The public rooms all face the bay and open on to a wide terrace scattered with comfortable garden furniture. Beyond, a wide lawn and gardens, shaded by tall palm trees, sweep down to the water's edge where a small jetty completes an ideal setting for an after-dinner stroll.

The menu has a good selection of rice dishes, a speciality of the Valencia region, as well as excellent sea food: Arroz Empedrado, rice with salt cod and haricot beans; Paella de Pato, paella made only with rice, vegetables and pieces of duck; Arroz con Costra, rice with mixed meats and chick peas and Dorada a la Sal, sea bream baked in salt, a delicious local method of cooking fish: coarse sea salt is heaped over the whole fish and baked until it forms a hard crust; when broken

The bay of Jávea seen from the Cabo de San Antonio.

open the fish inside is succulent and moist and not at all salty. Among the regional wines on the list Castillo de Murviedra is an excellent red from Valencia.

An interesting excursion can be made along a small road which continues beyond the southern end of the beach to Cabo San Martín and Cabo de la Nao. There are several small rocky coves and wonderful views of the impossibly blue sea from the steep pine-clad cliffs. The road continues to Playa de la Granadella, a small, pretty cove enclosed by steep headlands.

To the north of Jávea a road climbs over the headland to Denia. Almost at the top of this hill a narrow road to the right leads out on to Cabo de San Antonio, from where there are breathtaking views of the bay and mountains beyond. You can watch the toylike fishing boats far below making their way back to the harbour which nestles under the headland. Denia is an attractive resort town with a castle, a busy fishing port and a lively fish market.

EL SALER

THE FINAL STAGE of the tour is to the Parador at El Saler, about 80km further north along the coast. I have suggested an indirect scenic route which leads first into

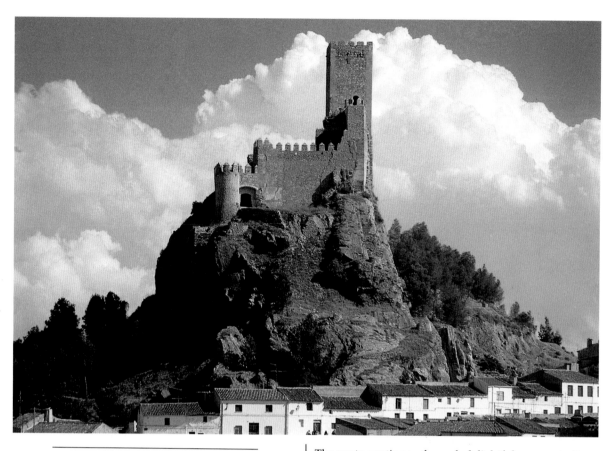

The Castillo of Almansa.

the mountains north of Guadalest and then along the coastal plain. From Jávea the route follows the N 332 to Benisa, an old town with stepped streets, small squares and a magnificent twin-towered Gothic church known as La Catedral de la Marina, the cathedral of the sea. It is set on a steep hill and surrounded by terraced vineyards with superb views towards the sea.

The route continues to Altea, a pleasantly situated resort dominated by a church with a large dome of blue azuleos. From here a road leads east into the mountains to the picturesque old town of Polop. A web of old streets surrounds a castle and there are some fascinating shops to explore. The route continues north to Callosa de Ensarriá, and then along the C 3318. The road follows a rocky valley filled with oleander bushes and climbs up to the village of Taberna. There are wonderful views from this road across the *huertas*, patterned with rows of orange and lemon trees, to the shimmering blue sea beyond. The road continues around the side of a towering mountain, a landscape of monumental proportions. The road ascends to the Col de Rates from here the views surpass any seen so far on this journey.

The route continues through delightful scenery to Pego and then westwards through the Vall de Gallinera. This too is strikingly beautiful. Steep-sided and narrow the dry river bed on the valley floor traces a pink and purple ribbon of oleander blooms along its course. Beyond is the picturesque village of Planes, surrounded by cherry orchards with a castle set above the old brown tiled houses. There are also the remains of a medieval aqueduct.

A short distance beyond, the road joins the N 340 where the route heads northwards to Albaida. The C 320 leads back to the coast to Gandía. There is a very long golden sand beach here backed by a promenade and dotted with *merenderos* (beach bars), sun shades and games areas. North of Gandía there are small market gardens scattered among the vast orchards of orange and lemon trees which carpet the Valencian plain. Continuing north along the N 332 you can see in the distance the massive rock of Cullera, crowned by a castle, below which the town spreads out beside the mouth of the Río Júcar, whence a road follows the coastline quite closely through a sequence of small beach resorts which become progressively less developed.

Here on the coastal plain the orange and lemon plantations give way to small market gardens often enclosed behind tall cane fences to protect them from the winter winds. The long sandy beach which runs along this part of the coast is backed by pine forests.

A few kms south of El Saler, the Parador Nacional Luis Vives is hidden among the pines between the long sandy beach of Dehesa and the lagoon of Al Albufera. A long low white building, its large bedroom balconies are framed by elegant arches. From these are lovely views over the pine trees and one of the best golf courses in Spain. A small footpath leads over sand dunes to a massive sandy beach which extends in both directions for many kms. It is one of the few places along this coast where there is no sign of development. The Parador interior is cool, spacious and elegant.

The first-floor restaurant has panoramic views of the dunes and sea beyond and there is an intimate bar and comfortable lounge on the ground floor. Extensive rice fields in the marshy region which surrounds the lagoon are the reason why Valencia is the home of *paella*. Paella Valenciana is the name given to the dish with which most people are familiar, a mixture of saffron-flavoured rice with pieces of chicken, fish and shellfish. The traditional Paella Valenciana, however, is made with snails, green beans and chicken or rabbit

The lagoon of La Albufera near El Saler.

and contains no fish. Another dish related to *paella* is Fideua, made in a similar way, but noodles are used instead or rice. Arroz Negra, black rice, is so called because it is made with squid and their ink sacks give the rice a dark colour. The wine list has a good selection from Valencia.

For those interested in the regional rice dishes it is worth taking a trip to the village of El Palmer, a short distance from the Parador on the edge of the lagoon. This curious village is almost surrounded by the rice fields and there are many excellent restaurants here, each with their own definitive version of *paella*, Arroz Abanda and Fideua as well as with excellent seafood.

The provincial capital of Valencia is only a short drive from the Parador. It is a large modern city with broad avenues, spacious parks, shaded squares and a lively and cosmopolitan atmosphere. However, it also has a well preserved, and quite compact, old quarter, centred around the cathedral. This was started in the 13th century but not completed until the 16th century. As a consequence it reflects three different architectural styles in its three portals, one Romanesque, another Gothic and the third Baroque. Its octagonal Gothic tower is a distinctive landmark. It contains many treasures including paintings by Goya and, legend has it, the chalice used by Christ at the last supper. This gem-studded agate vessel is carried through the streets of Valencia in a solemn procession on Maundy Thursday.

Adjacent to the cathedral, and linked by an archway, is the Baroque church of NS de los Desamparados. There are many other churches and mansions within the city. A particularly beautiful building is the Palacio del Marqués de Dos Aguas, a soaring flight of Baroque fancy with its entire façade intricately decorated with sculptures and an elaborate portal carved from alabaster. It houses Spain's most important museum of ceramics.

For those interested in ceramics the neighbouring town of Manises, near the airport, is the home of Spain's leading school of ceramics. The famous Lladró borthers attended here and the Lladró factory and shop is to be found in a suburb of the city called Tabernas Blanques. Valencia also possesses a fascinating botanical garden – one of the best in Europe.

About half an hour's drive north of Valencia along

The Cathedral of Valencia. Overleaf: The village of Casares.

the Autopista A 7 is Sagunto. Founded by the Iberians, the present town is set below a mountainous ridge of rock, over 2000ft long, which rises up abruptly from the plain. Surmounting the ridge are the remains of a Roman city. Massive castle walls encircle the mountain top with numerous gates, towers and squares. From the highest part, the Plaza Ciudadela, there are superb views looking down over the walls to the plain below and the sea beyond. Set just below the castle walls are the extensive remains of a theatre founded by the Greeks and later enlarged and improved by the Romans. The old town, on the slopes below the castle, is also interesting and atmospheric. There are two churches, 14th-century Santa María and 13th-century San Salvador.

To return to the Parador, follow the Autopista A 7 back to Valencia where you take the southern part of the city's ring road to join a brief section of the Autopista south to El Saler. The nearest alternative Parador to El Saler is at Benicarló, 150km north (page 152).

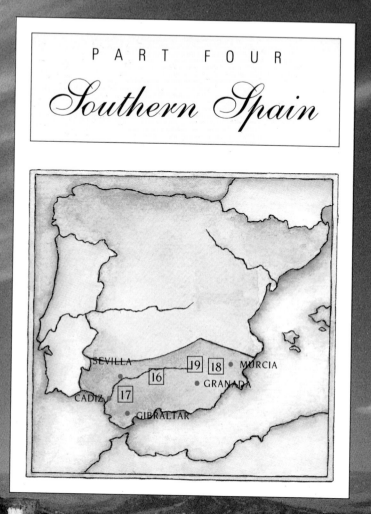

PART FOUR

Southern Spain

SEVILLA
CADIZ
GIBRALTAR
[16]
[17]
[19] [18] MURCIA
GRANADA

- TOUR 16 -
MICHELIN MAP NO. 446

CÓRDOBA

Carmona
SEVILLA

Antequera
MÁLAGA

MÁLAGA
ANTEQUERA
CÓRDOBA
CARMONA

*T*OUR 16 Explores the provinces of Málaga, Córdoba and
Sevilla in the central region of
Andalucía. Bordered in the north by the
Sierra Morena, the natural barrier which
almost isolates this part of Spain from the
rest of the country, the southern limit is the
Costa del Sol. The eastern extremity is the
maritime city of Málaga and to the west is
the delta of the great Andalusian river, the
Guadalquivir. Andalucía is the region of
Spain whose characteristics most colour the
visitor's expectation of the country. It is a
land of white hilltop villages threaded by
narrow Moorish streets, mountains covered
by silvery-green olive trees, shimmering
heat and the deep-blue Mediterranean sea.
The itinerary begins in the city of Málaga, heads north through
the mountains to Antequera and Córdoba and then follows
the course of the Río Guadalquivir to the historic hilltop town
of Carmona.*

MÁLAGA

MÁLAGA IS A BUSY CITY and seaport with the unmistakable atmosphere of the Mediterranean. Founded in
Phoenician times it gained its importance after its capture by the Moors in the 8th century. Its most notable
building is the cathedral begun in the early 16th century.
It has a most imposing façade with three portals flanked
by two large towers. Among the many fine features in
the interior are superb carved 17th-century choir stalls
and a gilded statue of the Virgin which was carried
during the wars against the Moors. The church of NS
de la Victoria occupies the site upon which Ferdinand
and Isabella were encamped during the seige of Málaga.

Set up on a hill above the cathedral is the Alcazaba,
the Moorish fortress, surrounded by beautiful terraced
gardens which cascade with flowers. It now contains
an archaeological museum. Nearby are the remains of
a Roman theatre. Other buildings of interest include
the 15th-century church of Santiago el Mayor, the 17th-
century church of Santo Cristo, and the 18th-century
Episcopal Palace with a magnificent Baroque façade.

On the eastern edge of the town, on a high wooded
hill overlooking the port, is the Castillo de Gibralfaro,
so-called because it had a beacon in one of its towers
to guide ships. During the seige of Málaga, at the time
of the reconquest, it took the Spanish forces 40 days to
overcome the stronghold.

The Parador Nacional de Gibralfaro, adjacent to the
castle and surrounded by pine and eucalyptus trees,
occupies the site of an old hostelry, parts of which have
been retained in the modern building. It has been constructed in traditional style of large blocks of stone and
tall elegant arches. The bedrooms are particularly large

and have furnished balconies from
where there are superb views of the
city and the sea. The Parador has a
delightfully peaceful, cool and slightly
remote atmosphere in spite of its proximity to the city. It is a popular place
for a drink or a meal with the
Malagueños.

The restaurant offers an aperitif to
diners called Trajinero, which is a
sweetish Oloroso-type wine made from
grapes grown on the hillsides around
the city. I chose Ajo Blanco Malagueño
to start my meal. It is a delicious and
unusual chilled soup – an interesting
alternative to the more familiar
gazpacho. It is made by combining
ground almonds, breadcrumbs, garlic, wine vinegar,
olive oil and water, garnished with small green grapes.
Of the bewildering choice of seafood in this region
chipirones and *chanquetes* are frequently seen on local
menus. The former are tiny squid fried quickly with
garlic until golden. The latter are minute anchovies
often prepared in a similar way but also sometimes
combined into an omelette.

ANTEQUERA

THE NEXT STAGE OF THE ITINERARY is north to the
Parador at Antequera, a distance of only 50km and I
have suggested an indirect route which leads through
the valley of the Río Guadalhorce and then through the
Sierra de Alcaparrín to the Embalse del Guadalteba-
Guadalhorce. From the centre of Málaga you should
follow the signs to Campanillas. This road, the MA 402,
leads across the fertile plain of the Río Guadalhorce to
Cártama, where there is a ruined Moorish castle.

This part of the journey is through vast plantations
of orange and lemon trees. Beyond Pizarra the road
continues through a progressively narrowing valley
called the Valle de Sol, the valley of the sun. Álora is
strikingly situated, the small white houses of the town
are grouped together in the saddle of a ridge above
which is a castle. Behind is an imposing backdrop of
rugged mountains. The narrow streets and alleys of
the town climb the hill upon which it is built at a dizzy
angle.

The road begins to climb into the mountains beyond
Alora and leads alongside a steep valley terraced with
olive groves. The scene is dominated by a vast ridge of
rock. This is the Garganta del Chorro. The Río Guadalhorce forces its way through a deep narrow crevasse and
beside it a railway tunnel is bored like a massive
mousehole into the rock face. Beyond, the road leads
through a narrow gorge with steep cliffs to Bobastro. A
few kms past this village, a small road leads to the

Antequera.

remains of a 9th-century Mozarabic sanctuary on rocky slopes covered by pine trees and clouds of yellow broom.

The little town of Ardales, overlooking the Embalse de Guadalhorce, is set in the midst of soft rounded hills dappled with beige, brown and green. The road continues, with constantly pleasing views of hillsides chequered by wheatfields, to Teba. This too is an attractive old town set on a spur of rock with a castle and the remains of battlements. The route continues, skirting the embalse, to Campillos, and then along the N 342 to the east. A few kms to the north of this road is the Laguna de la Fuente de Piedra, a limpid blue salt water lagoon, rich in bird life and surrounded by low olive-covered hills. 30km beyond Campillos along the N 342 a junction with the N 334 leads south to Antequera.

The town is attractively situated on the slopes of the Sierra de Chimenea and looks out over the plain of the Río Genil. Above the rooftops of the houses a Moorish castle commands superb views of the countryside. In the old part of the town is the church of El Carmen with a beautiful Baroque altarpiece and a Mudéjar ceiling. There is also the 16th-century hall church of Santa María la Mayor, and the 16th-century church of San Sebastián. Near the town there are three dolmen, of which the most impressive is the Cueva de Menga with a massive block of stone weighing nearly 200 tons forming its roof.

The Parador Nacional de Antequera, on the western edge of the town a few minutes' walk from its centre is a modern building set in a quiet location with lovely views over the plain. There is an attractive garden with a large pool shaded by palm trees. The rooms are spacious and airy with high, sloping ceilings.

The menu included Remon Antequerano, a local dish which is an unusual salad of salt cod, with orange, onion and garlic. I had Porra Antequerana to start my meal, a creamy gazpacho-like purée with ham, egg, tuna fish and tomato. From the good selection of seafood I chose Rape en Pimentón, monk fish cooked with paprika. A delicious sweet is Bienmesabe Antequerano, a tart filled with a mixture of honey and ground almonds.

A fascinating morning's excursion can be made from the Parador to El Torcal, a series of extraordinary

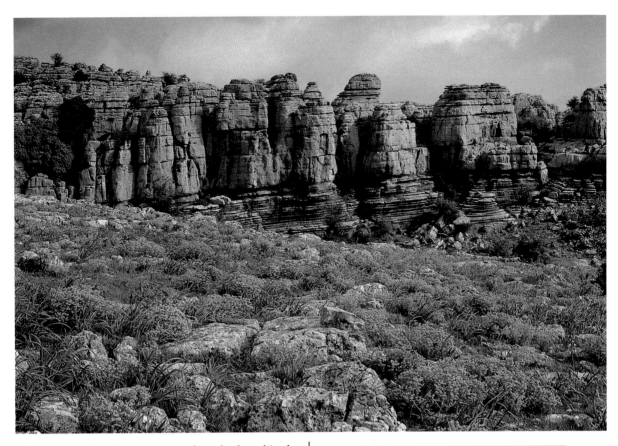

El Torcal.

ridged and striated silver-grey rocks to be found in the mountains 13km to the south of the town. They have been sculpted into strange abstract shapes, creating a quite bizarre landscape. Numerous small footpaths lead off into this curious region. It is reached along a road which climbs through a steep-sided green valley from where there are fine views of the old town.

A longer round trip can also be made from the Parador which explores the countryside and villages to the east of Antequera. The first place of interest is Archidona, reached by taking the N 342 to the east of Antequera. The road crosses a flat, fertile plain, patterned with olive groves and wheatfields and dotted with *cortijos* (farms). Archidona is set on a steep craggy mountain with a forest of small white houses clinging to its slopes. It has a charming old quarter with a pronounced Andalucían character. Here there is a very pretty, and most unusual, octagonal *plaza mayor*. There are also the remains of town walls and a sanctuary within the Moorish castle above the town.

A quiet road, the MA 214 leads north-east to Villanueva de Tapia through a virtual sea of olive trees, in peaceful countryside populated only by small isolated farms. Beyond is the picturesque town of Iznájar built on a mountainous rock overlooking the Embalse de Iznájar and threaded by steep narrow streets which rise precipitously to the small church at its summit. The road continues northwards along a very attractive scenic route, skirting the embalse to the old town of Rute, then leading north-east towards Priego de Cordoba, passing the strikingly situated village of Carcabuey, with a castle crowning the rocky crag upon which it is built. Priego de Córdoba is a very appealing old town with numerous Baroque churches as well as a castle and a *lonja*. The streets are lined with old houses which are festooned with flowers and decorated with ornamental grilles. There is also a beautiful 18th-century fountain, the Fuente del Rey, and from the town walls there is a wonderful view over the surrounding countryside.

From here the route back to the Parador can be made by returning along the C 336, past Carcabuey, to Cabra with the ruined castle of San Juan, formerly a mosque, and the 16th-century church of Santo Domingo. The C 327 then leads south to Lucena, a large lively town with the 15th-century church of San Mateo and a ruined castle. At a junction, the road meets the N 331 which leads south to Antequera.

CÓRDOBA

THE NEXT STAGE of the tour is north to the Parador at Córdoba. From Antequera the route is along the N 334 across a flat, undulating landscape covered by wheat-fields to Estepa, on a steep hill overlooking the plain and whose streets rise steeply towards the castle. The entire town seems to be built on a one-in-four hill with a tangle of narrow cobbled steps and alleys threading between the blindingly white houses. From the top, by the castle, there are staggering views over rooftops to the countryside beyond. Here too is the Convent of Santa Clara with a fine Renaissance portal, the Baroque churches of the Virgin de los Remedios and El Carmen and the Palacio de los Marqueses de Ceverales with an impressive Baroque façade. The town is also famous for its Pulvorones; sweet almond biscuits.

At Estepa the C 338 leads north-east to Puente Genil beside the Río Genil and then west towards Lucena. After 18km the CO 761 heads north to Moriles, a wine town amidst extensive vineyards. This is an important wine-growing region. Those produced with the Montilla/Moriles label are as highly regarded as the more well-known wines of Jerez further to the west. The CO 760 now leads to Aguilar, an attractive hilltop town surrounded by olive groves and vineyards with a broad octagonal plaza and a ruined Moorish castle. Of its several old churches the extravagantly decorated Baroque chapel of the Convento de Carmelitas Descalzas is of special interest. Here, at the junction with the main road, the N 331, the route continues north to Montilla and then through rolling vineclad hillsides to Córdoba.

Córdoba is a mellow city on the banks of the broad Río Guadalquivir with a backdrop of the wooded Sierra de Córdoba. The Moorish capital during their occupation of Spain, it retains a fine bridge and numerous buildings from this period along with a labyrinth of narrow shady streets.

Le Mezquita, the mosque, is one of the largest and most magnificent of those built by the Moors throughout their Empire and one of the finest buildings from

this period remaining in Spain. Started in the latter part of the 8th century, on its completion at the end of the 10th century, it was over 600ft long and 400ft wide with 19 aisles. It is surrounded by massive, buttressed walls and faces a square shaded by orange trees. After the capture of Córdoba in 1236 it became a Christian church and then a cathedral. The present building is a fascinating mixture of different architectural styles, resulting from 9 centuries of continual building. The interior has a quite mystical atmosphere with subdued daylight filtering through a forest of elegant columns and horseshoe arches.

You will need a guide book if you are to see all the city has to offer, but much pleasure can be derived from just strolling along its narrow, flower-laden streets and discovering it for yourself. It is particularly enchanting after dark when the mellow glow of street lanterns creates pools of yellow light and dark mysterious shadows.

Among its squares the charming Plaza del Potro (which contains an inn mentioned by Cervantes in *Don Quixote*), the Plazuela de los Dolores and the Plaza de la Corredera are particularly appealing. The latter was once used as a bullring and is now the setting for a lively and colourful street market. The Roman bridge is also lovely and one of the finest views of the city can be had by walking over it to the opposite bank.

The Parador Nacional La Arruzafa, in a quiet setting 3km to the north of the city centre on the slopes of the Sierra de Córdoba, occupies the site of the old Manor of Abderramán I who had the first palm trees in Europe planted in his garden. *Arrazufa* is Arabic for a garden of palm trees. From its hillside setting the modern Parador building commands extensive views of the city and the valley of the Guadalquivir. All the spacious bedrooms have large, furnished balconies with a beautiful outlook. A large sun terrace extends the full length of the hotel. Below this are attractive gardens with paths and steps leading to a large swimming pool surrounded by lawns. Beyond are tennis courts.

The restaurant offers a choice of à la carte meals or a grand buffet with a large selection of hot and cold dishes from which you serve yourself. Among the regional dishes on the menu during my stay was Salmorejo Cordobés, a chilled soup based on lean meat, garlic and olive oil; and Cazuela de Rabo a la Cordobesa, bull's tail braised in a wine-rich sauce with vegetables. Cazuela de Mollejas con Champiñón Jamón are sweetbreads cooked with mushrooms and ham.

From the Parador an enjoyable excursion can be made to the Medina Azahara, and into the wooded Sierra de Córdoba, by taking the C 431 to the west of the city. After 8km a road to the right leads to the Medina Azahar. Here on a hillside are the remains of the once beautiful palace and town of Caliph Abderramán III. Its construction, in the 10th century, was an epic venture employing many thousands of men, mules and camels for over 25 years. The complex included a mosque, baths, stables, gardens, lakes and accommodation for its large population. It was laid to waste in 1010 by Berber mercenaries and little remained. In 1944, however, the remains of the Royal apartments were discovered and these have now been extensively reconstructed and are the most impressive relic of the site. Nearby, high on the wooded slopes, is the 15th-century Monastery of San Jerónimo, built from the ruins of a Moorish castle and containing a particularly lovely Gothic cloister.

A small country road continues through beautiful woods high up into the mountains. There are extensive views over the Guadalquivir valley and the mountains beyond. You can see for miles and miles. It continues along the edge of the Sierra to Las Ermitas from where you can look down on to the city far below. It is a wonderful place to take a picnic lunch among the pine trees. At Santa María de Trassierra, a few kms to the west, a small chapel within the ruins of a castle was originally a mosque.

CARMONA

THE FINAL STAGE of this itinerary is westwards along the valley of the Guadalquivir to the Parador at Carmona. Leaving Córdoba along the C 431 leads to Almodóvar del Río, an attractive old hilltop town overlooking the river. At its summit is a most impressive castle with battlements and towers, around which steep narrow streets spread in a tangle. The road follows the river through fields of vegetables and orchards to Palma del Río. This too is an atmospheric old town with a castle and several interesting churches.

At Palma del Río a road to the south, the C 430, runs alongside the Río Genil to Ecija. This beautiful riverside town with shady squares, parks and fine old buildings is known as Ciudad de las Torres, the city of towers, and as you approach it across the plain at least a dozen lovely towers can be seen soaring above the rooftops. Many are decorated with colourful *azulejos*. It is also known, less attractively, as La Sartenilla de Andalucía (the frying pan of Andalucía) because of its searing summer heat.

There is a Moorish castle and a beautiful *plaza mayor* surrounded by arcaded houses and a fine *ayuntamiento*. Among its many churches the 16th-century Santiago el Mayor and the 18th-century Santa Cruz are of particular interest. The Palacio de los Marqueses de Peñaflor has a magnificent Baroque façade. There are also many

Córdoba seen from the Roman Bridge.

fine mansions to be seen along the Calle de los Caballeros. Many of the houses have beautiful patios.

The town of Osuna is about 30km to the south of Ecija along the C 430. This too is an atmospheric old town with numerous medieval mansions along its streets. The Calle Carrera and Calle San Pedro contain the best examples. At the highest point of the town is a 16th-century university and an imposing 16th-century Colegiata.

From Osuna the route continues westwards along the N 334 through quite flat countryside to La Puebla de Cazalla. Here the SE 701 leads north-west to Marchena, a rather faded and crumbling old town with considerable charm and character. Some 25km to the south is Morón de la Frontera, an ancient town with the remains of a huge Moorish fortress dominating the landscape from its hilltop setting.

From Marchena the C 339 leads to the north-east across an undulating plain the Carmona. Set high on a steep hill, it is visible from a great distance. Battlemented walls surround the town which is entered through imposing fortified gateways, the Puerta de Córdoba and the Puerta de Sevilla. Within stand three Moorish fortresses, the Alcazar de la Puerta de Córdoba, the Alcazar Puerta de Sevilla and the Alcazar de Puerta Marchena. One of the most prominent features of the town is the tower of the 17th-century church of San Pedro, a copy of the famous Giralda tower in Seville. The 15th-century Gothic church of Santa María la Mayor has a patio with horseshoe arches, a fine Plateresque retablo and 18th-century carved choir stalls. There is a lovely square, the Plaza de San Fernando, surrounded by Mudéjar houses and overlooked by an 18th-century *ayuntamiento*. Of the many other interesting buildings the churches of San Bartolomé, San Salvador and the Convent of La Concepción are outstanding.

On the western side of the town is a Roman necropolis. There are over 1,000 graves and several hundred burial chambers which have been excavated. They date from between the 2nd and 4th centuries and represent one of the most important archaeological sites in Spain.

The Parador Nacional Alcázar del Rey Don Pedro, within the remains of one of the Moorish fortresses, the Alcazar de Arriba is on the western edge of the town with fine views overlooking the fertile plain. It was used as a residence by King Don Pedro who converted it into a lavish palace. It was also used by the Catholic Kings during their final battles with the Moors in Granada. The castle was abandoned after an earthquake in 1504. It is only a few minutes' walk away from the centre of the town through a maze of narrow cobbled streets lined with white-washed houses.

An old house in Marchena.

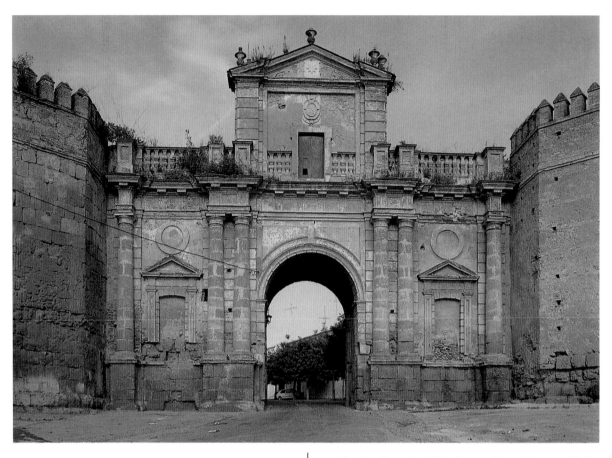

The Puerto de Córdoba in Carmona.

The Parador is a modern construction in traditional style and contained within massive walls several metres thick. Long castle-like corridors link the rooms and there is a lovely terrace ranged along the sheer side of the hill with splendid views. There is a beautiful patio decorated with blue tiles and elegant arches surrounding a fountain. Below the Parador, on the hillside, is a magnificent blue-tiled swimming pool. The building is a most successful combination of medieval ambience and modern comfort.

The restaurant is situated in a vast room with a high-vaulted ceiling supported by stone arches and wooden beams. I chose a typical dish of the region to start my meal, Espinacas Estilo Carmona, a highly seasoned purée of spinach cooked with chick peas. To follow I had Lomo de Merluza a la Sevillana, pieces of hake cooked in a rich sauce of ground almonds, olive oil, lemon juice and garlic.

The city of Seville is less than 40km away long the N 6 and the Parador makes a good base from which to visit the city for a day. For those who wish to avoid the traffic and parking problems of a busy city there is a good bus service from near Plaza San Fernando into the centre of Seville.

The Parador also makes a good base from which to make an excursion into the Sierra de Morena. From Carmona the route leads north-east along the C 432 to Lora del Río, where there is a ruined castle and an *ayuntamiento* with a Baroque façade. A quiet country road continues northwards to the attractively sited town of Constantina. It winds through hilly, open heathland which is dotted with oak and pine trees and carpeted with gorse, broom, wild flowers and herbs. In Constantina is the 18th-century church of Las Navas de la Concepción which contains a fine Baroque retablo. Beyond, towards Alanís, where there is a 14th-century church and the ruins of a castle, the landscape becomes more hilly and quite densely wooded.

From Alanís the route continues to the south, along the C 421, through a wild and remote landscape to Cazalla de la Sierra. The town church of Santa María de la Consolación is built in a blend of Mudéjar and Gothic styles. Just beyond, a small road leads westwards across an even more lonely and beautiful landscape to El Real de la Jarra. Here wild asparagus grows by the roadside and the hillsides are covered in clouds of yellow broom and a sea of rockrose. A few kms further on, the road crosses the very pretty valley of the Río Calla, the scene of a Romería at the end of April. There is also an idyllic spot for a picnic lunch on the banks of the small river. Beyond is the attractive old town of Olalla del Cala where narrow streets and ancient houses surround a hilltop castle and a 15th-century church.

From here a small road continues westwards to the enchanting village of Zufre, one of the prettiest white villages in Andalucía. It is ranged along the edge of a sheer cliff and its narrow cobbled streets and alleys are lined with immaculately white houses which literally cascade with floral colour. It is completely untouched by tourism and I felt that this was how the narrow streets of Córdoba and Sevilla must have looked centuries ago. There is a 16th-century Mudéjar church and *ayuntamiento*.

Beyond Zufre the road joins the N 433 where the route continues north-east to Aracena, an attractively-sited town crowned by a Moorish castle and an imposing 13th-century church. Nearby is the Gruta de las Maravillas, one of the largest stalactite caverns in Spain.

From here a road climbs into the highest parts of the Sierra Morena. It is surprisingly green and wooded; massive chestnut, walnut and oak trees cover the mountainsides and below them velvety brown pigs forage contentedly. This is the country of jamon serrano, mountain ham, and region where many would claim the best Spanish ham is produced. Jabugo is the village which gives its names to these hams, the huge curing factory almost dwarfs the small community. The route continues south from Jabugo and after a few kms a small road leads east back towards Aracena. There are superb views to the south along this road from a viewpoint called La Peña de Arias Montano, just above the pretty village of Alajar. Upon returning to Aracena the route back to the Parador is south along the N 630 to Seville and then the N 4 east to Carmona.

From Carmona you can continue to the Parador at Ayamonte, 165 km (page 188), to join Tour No 17) and complete a round trip back to Málaga. The nearest alternative Parador is at Zafra, 140km distant (page 128).

La Mezquita in Córdoba.

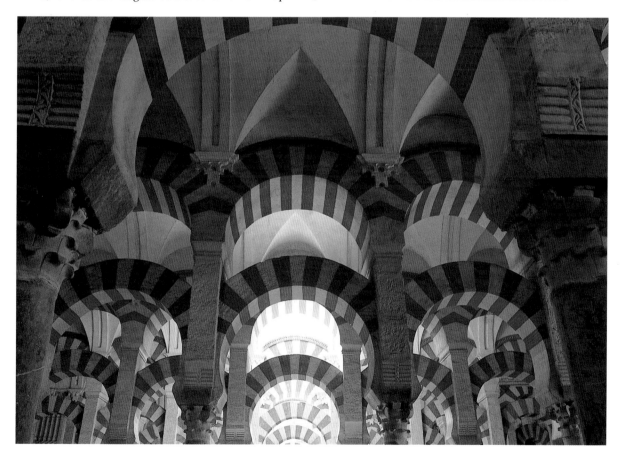

OUR 17 Centred in the western region of Andalucía in the provinces of Sevilla, Huelva, Cádiz and Málaga, it explores the coastal regions of the Costa del Sol and the Costa de la Luz as well as the Guadalquivir Delta and the mountain ranges of the Sierra de Ronda and the Sierra de Bermeja. The landscape is immensely varied since it ranges from the marshy lowlands of the Coto Doñana and the vine-covered sandy hills of Jerez to the vast beaches of Spain's Atlantic coast and almost alpine-like valleys hidden among the country's southernmost mountains. The itinerary also provides an interesting and scenic route from the Portuguese border to Málaga and,

AYAMONTE – MAZAGÓN
CÁDIZ – ARCOS DE LA
FRONTERA
TORREMOLINOS

combined with Tour No 16 (page 176), can create a round trip. The Paradors which link the tour include one in an evocative hilltop village, another overlooking the finest and quietest, beach in southern Spain and a third in the atmospheric maritime city of Cádiz.

AYAMONTE

AYAMONTE IS THE STARTING POINT of this route, although of course it can be followed in reverse, starting from Torremolinos. The nearest airport is at Sevilla, 150km. The closest alternative Parador is at Carmona, 165km (page 186). Ayamonte is the border town lying beside the broad estuary of the Río Guadiana which separates Spain and Portugal. On the opposite bank is the Portuguese town of Villa Real de Santo Antonio which is linked by car and passenger ferries. The town contains a number of interesting buildings. The church of NS de las Angustias dates from the 16th century. The convent church of San Francisco, with a superb panelled ceiling and Mudéjar tower, is also from this period and so too is the convent of Santa Clara. There is also a 15th-century palace in the *plaza mayor* with an attractive façade.

The more modern parts of the town are centred around the mouth of the river but the old town extends in a series of narrow streets to the summit of a hill. This was the site of the ancient castle and is now that of the Parador Nacional Costa de la Luz. It commands magnificent views over the river estuary, the sea and the Portuguese countryside beyond. The sunsets seen from the Parador are simply spectacular. It is a single-storey building, in a hilltop setting. There is a swimming pool and terrace adjoining the restaurant, all enjoying the same sweeping views. The interior is cool and welcoming with green foliage cascading down the walls of the tiled corridors and rooms.

The restaurant has an excellent selection of seafood on the menu. I chose Pez Espada Parador, a swordfish steak cooked with a delicious orange sauce. Arroz a la

Ayamontina is a seafood *paella* and La Raya en Pimentón is ray cooked with paprika.

MAZAGÓN

THE NEXT PARADOR at Mazagón is only 85km away on the other side of the estuary of the Río Odiel beyond Huelva. Since it is set beside a superb beach it is a more attractive base for those wishing to spend some time by the sea which is the main attraction in this part of Spain. The landscape here is very flat and the coastal plain is heavily cultivated with vast fields of strawberries and citrus fruits. The stretch of coast between the estuaries of the Guadiana and the Odiel provides some excellent beaches. The most attractive region is between the village of El Rompido and the resort of Punta Umbría. This is reached by taking the N 431 to the east of Ayamonte to Lepe and Cartaya. A short distance further a small road leads south to El Rompido, an attractive small fishing community sheltered by a long bar of sand.

The road follows the coastline closely, and the long quiet beach is backed by sand dunes and pine trees. Access to the sea is possible in many places. Towards the large and heavily developed resort of Punta Umbría the beach becomes a vast and smooth expanse of fine golden sand.

The Odiel estuary is crossed at Huelva, a busy port at the junction of the Río Odiel and Río Tinto. Although a town of ancient origins few buildings survived an earthquake in 1755. Of these the most interesting are the 16th-century cathedral and the 16th-century church of San Pedro.

Beyond Huelva and its industrial suburbs, the C 422 leads south-east along the Paseo de los Piñones to La Punta del Sebo and then crosses the mouth of the Río Tinto. Here on a promontory is a monolithic monument to Christopher Columbus, a gift to the town from the United States of America, perhaps to thank them for discovering it. It was from the small town of Palos de la Frontera, a few kms up-river, from which Columbus sailed with his small fleet of three ships on 3 August 1492, returning on 15 March 1493. The water has now retreated far from the town and there is no longer a harbour. Nearby is the 15th-century Monasterio de la Rábida from where Columbus made the preparations for his voyage. It contains a small museum of relics associated with the expedition.

A few kms north of Palos is Moguer, a neat, orderly town with shady squares and blindingly white houses lining its streets. It has a splendid *ayuntamiento* decorated with arches and columns. There are two interest-

The coastline near El Rompido.

ing churches, NS de la Granada and the convent of La Esperanza with a fine Baroque retablo. On the northern edge of the town is the 14th century Mudéjar convent of Santa Clara.

Returning to the main road, the C 442, the route follows the coast eastwards to the resort of Mazagón through a forest of umbrella pines. The Parador Nacional Cristóbal Colón, hidden among the pine trees 6kms to the east of Mazagón is a low white building spread out in an L-shape over a broad expanse of lawn and garden shaded by pine and palm trees. The gardens reach down to the edge of a cliff below which a vast beach of firm yellow sand stretches away in both directions for several kms. Close to the cliff edge is a swimming pool. The bedrooms are large and airy and open on to spacious verandahs which over-look the garden. The Parador has a remote and peaceful atmosphere with only the rumble of the Atlantic surf breaking on the beach below to disturb the silence.

The restaurant is an attractive L-shaped room on the first floor with a pretty, tiled floor and a wooden-beamed ceiling. It opens on to a balcony overlooking the garden. Seafood is understandably a strong feature on the menu. I had Sopa de Rape to start my meal, a delicately flavoured fish soup with monk fish, calamares, prawns, rice and tomato. Rape a la Andaluza is pieces of monk fish sautéed with paprika. I chose Solomillo a la Sevillana for my main course; fillet steak cooked with olives. An excellent local white wine is Viña Odiel from the Huelva vineyards.

The road continues close to the sea beyond the Parador to Matalascañas, a huge unattractive resort. For most of this distance the sea is hidden beyond pines and access to the beach is limited. Just before reaching Matalascañas a road to the north leads along the western edge of the Coto de Doñana to the village of El Rocío. This countryside is one of the most important nature reserves in Europe. Known as Las Marismas (the marshes) it is a flat, sandy terrain dotted with lakes, pools and waterways fringed by reeds. It is especially important to ornithologists since it is a resting place for birds making their migratory flights between Africa and Northern Europe. In addition, animals such as red and fallow deer, lynx, wild cat and wild boar are also found. It is possible to make trips into the national park by applying to the Park centre on the road between Las Matalascañas and El Rocío.

El Rocío is a small, curious town on the edge of the marshes. Little more than a collection of shanty-like buildings lining dirt roads, it is dominated by the enormous white church of NS del Rocío, Our Lady of the Dew. It is the scene of one of the largest and most famous *romerías* (pilgrimages) in Spain which is held at Pentecost. People from all around, Sevilla, Huelva and Cádiz, make their way to the village on horseback, in decorated wagons and by the busload to commemorate a statue found here to which mysterious and miraculous powers are attributed.

The route continues north of El Rocío through the wine-growing towns of Almonte and Bollullos par del Condado to Palma del Condado where there is a 16th-century Plateresque church and an attractive *ayuntamiento*. Here the route joins the main road, the N 341. Before continuing eastwards it is worth making a brief detour to the west to Niebla, a Roman town and later the capital of a small kingdom. It is encircled by massive walls, punctuated by over 40 towers. Four of the original gateways have survived. The church of Santa María de la Gran dates from the 10th century and there are also the ruins of a 15th-century church.

From Palma del Condado the route follows the N 431 eastwards to Sevilla and then the N 4 south to Dos Hermanos, where you can join the Autopista A 4 and

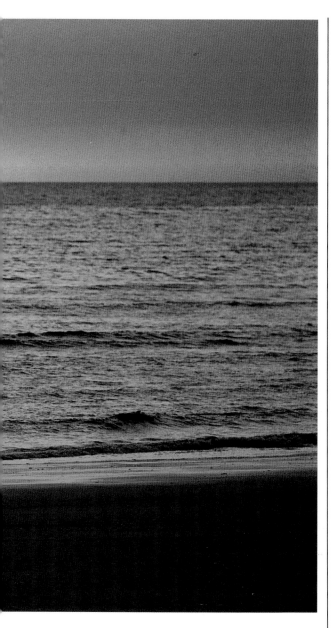

century retablo. Among the other churches worth seeing is the monastery of Santo Domingo with a fine Gothic cloister. The town's medieval mansions include the Palacios of Duc de Monnpensier and the Duque de Medina de Sidonia.

The small port of Bonanza, a few kms to the north of the town has numerous small bars where you can drink Manzanilla and there are some good simple fish restaurants with plenty of local atmosphere. From Sanlúcar the road follows the coastline south to the pretty flower-decked town of Chipiona whose church of NS de la Regla has a 17th-century Gothic cloister.

Rota is a lively, rather chaotic American base, and further on, El Puerto de Santa María, an appealing old town with a busy port engaged mainly in wine exporting, has numerous *bodegas,* those of Osborne and Terry being particularly impressive. The 14th-century Moorish castle of San Marcos lies in the centre of the town and nearby is the 13th-century church of NS de los Milagros with an impressive Gothic façade and a beautiful Plateresque portal. There are many other churches and mansions to see and the town is well worth exploring.

CÁDIZ

THE ROUTE CONTINUES past the busy commercial port of Puerto Rea to Cádiz, a city built on a slender 9km long promontory whcih juts out into the Bay of Cádiz. The old part of the city is built on a rock at the very tip and is almost surrounded by water.

The Hotel Atlántico is the Parador of Cádiz and overlooks the sea. The gardens and pool in front of the hotel extend to a promenade which runs along the water's edge. It is a large modern building in the established style of Mediterranean hotels. The bedrooms are angled and staggered, giving the large balconies good views of the sea. The interior is spacious and luxurious with polished marble floors and elegant columns. The hotel is famous for its spectacular sunsets. Whenever travellers swop tales the question of the best place for a sunset is often mooted. Those seen from the hotel terrace are equal to the splendid displays on Kuta beach in Bali and on the Serengeti plain.

The restaurant shares this fine outlook. The menu is understandably centred on the superb seafood of the region. I chose Fritura Gaditana which was quite simply the best dish of mixed fried fish I have ever tasted. It contained tiny sole no more than 5in long, hake the size of a fish finger, miniscule anchovies, squid that would fit into a teaspoon and red mullet no longer than a small sardine. Urtas Asadas al Vinagre de Jerez is a type of sea bream, filleted, grilled and served with a light sauce flavoured with sherry vinegar. The wine list

continue to Exit 3. Here a road leads south-west to Lebrija, an attractive old town whose church of Santa María, once a mosque, has a tower reminiscent of the famous Giralda tower in Sevilla.

The road continues through low chalky hills ridged by the vines from which the wines of Jerez are made. Sanlúcar de Barrameda beside the estuary of the Río Guadalquivir where it flows into the Atlantic ocean, known for its Manzanilla wines, like the *fino* sherries but with a distinctive flavour attributed to the nearness of the sea. The church of NS de la O has a fine Mudéjar portal with *artesonado* (moulded) ceilings and an 18th-

The beach at Cádiz.

Vineyards near Jerez de la Frontera.

includes Castillo de San Diego, a crisp, fruity white wine made from the vines grown on the Albarizo soil around Jerez.

The city of Cádiz possesses many fine buildings. The New Cathedral, not completed until the early 19th century overlooks the sea and has a magnificent dome nearly 200ft high. The original 13th-century cathedral, the church of the Sagrario was reconstructed at the beginning of the 17th century in the Renaissance style. The 19th-century *ayuntamiento* is a massive building with an imposing and elaborately decorated façade. The 18th-century Baroque church of NS del Carmen contains a retablo by El Greco and a fine patio.

The old part of town is a warren of narrow tunnel-like streets and alleys. To stroll through these at night evokes a strong sense of the past. The cobbles glisten as if wet, lit only by small pools of yellow lamplight cast by hundreds of lanterns. As well as its historic buildings and busy city life, Cádiz also has superb sandy beaches which extend along the southern edge of the promontory for many kms.

An interesting circuit can be made from Cádiz along the coast towards Gibraltar and then inland through the Sierra de los Melones. The route is initially southwest along the N 4 which runs alongside the magni-

ficent sandy beaches of Victoria and Cortadura to San Fernando. Here there is a Roman bridge and an 18th-century *ayuntamiento*. At Chiclana de la Frontera, where there is a large 18th-century church, a road leads eastwards to the coast to Sancti Petri. The remains of a 13th-century castle can be seen on a small offshore island. From Chiclana the N 340 continues south to Conil de la Frontera, an old fishing town with a 16th-century church and the remains of a Moorish fortress.

Beyond is the white hilltop town of Vejer de la Frontera which has retained a strong Moorish atmosphere. It has a tangle of steep narrow streets lined by white-washed houses, a castle and an interesting Gothic church. From here a small road leads out to the Cabo de Trafalgar. Little more than a spit of sand marked by a lighthouse, it is the place where Nelson defeated the combined French and Spanish fleets. The road continues alongside a series of good sandy beaches to Barbate de Franco, a busy fishing port.

The route continues through peaceful countryside close to the sea to Zahara de los Atunes, a small fishing village set on a large sandy beach on the edge of a small creek. Although unexceptional it has an agreeably relaxed and unhurried atmosphere. There are a number of excellent seafood restaurants with a tempting array of locally caught fish and shellfish. From here a road leads back to the N 340 whence the route continues south-east towards Tarifa. After 15kms a road to the right leads to the ruined Roman town of Bolonia.

Tarifa is a town of considerable atmosphere and character. It is entered through a fortified gateway and inside is a fascinating web of narrow streets and alleys. The town is set at the narrowest point of the Straits of Gibraltar and has a 10th-century Arab fortress built to defend its vital position. Superb views of the Straits can be seen from the ramparts. There is also the medieval Torre de Guzmán and a 16th-century Gothic church with a fine Baroque façade.

The landscape changes now from the flat coastal plain surrounding Cádiz and becomes progressively more interesting as the road continues towards Algeciras. It climbs around steeply indented mountainsides to the Puerto de Cabrito from where there are sweeping views to the sea. Beyond, at the Puerto del Bujeo, there are impressive views of the rock of Gibraltar rising up from the sea like a massive iceberg.

The route continues beyond Algeciras, an unattractive modern town, towards San Roque. A few kms before reaching the town the C 331 leads north to Almoraima, where there is a 17th-century convent in a peaceful wooded setting. Here a road leads to the left, winding up a steep and dramatic hill to Castellar de la Frontera. On its rocky crest is a castle and below a small Moorish village of ancient whitewashed houses. There are fine views over the craggy wooded hillsides and of the Embalse de Guadarranque from the village.

Beyond Almoraima the road begins to climb into the mountains to Jimena de la Frontera, an attractive hilltop village crowned by a ruined castle from where there are sweeping views over the surrounding landscape. The road continues high along the side of the precipitous valley of the Río Hozgarganta. It is a remote and wild region with only an occasional isolated farmhouse to be seen between the villages. Deep woods with gorse, rosemary and broom cover the hillsides. The road climbs to the Puerto de Galiz. Here the CA 511 descends into a green and pleasant valley to Alcalá de los Gazules. The village is set on a knoll on the side of the valley, its cluster of small white houses stacked like boxes on its slopes.

The road continues westwards for 24km to Medina-Sidonia, a picturesque old town set high on a hill. It was founded by the Phoenicians and has been home to Greeks, Romans, Visigoths and the Moors. It possesses a Gothic church with a particularly fine 16th-century Plateresque retablo. There is a gateway decorated with horseshoe arches, an interesting *ayuntamiento* and the remains of the Arab fortress. From here the return to Cádiz is made by following the C 346 back to Chiclana de la Frontera.

ARCOS DE LA FRONTERA

THE NEXT STAGE of the tour is north-west to the Parador at Arcos de la Frontera. The first part of the route is along the N 4 to Jerez de la Frontera. The town is of course famous for its wines which are grown on the white chalky hillsides known as *albarizas*. It is possible to visit a *bodega*, of which there are many, and have the process of sherry-making explained. The cellars of González Byass are to be found right in the centre of the town next to the remains of the 11th century Moorish Alcázar but there are many others to choose from. The town also contains some interesting buildings. There is a 17th-century church, San Salvador, and the 15th-century Gothic churches of San Miguel and Santiago; the 16th-century Renaissance Casa del Cabildo Viejo now houses a library and an archaeological museum. The Palacio de los Marqueses de Monatana has an impressive Baroque façade and a beautiful patio. The Casa de Bertemati, the Casa de Riquelme, the Casa del Marqués Domecq and the Palacio de los Marqueses de Campo Real are also notable.

Perhaps the most beautiful building is to be found on the outskirts of the town. This is La Cartuja de NS de la Defensión, 5km to the south of Jerez. The building, a 15th-century Carthusian monastery, abandoned in the 19th century and re-established in the middle of the present century, is entered through an imposing doorway which reveals an exquisitely decorated façade of golden stone. Not all of the building is open to the public but its exterior is exceptionally beautiful.

Leaving Jerez the N 342 leads eastwards to Arcos de la Frontera. The town is strikingly set on a precipitous crag overlooking the Río Guadalete. Sheer cliffs rise from its banks and vineyards, olive groves and orchards spread out beyond. The streets are so narrow they feel like tunnels as you drive through and so steep that walking down the rough cobbles needs considerable care. Blindingly white houses brim with flowers and the atmosphere is profoundly Andalusian. One of the narrowest and steepest streets leads into the Plaza de España. Here the 16th-century church of Santa María de la Asunción looks over the square with an impressive Plateresque façade and soaring bell tower. Nearby is the Gothic church of San Pedro, containing paintings by Zurbarán and Pacheco and a magnificent Gothic retablo. The western side of the square is dominated by an Arab fortress and to the south a balcony overlooks the river with sweeping views.

On the fourth side of the square is The Parador Nacional Casa del Corregidor. Formerly the mansion of González de Gamaza and today a comfortable hotel,

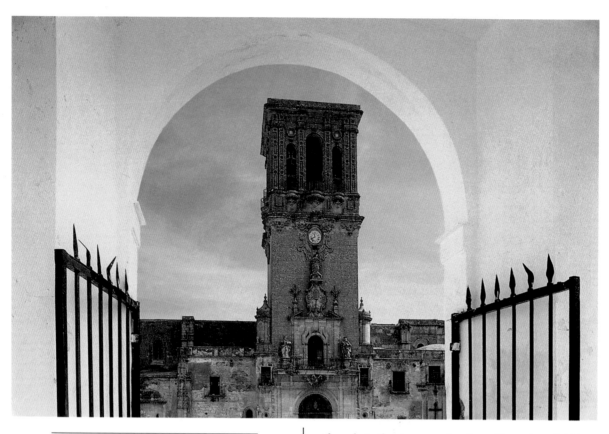

Left: A street in Arcos de la Frontera. Above: The church of Santa María de la Asunción in Arcos de la Frontera.

sitting right on the very edge of the cliff in a setting which makes it one of the most memorable of the Paradors. The bedrooms have balconies from which you can watch the sun go down. Long corridors connect the rooms with wooden-beamed ceilings, stone arches and terracotta-tiled floors. There is a small, charming patio filled with plants and set out with tables and chairs. Breakfast is served here. The restaurant opens on to a broad semi-circular terrace from where you can watch red kites wheeling around the cliff face.

Among the Andalusian specialities on the menu I tried Rape Sanlugueña, pieces of monkfish cooked in a sauce with peppers, asparagus and peas. The delicious fresh peas which were in season also featured in Guisantes con Jamón, in which they are cooked in a casserole with *serrano* ham and garlic. Cordero Quisado al Estilo de Arcos is small pieces of lamb on the bone cooked with potatoes, onions and carrots in a sauce flavoured with garlic and thyme. An excellent local wine on the list was Viñedos Regantío Viejo, a deep

red made in the Arcos region from Cinsault and Cabernet Sauvignon grapes.

Arcos is a good base from which to explore some of the pueblos blancos (white towns) of the region. A day's round trip can be made by first taking the N 342 north-east through open rolling countryside to Bornos, an appealing old town attractively situated on the banks of the Embalse de Arcos. There is a large 16th-century convent and the streets are lined with old houses and mansions.

The road continues to Villamartín and Algodonales. The landscape becomes progressively more hilly as the contours of distant mountains draw nearer. A fiesta was in progress during my visit to Algodonales. I watched a solemn procession in which a statue of the Virgin was carried through the streets on the shoulders of a dozen or so brawny village maidens dressed in white gowns. A drum beat out time to their slow, swaying march. The statue was placed on a dais in front of the church. Throughout the day the villagers, family by family, brought large bunches of carnations and carefully arranged them in vases around the figure. Gradually the flowers formed a small mountain of brilliant colour.

The road leads further westwards through craggy hills to the Puerto Cabañas where a distant view of the

Olvera.

hilltop town of Olvera is dramatically revealed. Shimmering white houses are scattered on the slopes and above a church and a Moorish fortress appear almost to be sculpted from the rock.

A quiet country road leads through a small green valley to the south of Olvera and then passes through a gorge created by the Río Trejo to Setenil. It is a small, curious town built on and around an outcrop of tufa rock. Into this many homes have been tunnelled. Entire streets of cave dwellings with quite normal house fronts and small tiled roofs protruding from the rock have been built. There are also the remains of a castle and a 15th-century Gothic church. The 16th-century *ayuntamiento* has a fine *artesanado* (moulded) ceiling.

A road leads westwards from Setenil through a broad valley to Ronda, a town worthy of an extended visit. Its most famous sight is the deep cleft in the rock upon which it is built. A bridge crosses the ravine and houses are built along the sheer sides of the cliff. There is much more to see, however: the bullring dates from 1785 and has an extravagant Baroque façade. The collegiate church of Santa María la Mayor was formerly a mosque and has a wealth of interesting features in Gothic, Moorish, Renaissance and Plateresque styles. The Casa del Rey Moro has delightful gardens from where steps descend to the bottom of the gorge. The 14th-century Mudéjar Casa del Gigante has a patio surrounded by elegant marble columns and an *artesanado* ceiling. There are also fascinating streets and alleys in which to wander and squares with pavement cafés where you can linger over a drink.

From Ronda the route continues north-west along the C 339. After about 15km a small road leads west along a dramatic valley bordered by soaring pinnacles of rock to Montejaque. The road continues to the Cuevas de la Pileta where a cave nearly a mile long has been carved by an underground river. Here there are cave paintings of animals from the paleolithic age which are reminiscent of those at Altamira. Back on the main road the route continues north towards Algodonales along the side of a deep mountain valley. After about 15km a small road leads eastwards to the village of El Gastor. Nearby is a dolmen known as the Giant's Tomb. Continuing north along the main road for another 10km the route leads westwards along a quiet road to Zahara de la Sierra, strikingly set upon a steep ridge of rock – a very pretty village with an Arab castle and a 16th-century Baroque church. There are impressive views of the Sierra de Grazalema from the castle walls.

The road leads deeper into the mountains to the Puerto de las Palomas. The scenery around this pass is breathtaking – and as dramatic as any in the Alps. The road continues over the Puerto del Boyer to El Bosque and then through hilly farmland back to Arcos.

TORREMOLINOS

THE NEXT STAGE of the tour is south-east to the Parador at Torremolinos. From Arcos the route is first west-wards along the C 344 to El Bosque and then south along the CA 524 to Ubrique. A large, lively town in an impressive mountain setting, Ubrique is well-known for its leather-work. There is also an interesting Gothic church here.

From here the route continues along the C 344 through the Sierra Ubrique to Grazalema, an isolated little town with a lovely Gothic church. Beyond, the road joins the C 339 where the route continues south-east to Ronda. A few kms south of Ronda the C 341 forks right through impressive mountain scenery, passing a sequence of attractive small villages. From a distance the clusters of brilliant white and red-roofed houses stud the green mountainsides like gemstones. Gaucín has an impressive Arab castle set high on a ridge above the town. It is possible, on a clear day, to see both Gibraltar and the Moroccan coast from the ramparts of the castle.

Here the MA 539 leads south-east through a remote and beautiful mountain landscape towards Estepona. A brief detour leads to Casares. It is one of the most picturesque and strikingly situated of the white hilltop towns, its small white houses clinging to the sides of a steep conical rock, the top of which is crowned by a castle. The road continues through Manilva, set among vineyards, to join the main coast road, the N 340, 11km west of Estepona.

The route now leads east along this road to Torre-molinos through a succession of Costa del Sol holiday resorts, Estepona, San Pedro, Marbella, Fuengirola and Benalmádena Costa. Driving along this road offers little pleasure. It is fast, very busy and in the summer it can be quite dangerous. The scenery too is swamped by gross development. Towns like Estepona, San Pedro and Marbella still retain attractive old parts but they are places to stay for a seaside holiday more than sightseeing destinations.

The Parador Nacional del Golf is situated about 1km to the east of Torremolinos along a small road to the

A finca near Tolox.

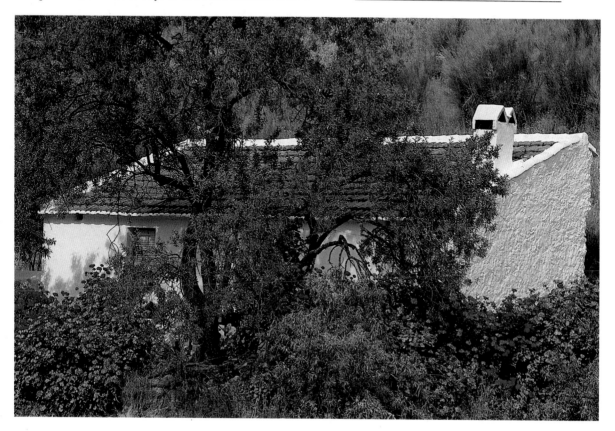

right of the main road. It is clearly signposted. The approach is along an avenue lined with palm trees, oleander and bougainvillea. It is a long, low building of white brick built in regional style. The bedrooms have large sun terraces facing an enormous lawn, in the centre of which is a swimming pool. Beyond, low sand dunes border a long, quiet, sandy beach. The Parador is virtually surrounded by a splendid golf course. Leisure and relaxation are the essence of this Parador. The proximity of Málaga airport, however, makes it less than quiet on occasions.

Regional dishes on the menu include: Riñones a la Jerezana, lambs' kidneys cooked with onions, garlic, parsley and sherry; and Huevos a la Flamenca, eggs baked on a bed of sautéed mixed vegetables with *serrano* ham and *chorizo* sausage.

An interesting excursion can be made from the Parador into the Sierra de Mijas. From the main road the C 344 leads west through orange and lemon groves to Alhaurín el Grande. Here a road leads south over the Puerto de los Pescadores, with splendid views, to Mijas. This once remote Moorish village is now encroached upon by the Costa del Sol developments. Nevertheless it still has considerable charm. It possesses a 16th-century church, formerly a mosque, the remains of castle walls and an ancient rectangular bullring.

From Alhaurín el Grande the route continues to Coín. Here you have two choices. A full day trip can be made by continuing north-east through the valley of the Río Grande to the pretty hilltop village of Tolox. Continuing north to Alozaina, a road to the left leads through dramatic mountain scenery to the Puerto de las Abajes. Beyond is El Burgo, another delightful mountain village. The route continues with spectacular mountain views to the Puerto de Viento, where the road descends to Ronda. The return to the Parador can be made by taking the C 339 south to San Pedro where the N 340 leads back to Torremolinos.

The alternative, and shorter, journey from Coín is along the C 337 to Marbella. This leads over the Puerto de Ojén with stunning views of the coastline. A short detour can be made higher into the mountains to the Refujio de Juanar. Once a Parador, this charming mountain retreat is set in the midst of wooded mountains. It's hard to believe this peaceful and remote place is only a few kms from the hectic chaos of the Costa del Sol. About 1km beyond is a *mirador* with a breathtaking view of Marbella. Back on the main road the route descends to Marbella where the N 340 is joined.

The nearest alternative Parador to Torremolinos is at Málaga, 10km (page 176).

Gaucín.

TOUR 18 Explores the eastern region of Andalucía, starting in the province of Málaga and then following the eastwards into Granada, Almería and Murcia before turning inland to the province of Jaen. The route explores an excitingly varied countryside. The most lovely of all Spain's southern coastal scenery is found to the east of Málaga and also some of its most barren. There are landscapes of desert-like hills, hidden green valleys and mountain ranges covered in dense pine forests – all within the space of a few hours' driving. Some of the most picturesquely sited villages in Spain are to be found on this trip, along with curious troglodyte villages and towns rich in magnificent architecture. The Paradors featured include two beside the sea, one in a unique mountain setting and another in a palace in the heart of a beautiful historic town.

— TOUR 18 —
MICHELIN MAP NOS. 446 & 445

NERJA – MOJÁCAR –
PUERTO LUMBRERAS –
CAZORLA – ÚBEDA

NERJA

THE ITINERARY BEGINS at the Parador Nacional de Nerja, a short distance from the Málaga–Almería road, the N 340, and about 55km from Málaga. The nearest airport is at Málaga, about 1½ hours by car, and the nearest alternative Parador is also at Málaga (page 176).

The Parador is in an enviable setting on the eastern edge of the town of Nerja, built on a clifftop overlooking the splendid beach of Burriana – one of the loveliest on the Costa del Sol. The reception area of the Parador opens on to a beautiful garden cascading with tropical blooms and shaded by palm and lemon trees. Beyond is a swimming pool set in a wide green lawn which extends right to the edge of the cliff. From here there are superb views of the beach and the coastline beyond, which curves away for many miles with the lovely Sierra de Almijara creating an imposing backdrop. An elevator whisks you effortlessly down to beach level. The restaurant, bar and lounge are in a separate wing and open on to a paved sun-terrace which overlooks the sea.

The local cuisine includes excellent fish dishes like Fritura Malagueña, a mixture of fried fish which includes *calamares* (squid), *gambas* (prawns), *merluza* (hake), *lenguado* (sole), *boquerones* (anchovies) and *sardinas* (sardines). Another local speciality is Pollo con Ajillo, small pieces of chicken on the bone sautéed in olive oil until golden with whole cloves of garlic.

Nerja is set at the foothills of the Sierra de Almijara. The coastline here is the most beautiful of the Costa del Sol. The town is built on a cliff and a famous local landmark is the Balcón de Europa, a semi-circular terrace which juts out over the sea with superb views along the coast. Here in the evening people stroll or sit at the café tables which line the small square. Below is a pretty, sheltered beach dotted with fishing boats.

A fascinating excursion is to the nearby Cueva de Nerja, an impressive stalactite cavern which was not discovered until 1958 and is known as the Prehistoric Cathedral. It is over half a mile in length and contains paintings of animals. Numerous other finds from the Stone Age have also been made here and there is a small museum. The cavern is also used for concerts. Near the cavern is the attractive small village of Maro set between fertile green headlands. There is a secluded beach at the foot of the cliffs which can be reached by a small road zig-zagging down between fields of fruit and vegetables.

About 7km from Nerja is the charming Moorish village of Frigiliana, at the head of the small green valley of the Río Higuerón. Its small white houses are clustered around narrow, stepped and cobbled alleys which only people and donkeys can negotiate. It has an enchanting atmosphere and evokes an impression of a centuries-old way of life.

Nerja is also an ideal base from which to make an excursion along the coast to the west. A delightful scenic circuit can be made into the Sierra de Tejeda by following the N 340 towards Málaga and then taking the MA 137 north to Torrox, a little white town set in a valley filled with small market gardens. From here the road climbs higher into the mountains with increasingly impressive views. The region is known for its wines and the hillsides are covered with vineyards, olive groves and almond trees. Many of the fincas, small farms, have curious stone-edged 'beds' for drying the fat, sweet grapes. If you are visiting in the autumn a sprig or two of these freshly made raisins make a delicious accompaniment to the local wine. At this time too you will find small baskets of *higos* in the shops. These are juicy, just-dried figs – totally different from, and far superior to, the supermarket variety.

The road continues further into the mountains to the village of Cómpeta. This small town of white houses with red-tiled roofs is set in the middle of quite spectacular mountain scenery. From here the road winds back down towards the coast through the attractive villages of Sayalonga and Algarrobo to Algarrobo Costa from where you can return along the N 340 to the Parador.

MOJÁCAR

THE NEXT STAGE of the journey is eastwards along the coast to the Parador at Mojácar following the N 340 for much of the way. The first part of the journey is

A beach near Nerja. Overleaf: The Sierra de Tejeda near Cómpeta.

through magnificent coastal scenery. The road follows the steep and deeply indented mountainsides in a series of sweeping curves with superb views of the sea. A brief detour can be made along the old coast road around the headland of Cerro Gordo. This is signposted to the right just before entering the tunnel of Cerro Gordo, which carries the new wide road. The rocky headland is covered in vivid green pine trees and the views through these into the paintbox-blue water is nothing less than breathtaking. Just before reaching the resort of La Herradura another short loop of the old road leads around the beautiful villa-scattered headland of Punta de la Mona. From here are sweeping views of the long, curving beach of La Herradura.

Almuñécar is the next town, a heavily developed and unattractive resort which hides an old town in its midst with the remains of a castle. The road then follows the steep winding coastline until the town of Salobreña is suddenly revealed around a bend. This old Moorish town is set on a ridge about 1km inland in the midst of a vast plain planted with sugar cane. Its white houses cover the rock like a snow-clad mountain peak and sparkle in the sunlight in brilliant contrast to the surrounding sea of green. Above the town is an impressive castle.

From Salobreña the road crosses the wide plain of Motril where fields of carnations mingle with plantations of tropical fruits and sugar cane. The coast is regained at Torrenueva, a large resort, and the road once again winds sinuously around steep mountainsides. Here they are arid and barren. However, extensive cultivation of vegetables and fruit is carried on under vast plastic greenhouses which shimmer in the distance like a mirage. Calahonda is an attractive fishing village which has become a relatively unspoilt, and undeveloped resort. So too has Castell de Ferro a few kms beyond.

The route continues through La Rábida to Adra, a large modern town with a busy fishing port. Beyond Adra you can make a detour into the Sierra de Gádor. This will add two hours or so to your journey to Mojácar but is a rewarding alternative to continuing along the N 340 between Adra and Almería.

At Puente del Río the C 331 leads north into arid brown mountains towards Berja. Shortly a broad green valley is suddenly revealed in the midst of which is Berja. Here the valley floor is planted with vineyards.

The Moorish town of Mojácar.

The vines grow 8ft high or more, supported on large trellises. These are desert grapes, fat, juicy and golden. Berja is a nice old town with a small arcaded market square.

The road continues northwards, climbing higher towards Lújar de Andarax, on a mountainside over-looking the fertile valley of the Río Andarax. Grape vines and fruit trees are planted extensively here. As well as desert grapes these vines also produce a wine for which the town is known. There is an arcaded *ayuntamiento* in the plaza and a fine old church.

The road now continues eastwards high along the side of the valley. A small detour can be made further north, and higher still, to the enchanting village of Ohanes, high in the steep mountain slopes with wonderful far-reaching views. The village is com-pletely unspoilt, with a warren of steep cobbled streets and stepped alleys threading between the small white-washed stone houses. This region was one of the last places where the Moors remained after their expulsion from Granada. Until only a decade or so ago it was commonplace for women of all ages to cover their faces when men were present in these remote communities.

The road continues beyond Ohanes back down the mountain with stunning views and then continues to follow the valley. As the road proceeds further east so the landscape becomes more arid. The valley is still green and fertile but beyond the landscape is brown and tree-less. There are two choices here: one is to continue along the valley rejoining the N 340 some 12km north of Almería where the route continues north-east to Tabernas. It is in this region that the most dramatic landscape of Almería may be seen. Here the bare red rock mountains are covered only with huge thickets of prickly pear cactus. It has been the location of many a 'paella' Western movie and just to the south of Tabernas is a replica Western town built as a film set and now used to stage gunfights for tourists to watch. Tabernas has an impressive Arab fortress and nearby is a futuristic solar-energy plant.

The longer alternative is to take a small road to the south beyond the village of Alcún. This leads over the Sierra de Gádor with breathtaking views and rejoins the coast at Aguadulce from where it is 10kms along the N 340 to Almería. There are two attractive moun-tain villages along this route which are worth a visit, Enix and Felix.

From Tabernas the road continues through similar scenery for about 30km or so to Sorbas, a strikingly situated town where the houses rise sheer from the side of the ridge on which it is built. About 20km beyond Sorbas a road leads south to Mojácar, a village built in the foothills of the Sierra Cabrera, 3km from the sea.

This too is a spectacularly sited town. Its brilliant white cube-shaped houses seem to trickle down the sides of the red-brown rock on which it is set, like a carelessly iced cake. It has been a settlement since the Bronze Age and has housed the Phoenicians and Romans in its time. Its present form, however, was created by the Moors with typically narrow streets, cobbled alleys and small squares. What was, not so long ago, a remote and undiscovered village is now a lively and atmospheric holiday town. The village has been extended to include several large holiday hotels, and numerous villages dot the surrounding mountainsides.

The Parador Nacional Reyes Católicos is situated beside the road which runs along the seashore between Garrucha and Carboneras. It is 2½km from Mojácar and just a few strides from the beach. It is a very large, low building which extends in several wings and provides most rooms with a sea view from their roomy balconies. Long, cool corridors connect the bedrooms with the restaurant, bar and lounges, and small furnished areas are scattered throughout. The public rooms open on to a large tiled sun terrace – grass does not grow very well in Almería. It is dotted liberally with straw parasols and sun-loungers and in the centre is a spacious pool.

Regional dishes on the menu include: Conejo con Gurullos, casserole of rabbit in a rich sauce, served with a small rice-shaped pasta; Merluza en Salsa de Almendras, fillets of hake, served in a creamy almond sauce; and Gazpacho Almeriense, the familiar Andalucían cold soup but with small pieces of fried bread added just before serving. I chose a regional wine from the list, Viña Amalia, a crisp dry white from the vineyards of Montilla-Moriles.

A day's excursion can be made easily from the Parador to the Cabo de Gata, a dramatic coastline of purple-tinged mountains which plunge precipitously into an intensely blue sea. First, however, it is worth making a brief detour to the north to Garrucha. This is an attractive fishing town 6km to the north of the Parador with a busy harbour and an atmospheric seafront lined with some excellent fish restaurants and small bars. There is also a 16th-century castle overlooking the sea.

Landscape near Tabernas.

The coastline near Carboneras.

The route to Cabo de Gata first returns to the Parador and then continues south along the coast road towards Carboneras. The first part of the journey runs close to the sea through a region of quite extensive development. Further south, however, the road begins to climb higher into the mountains with increasingly exciting views. There is little vegetation here apart from monumental cactus plants, which grow in some places like small forests. A few kms before reaching Carboneras the road climbs high around a steep headland revealing sensational views. From this point the road descends again to the sea and runs alongside a long, empty sandy beach. Carboneras is a large, modern-looking town but it has an appealing old quarter centred aroung the Castillo of San Antón. A busy market is held here on Thursdays.

The road now turns away from the sea. After a few kms a road to the left leads back to the coast through a parched landscape scattered with small white houses and farms. Here the attractive little fishing village and secluded resort of Agua Amarga, has a good beach and a quiet and intimate atmosphere. Joining the main road, the N 332, the route leads south-west towards Almería.

After a few kms a road leads north to Níjar, on a steep mountainside. It is an evocative old town with small squares and a maze of narrow streets. The centre of an active craft industry of ceramics, rugs and baskets made from esparto grass, Níjar is a good place to buy inexpensive and authentic gifts or souvenirs.

Back on the main road another small road leads south to San José, a fishing village and resort prettily situated in a small bay of crystal-clear water enclosed by steep domed headlands. Just before reaching San José, however, a road leads west to the villages of Los Escullos, with the remains of a castle, and Isleta del Moro. These are two tiny isolated fishing communities just with a few small bars and large unpopulated beaches.

A few kms beyond San José there is a fine long sandy beach backed by pine and eucalyptus trees. The road continues close to the sea towards the Cape, climbing steadily higher into the mountains. This section of the road is unsurfaced and a little rough in places but quite serviceable. All along this route there are small deserted coves and quiet beaches to scramble down to. The road continues to the lighthouse from where there are sweeping views down to the town of Cabo de Gata and the salt pans of Acosta.

Almería is a city well worth a visit but needing a separate trip to do it any justice. It has a massive 8th-century reddish stone fort on a ridge, an imposing 16th-century cathedral and there are many interesting churches and mansions. From Almería the route back to the Parador is along the N 340 as before.

PUERTO LUMBRERAS

THE NEXT LEG of the tour is to the Parador at Puerto Lumbreras. It is a direct journey of only 62km and I have suggested an en-route excursion which takes you into the Sierra de los Filabres. From Mojácar you need first to return to Sorbas. A short distance to the west of the town a road leads north through open, undulating countryside to Uleila del Campo, attractively situated in the foothills of the Sierras. The road now begins to climb into the mountains, bare and rocky with little vegetation other than huge thickets of prickly pear cactus. Beyond, however, on the northern slopes there are plantations of almond and olive trees. It is a sparsely populated region with only the occasional isolated farmhouse to be seen.

The road now begins to descend to Cobdar, a village with narrow streets and little whitewashed houses, in a small fertile valley above which towers a monumental dome of red rock. Beyond, the road continues along the valley to Albánchez, an equally unspoilt village. The valley here is filled with fruit trees, almonds and fields of vegetables. From Albánchez the route turns westwards to Líjar along a dry riverbed filled with oleander bushes; a harsh and bleak landscape with a kind of gaunt beauty. Charcos is a small village of ancient, crumbling houses scattered down the mountain slope. At the attractively situated village of Alcudia de Monteagud the route leads northwards towards Macael. The road descends from here through a region dominated by vast quarries where the mountain is progressively blasted and hacked into manageable chunks. Below in the valley, the towns of Macael and Olula del Río seem almost entirely devoted to huge factories and workshops cutting and polishing the marble into all manner of shapes and sizes.

The route eastwards along the valley of the Río Almanzora joins the N 340 a few kms south of Huércal Overa where it heads south towards Vera. After about 10km a road leads westwards to Cuevas de Almanzora. Near the town in the rocky hillsides are prehistoric dwellings, some still in use. The 16th-century castle belonged to the Duke of Alba. The road continues to the coast at Palomares, famous for nearly having been the scene of a major nuclear disaster in 1966 when the American air force accidentally dropped four atomic bombs – which didn't go off.

A road follows the coast with constant views of the sea to Águilas with an extraordinary coastline of bare red rock which simply plunges straight into a deep blue and very clear sea. Águilas is a large town with

quite extensive development dominated by a massive domed headland upon which there are the remains of a castle. Beyond, the road continues to Cabo Cope where another sea fort is set beside the beach.

The route from Águilas is inland now along the C 3211 to Lorca, an ancient town on the slopes of a steep ridge upon which is an imposing castle. There are numerous churches, palaces and mansions including a 17th-century *ayuntamiento* and the 16th-century church of San Patricio. The town is also famous for its distinctive, and stylish, rugs as well as its spectacular Holy Week processions. It has now been designated a national monument.

The Parador Nacional de Puerto Lumbreras, on the eastern edge of the town, 18km south-west of Lorca beside the N 340 is quiet, comfortable and cooled by air-conditioning. The restaurant is an attractive semi-circular rooms which looks on to a garden shaded by lemon trees. Beyond is a swimming pool. The interior is decorated with a variety of Lorca rugs used effectively as wall-hangings.

The local cuisine offered on the menu included: Ensalada de Pimientos Asados y Tomate, a refreshing salad of cooked peppers and chopped raw tomatoes; Costillos de Cabrito en Ajo Cabañil, succulent cutlets of kid cooked with garlic, paprika and wine vinegar; and Berenjenas a la Crema con Gambas y Jamón, aubergines cooked in a creamy white sauce with prawns and ham. The regional wines on the list are those of Castillo Jumilla.

CAZORLA

THE TOUR NOW CONTINUES north-west to the Parador at Cazorla. The first part of the journey is along the N342 through quiet, open countryside to Vélez Rubio, below a steep ridge with a massive and extravagantly decorated 18th-century church. Its ornate façade is flanked by two enormous Baroque towers and surmounted by a dome. A small road leads north, skirting the mountain, to Vélez Blanco, an atmospheric old town with an imposing castle high on a rock above the houses. Nearby are the Cuevas de los Letreros. In these caves the Neolithic painting of Indalo Man was discovered – a figure with outstretched arms holding a rainbow. The image is now used as a symbol for the region.

From Vélez Blanco the road passes through the Sierra de María, an attractive landscape of dry, ochre mountainsides dotted with pine and almond trees. Beyond, the road passes through a dense pine forest and then across a vast bleached plain of wheatfields, bordered by distant hazy ridges and dotted with occasional isolated farms.

The village of Jata at the opening of a shallow, green valley consists almost exclusively of troglodyte dwellings, tunnelled into the ridge of sandy stone which

borders it. Some are quite elaborate with tiled half-roofs projecting from the cliff face; others simply have a door and window opening directly into a cave. It is most peculiar to see chimney pots and even TV aerials rising straight out of the ground.

The road continues to Orca, where there are more troglodyte dwellings, many occupied. In the centre of this atmospheric old town is the 11th-century Alcazaba de las Siete Torres, the castle of the seven towers. Nearby is the 17th-century Palacio de los Marqueses de dos Fuentes and a lovely old church with a Mudéjar tower.

The road follows the course of a shallow green valley planted with maize, vegetables and sunflowers to Galera. Here the route continues north along the C 3329 to Huéscar, an appealing old town with a magnificent 16th century hall church around which are a web of picturesque tiled alleys called Las Santas.

The C 330 leads west across an exposed plain planted with wheatfields and almond trees, bordered by the imposing ridge of the Sierra de Marmolance. A bridge crosses a quite spectacular chasm hundreds of metres deep through which the Río Guardel flows fast and furious over the rocks. The road continues to the village of Castril, strikingly set between two towering peaks of rock. Upon one is a huge statue of Christ to which a footpath ascends to a *mirador*. Below is the Río Castril, a fast-running river known for its trout fishing.

Beyond, the route continues into the Sierra de Segura, a beautiful mountain range thickly covered in pine trees, to the Pantano de la Bolera, an expanse of water so intensely blue it looks as though it has been squeezed from a paint tube. At Pozo Alcón the route continues north-west along the C 323 climbing higher into the Sierras towards Tíscar. The views from this road are staggering: ridge after ridge recede hazily into the far distance.

Suddenly a bend in the road reveals the village of Tíscar. Its small houses are scattered down the steep mountainside beneath a jagged cockscomb of rock. Upon one a castle tower juts up like a pointing finger to the sky. It is an unforgettable sight. The road continues through a tunnel, climbing beyond the village to the Puerto de Tíscar from where there are sweeping views of the mountains beyond.

The distinctive candlewick pattern of millions of olive trees quite suddenly dominates the landscape – the unmistakable appearance of the province of Jaén. The road descends in a series of gentle curves to the valley where Quesada is set above it on a knoll. The town is the birthplace of the painter Rafael Zabaleta and a small museum is devoted to his work.

A view from the Sierra de Cazorla towards Quesada.

The route leads on north-east to Cazorla a picturesque town in a beautiful setting, cradled in an amphitheatre formed by the surrounding peaks of the Sierra de Cazorla. The small white houses of the old town spill down the mountain slope and above, on a ridge, is an Arab fortress. There are also the remains of a ruined Plateresque church. From the centre of Cazorla a road leads up into the Sierras passing the village of La Iruela, with the remains of a castle on a towering pinnacle of rock.

The road continues to climb higher towards the Puerto de las Palomas with sweeping views over the patterned plain below. The mountainsides are thickly covered with pine trees and carpeted with flowers, shrubs and aromatic herbs. From a *mirador* you can look down into a green valley far below where the youthful Río Guadalquivir is beginning its long journey to the sea. This region is one of Spain's richest wildlife reserves with large populations of animals like ibex, moufflon, wild boar, eagles and ospreys. There are also species of flowers and butterflies found nowhere else in the world.

The Parador Nacional El Adelantado, on a small road leading higher still into the mountains a few kms beyond the summit of the pass, is set on the edge of a rocky ravine 1400m above sea level and surrounded by pine forests. Beyond are the imposing ridges of the Sierra de Cazorla. It is hard to imagine a more peaceful and remote setting in which to stay. The silence at night was total except for the strident squealing of a wild boar somewhere in the forest. The Parador is built in the style of a traditional Andalusian *cortijo*, or manor house. There is a long sun terrace which extends along the first floor of the building and, below, another is enclosed behind large windows for the colder winter days. In front is a large natural lawn with sun-loungers scattered below the shady pines.

The restaurant and bar open on to the terrace, providing a memorable setting for a pre-dinner drink as the sun dips below the distant peaks. The menu offers appropriately hearty fare. I began with Olla Gitana, literally gipsy's stew pot, a knife-and-fork soup containing chunks of salt pork, *chorizo*, green beans, potatoes, chick peas, peppers and spinach, and followed this with Chuletas de Venado en Adobe, venison cutlets marinaded before grilling. Other delicious regional dishes were Tortilla de la Serrana, an omelette filled with finely chopped meat and ham and Trucha a la Cazorlena, trout sautéed with small pieces of serrano ham, salt pork and mushrooms.

The Parador is an excellent base for ramblers, with many signposted walks into the Sierras. Another, less energetic, possibility of exploring the more remote regions is in small groups by Landrover. Such trips are conducted by the park authorities and can be arranged by the Parador.

An enjoyable and varied round trip along the Embalse de Tranco begins by returning to the junction of the Parador road. The route continues to the left and quite soon after to the right – it is signposted to El Tranco – then along the shady valley of the Guadalquivir to Torre del Vinagre, where there is a museum explaining the region and its wildlife. There is also a botanical garden, and nearby a fish farm can be visited. The valley becomes progressively wider and the road begins to run quite close to the river with numerous spots where you can walk down through the trees to its banks.

At the opening of the lake, near Bujaraiza, is a wildlife park called the Parque Cinegético where many of the region's animals and birds can be observed. It is best to visit either early or late in the day when they come to feed. The road continues around the edge of the large, impressive lake to the dam itself at Tranco. Here the road climbs high above the lake with superb views to Cañada Morales where it follows a rich green valley dotted with small white farmhouses. There is soon a road junction with the C 3210. The route continues to the left but a brief detour to the right leads 4km to Hornos, a very pretty, unspoilt village set dramatically on a sheer spur of rock and overlooked by the remains of a castle. In the tiny square, by the church, a doorway leads through on to a balcony which overhangs the cliff. From here there are stunning views of the valley, the lake and the mountains beyond.

The route continues back along the C 3210 to Cortijos Nuevos where it follows a fork to the right. Soon another turning to the right leads across a fertile valley planted with wheatfields, vegetables, fruit and olive trees to Segura de la Sierra. You will see the town long before you reach it. The small white houses are tiered up a perfectly conical peak crowned with geometrical precision by a castle – like the fairy on a Christmas tree. Segura de la Sierra is completely encircled by crenellated walls and towers. Inside the fortified gateway is an enchanting web of stepped, tunnel-like alleys. There is an ancient *ayuntamiento*, Moorish baths, a medieval fountain and the house of a famous Spanish poet, Jorge Manrique.

From Segura the route continues north-west through Orcera and La Puerta de Segura to join the main road, the N 322, where it turns south-east towards Villacarillo. Just before reaching this town a small road leads to the right to a village which is as picturesque as its name promises, Iznatoraf.

At Villacarillo there is an 18th-century *ayuntamiento* and a church attributed to Vandelvira. An attractive

Above right: The Puerto de Tíscar. Right: The Castillo and old town of Cazorla.

scenic road leads south-east through Mogón and Santo Tomé back to Cazorla.

ÚBEDA

THE FINAL STAGE of the tour is to the Parador at Úbeda, a direct route of about 80km. The more circuitous journey I have suggested takes you first to the birthplace of the Río Guadalquivir and then through some of the wilder regions of Sierra de Segura.

After returning to the beginning of the Parador road a turn to the right leads shortly to Vadillo. A small road continues beyond through a park checkpoint and then alongside the Río Guadalquivir. Here it is no more than a small, mountain river. The valley begins to narrow and the road climbs higher into the mountains. It is thickly wooded and there are many delightful spots beside the river to take a picnic lunch or relax in the shade. The old bridge at Puente de las Herrerías is particularly attractive. From this point the road is unsurfaced and continues to climb high along the side of a narrowing rocky valley. The river is now no more than a trickle below over the boulder-strewn bed.

The birthplace of the river is a tiny wooded valley high in the mountains. A dribble of water seeps from a crevice in a large rock and moves almost imperceptibly from one small pool to another. It is hard to believe that this seemingly insignificant spring grows into a mighty river which moulds the character and appearance of the province of Andalucía, generates a livelihood for millions of people and has created the cities of Sevilla and Córdoba.

The road climbs steadily to the summit of the pass where the views to the south are simply sensational. Distant Quesada appears as if in an aerial photograph. From here the road descends gradually to meet a tarmac road and after 1km or so to the left it joins the main road from Quesada, the C 323. The route continues north-east through Peal de Becerro to Torreperogil, an attractive town set in the midst of vineyards. The table wines produced here are dry and strongly alcoholic – quite unusual in Andalucía. There is also an interesting church, Santa María, built in a mixture of Renaissance and Gothic styles.

Beyond Torreperogil the main road, the N 322, is joined and Úbeda is just 10km away to the west. However, a short detour can be made to the north to the atmospheric old hilltop town of Sabiote. Here there are cobbled streets, entrance gates, a castle palace, several old mansions and a fine old church.

Parador Nacional Condestable Davalos in the old part of Úbeda in the Plaza de Vázquez de Molina, is the

The church of Sacra Capilla del Salvador at Úbeda.

Palacio de los Ortegas and at one time belonged to Don Fernando Ortega Salido, the Dean of Málaga. Built in the 16th century it was completely restored in the 17th century.

An imposing entrance and a stone staircase lead into a beautiful two-storey patio, shaded during the summer by a canvas awning. It is furnished with clusters of garden chairs and tables enhanced by palm trees in huge pots. It makes an evocative place for a pre-dinner drink. Another grand staircase, guarded by suits of armour, leads up to the bedrooms, some of which look out on to another small courtyard. The restaurant is an attractive L-shaped room decorated with arches.

From the local dishes on the menu I chose Ensalada de Perdiz as a starter, a delicious salad with slivers of marinated partridge combined with finely chopped onions, lettuce and diced tomatoes. Cabrito Guisado con Piñones is a casserole of kid with pine nuts. For those who like sweet things Natillas con Borrachuelos is a delicious concoction of a chilled creamy egg custard spiced with cinnamon and vanilla and served with small crispy fritters.

Next to the Parador is the Sacra Capilla del Salvador, an imposing church with an extravagantly decorated Renaissance façade, built by Andreas de Vandaelvira in the 16th century and containing a superb altar and choir stalls. On the other side of the Parador is the Palacio de las Cadenas, now the *ayuntamiento*, also built by Vandaelvira. Opposite this building is the 13th-century church of Santa María de los Reales Alcazares, built on the site of a mosque. Adjacent is the 16th-century Palacio del Marqués de Mancera. The town is filled with beautiful Renaissance buildings and, armed with a map from the Parador, wandering through its ancient streets will provide many hours of pleasure. Don't miss seeing the ornate Casa de las Torres, the Huerta de Granada, the 14th-century church of San Nicolás and the massive Hospital de Santiago.

Just 9km to the west along the N 321 is Baeza. This too is a town rich in architectural masterpieces. The 16th-century Gothic cathedral of Santa María has a beautiful wrought-iron pulpit and gallery as well as a cloister. Perhaps the most appealing corner of the town is the Plaza de los Leones, a beautiful square overlooked by the old abattoir, the Casa del Pópulo and the fortified gateways of the Arco del Pópulo and the Arco de Jaén. In its centre is the Fuente de los Leones, a romantically ornate fountain with four lions surrounding a female figure. Nearby is the 16th-century Arco de Baeza, and an attractively decorated *ayuntamiento* from the same period. Other fine buildings include the church of Santa Cruz and the nearby Seminario de San Felipe Neri, with a fine patio.

The nearest alternative Parador to Úbeda is at Bailén (page 214) where tour No 19 will provide a route back towards Málaga.

*T*OUR 19   *Based in the central region of Andalucía in the provinces of Jaén and Granada, the area covered is bordered in the north by the Sierra Morena and to the south by Las Alpujarras. To the east lies the Sierra de Cazorla and to the west the Sierra de Jabalcuz. The landscape ranges from the wide valley of the Río Guadalquivir to the stark mountain peaks of the Sierra Nevada. It is a region chequered by fields of ripening grain where shades of brown, ochre and white blend like shadows cast by clouds. There are vast hillsides patterned by millions of olive trees, deep green valleys and mountainsides terraced with almond trees and vineyards. Two great Andalusan cities are included, Jaén and Granada, the former dominated by a magnificent hilltop castle and the latter possessing one of Europe's architectural wonders, the Alhambra.*

The tour provides a scenic route connecting Andalucía and the coast with La Mancha and Madrid. It can also be used to create a round trip in conjunction with tour No. 18 (page 200). The paradors featured include one situated at over 8,000ft above sea level, one in a convent within the Alhambra and another in a dramatically sited castle.

BAILÉN
JAÉN
GRANADA
SIERRA NEVADA

BAILÉN

THE PARADOR NACIONAL DE BAILÉN is beside the main road between Madrid and Andalucía, the N 4, which crosses the Sierra Morena through the Desfiladero de Despeñaperros. Nearby is the junction with the road to Granada, the N 323. It is a spacious and airy building in the motel style with air-conditioning, a shady garden and a swimming pool providing a welcome respite from the searing summer heat. The restaurant is a large room with a high, sloping ceiling and a polished marble floor.

The menu includes a selection of local dishes, such as Cazuela de Espárragos Jaenenses, a casserole of slender wild asparagus; and Gazpacho Andaluz, a perfect example of a dish suited to a region's climate – a refreshing chilled soup made by liquidising cucumbers, peppers, tomatoes and garlic with olive oil, wine vinegar and water, served with small dishes of croutons and a selection of its ingredients cut into small dice as a garnish.

JAÉN

THE NEXT STAGE of the tour is south to the Parador at Jaén, only 40km away. There are however two interesting short excursions which can be made en route from Bailén. The first is only a few kms along a small road to the north of Bailén through olive groves to the hilltop village of Baños de la Encina whose impressive 10th-century Arab fortress has massive walls, punctuated by a dozen or more large square towers. There is also a nice old church.

The second excursion is first along the N 4 to Andújar, on the banks of the Río Guadalquivir, with a Roman bridge and some interesting churches and old mansions. It is also noted for its ceramics. A quiet country road leads north towards Las Viñas through a region of steep, rounded hills covered with oak trees. Further to the north the countryside becomes more mountainous and craggy with large outcrops of rocks and pine trees. The Río Jándula, a wide river with grassy banks is crossed and a rough road runs alongside it for some distance with numerous shady picnic places under the pines. Stone benches and even some barbecue areas are provided. It is a beautiful spot for an alfresco lunch and the river is deep and clear enough to bathe in. The road winds sinuously round the boulder-strewn mountainsides to the remote sanctuary of the Virgen de la Cabeza, site of a heroic siege during the Spanish Civil War.

From Andujar the C 3219 leads south through olive-covered hillsides to Arjona and meets the N 324 at Pilar de Moya. Here the route continues eastwards to Torredonjimeno and then along the N 321 to Jaén.

A short detour to the south can be made from Torredonjimeno to Martos, at the foot of a large mountain. The town contains two fine churches, the 13th-century Santa María de la Villa and the 15th-century Santa Marta with a Gothic portal. There is also a medieval *ayuntamiento*, once a prison, and the ruins of the Moorish fortress of La Peña. The town is the largest olive-growing centre in Spain.

24km to the south of Martos is Alcaudete with an impressive castle above the town and the small Cathedral of Santa María with two Plateresque portals and the Mudejar church of San Pedro.

The Parador Nacional Castillo de Santa Catalina, high on a mountain beside the Alcázar de Santa Catalina overlooking Jaén, is 3.5 km from the city centre. The Alcázar was built by King Alhamar who was also responsible for the Alhambra in Granada.

The Parador is, however, a modern construction built in traditional style to create harmony with the historic castle. Indeed the interior gives an initial im-

Solera. Overleaf: The Castillo of Santa Catalina, Jaén.

pression of an authentic medieval castle. There are massive stone staircases, open fireplaces, galleries and corridors with flagstone floors. Heraldic flags, tapestries and huge wrought-iron candelabra decorate the walls and ceilings. The bedrooms have balconies with far-reaching views of the mountain ranges which surround Jaén. So too has a large terrace in front of the bar and restaurant. The latter is an enormously long room with high stone arches, next to another vast hall with a soaring vaulted roof.

A popular feature of the menu is Cena Jocosa, a tempting selection of regional dishes, different meats in sauces, for example, as well as various salads, vegetables and sweets. It includes Espinacas al Estilo de Jaén, a spicy, creamy puree of spinach, and La Piperana, a salad of finely chopped cucumber and tomato marinaded in a tangy dressing. The house wine, red and white, is from neighbouring Torreperogil.

The city of Jaén is an appealing mixture of old and new, built on the slopes of the Sierra de Jabalcuz, a rugged grey-green mountain range which creates a dramatic backdrop to the silvery-white buildings clustered below. The lower town, spread across the olive-patterned plain, is modern with broad avenues and shady parks and squares. However, on the slopes

The water garden at the Generalife, Granada.

of the Cerro de Santa Catalina, and extending up to the castle walls, is a tangle of narrow streets, an inheritance of Jaén's Moorish past. Indeed the city's name is derived from the Moorish word *geen* (caravan route), since it lies at vital crossroads linking Andalucía with Castilla-La Mancha.

The most notable building is undoubtedly the Cathedral, the work of Andrés de Vandelvira and considered by many to be his masterpiece. Built on the site of a former mosque, work commenced in the year 1500 but it was not completed until the end of the 18th-century thus combining Gothic, Renaissance and Baroque elements. Of impressive scale with a lavishly decorated main façade flanked by twin towers, among its many treasures is the relic of Santo Rostro which legend claims to be the veil used by Saint Veronica to wipe Christ's brow. There are richly carved 15th-century choir stalls and the museum contains many fine paintings.

Other historic buildings in the city include the 18th-century church of El Sagrario containing a statue of Christ which is carried in the Easter procession; the fortress-like 14th-century church of San Idelfonso, part of the city wall, has fine Gothic and Plateresque portals; the Gothic church of Santa Magdalena, the oldest in the city occupying the site of a former mosque; the 17th-century monastery of Santo Domingo with a magnificent Renaissance façade by Vandalvira and a Plateresque cloister decorated by Corinthian columns. The 13th-century Monastery of Santa Clara has a cloister; the 16th-century Mudéjar chapel of San Andrés; the 17th-century *ayuntamiento*, near the cathedral, and the 15th-century Arco de San Lorenzo.

An interesting excursion can be made from the Parador into the countryside to the east of the city. From Jaén a country road leads south-east towards La Guardia de Jaén. It meanders through olive groves and wheatfields with striking views of the distant city and the towering mountain range above it. La Guardia is a jumble of small whitewashed houses spilled over a rocky hillside and surmounted by an 8th-century castle. There are the remains of a Dominican monastery and a church, both designed by Vandalvira. The route continues south along N 323 and then, after about 10km, to the east along the N 324 to Huelma.

This is a quiet scenic route winding through gentle hills with olive plantations and almond trees alternating with wheatfields and rocky uncultivated land. Far beyond is a constant vista of the lofty Sierras. After Huelma the route turns north along the C 325 towards Jódar and a few kms further on a road to the east leads to the village of Solera, on a steep hillside high above the valley floor. Its tiny white houses are clustered around a towering spike of rock upon which is a ruined castle, with the broad-patterned valley and distant mountains creating a dramatic perspective.

Upon returning to the main road the route proceeds north to Jódar through a peaceful valley scattered with fields of grain, almond and olive groves and the occasional small farmhouse. The roadside is lined by locust and pomegranate trees as well as wild grasses, cacti and tree-like thistles. At Jódar there are the remains of a massive fortress. There are two alternative routes back to the Parador. One is to continue to Úbeda and then follow the N 321 through Baeza back to Jaén. A more direct route is to return a few km south where the C 328 can be followed westwards to join the N 321 14km to the east of Jaén.

GRANADA

THE NEXT STAGE of the itinerary is south to Granada, direct journey of only 97km. I have outlined a route which offers an interesting and scenic alternative to the rather busy main road. The road which descends from the Parador joins the C 3221 and this leads south towards Valdepeñas de Jaén, winding around the lower slopes of the Sierra de Jabalcuz, with sweeping views, to the small thermal spa of Balneario de Jabalcuz. Beyond, the road begins to climb into the Sierra de la Pandera, a region of steep ridges of red rock bordering

a valley patterned by the ubiquitous olive groves. The route continues through a green fertile valley and then climbs up over the mountain and down again to Valdepeñas de Jaén, a town surrounded by fields of fruit, grain and vegetables.

The road climbs again, with enormous views, through rugged mountain scenery and over a remote and rocky pass; then descends through a small valley planted with vines and almond trees to Frailes, surrounded by large fields of sunflowers. The road continues to the attractive and lively town of Alcalá la Real. Set above it is the Fortaleza de la Mota, a huge 14th-century fortress. A Gothic church and several old towers are enclosed within the ramparts which encircle the steep sepia-toned hill upon which it is set.

The route leads south now along the N 432 through an open landscape of steep rounded hills. In the distance is the massive hazy ridge of the Sierra Nevada, snow covered for much of the year. At Puerto López a small road leads up into the mountains to a rocky valley. Here on a steep ridge is the strikingly situated Moorish fortress of La Mota, set above the small white town of Moclín. Just beyond is a *mirador* from where there are spectacular views of the village and castle and over the vast variegated plain which reaches away to the Sierra Nevada.

The road continues south through Tiena and Bucor to rejoin the main road at Pinos-Puente. Here there is an ancient fortified bridge over the Río Cubillas with a horseshoe arch and a gateway. A few kms along the N432 towards Granada a road leads south to Santa Fé. This curious old town is composed in a square and entered through four gates in its enclosing walls. It was built on the site of a Roman camp by King Ferdinand during the siege of Granada in 1491 and the Moorish surrender was signed here. The agreement between Christopher Columbus and Ferdinand and Isabella for their sponsorship of his voyage to America was made in the town. Santa Fé is also famed for its *piononos*, a creamy confection made from eggs, white wine and sugar. The city of Granada is just 10km or so to the east of Santa Fé along the N 342.

The Parador Nacional San Francisco is within the Alhambra precinct on a hill overlooking the city of Granada. You need only to follow the well-placed signs to the Alhambra to find it. The building was formerly a Franciscan convent founded by the Catholic Monarchs. It was built on the site of a mosque and palace founded in the 14th century. The convent retains some of the original Moorish construction. The bodies of Ferdinand and Isabella were laid to rest in the convent's crypt before they were taken to the Royal Chapel in the Cathedral of Granada.

It is surrounded by extensive and secluded gardens with an ornamental pool and shaded by trees. At the rear of the Parador there is a broad terrace from where

The Patio de los Leones in the Alhambra, Granada.

the old Moorish district of the Albaicín and the gipsy quarter of Sacromonte can be seen on the opposite hill. Lit by mellow lamplight in the evening it provides a romantic setting for a pre-dinner drink. The most distinctive feature of the Parador is its elegant two-storey patio. The mosaic-cobbled courtyard is dotted with plants and a fountain plays in the centre. The interior is furnished and decorated with antiques and local craftwork, creating a luxurious and welcoming atmosphere.

The restaurant is an attractive room which looks out on to a small courtyard filled with plants. The menu offers a number of local specialities of which the most renowned is Tortilla de Sacromonte, an omelette filled with a mixture of finely chopped calves brains, sweetbreads and liver. A delicately flavoured soup is Sopa de Picadillo, a chicken flavoured broth with chopped hard-boiled eggs and *serrano* ham added. Cordero a la Andalucía is a casserole of small pieces of lamb on the bone with potatoes and flavoured with garlic, paprika and herbs. An unusually flavoured fish dish is Lenguado al Hinojo y Jerez, fillets of sole cooked with sherry and fennel. For pudding there is an opportunity to try the Piononos de Santa Fé.

One of the great pleasures of the Parador San Francisco is that it is, quite literally, on the doorstep of both the Alhambra and the Palacio del Generalife – which means the architect's garden. They are the vast and extraordinarily beautiful gardens which cover the summit of the hill upon which the Moorish palace is built. The most photographed feature is the water garden, a long rectangular pool surrounded by trees and tropical blooms and along which rows of jets project a tunnel of silvery spray over the lake. It sounds just as delightful as it looks. At each end there is a pavilion where you can sit and contemplate the idyllic scene. The remainder of the gardens are equally beautiful. There are long avenues of trees and bushes, flower borders laid out with geometrical precision, and numerous pools and fountains shimmering and rippling in the sunlight.

I'm not sure if the current list of the seven wonders of the world includes the Alhambra – but if not it should. It is a magical place where you can easily become hypnotised by the sheer beauty of the buildings and decorations. A map and guide book are really essential as there is so much to see. The undoubted highlight is the Patio de los Leones the court of the lions, an exquisite courtyard surrounded by arcades supported by slender marble columns. At each end are pavilions of astounding beauty. The golden stone is minutely carved into the most intricate decoration. It is like a superb jewel on a massive scale.

Granada seen from the Mirador of San Cristóbal.

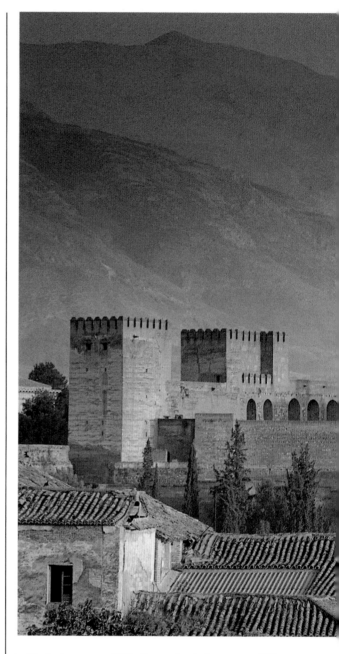

Granada has much more to offer than the Alhambra alone. Don't miss a visit to the Albaicín where a honey-combe of steep, narrow streets cover the hillside opposite the Alhambra. Here too is the hill of Sacromonte where the gipsy homes are carved into the rock and where *zambras* (parties), are held for tourists. From this region there are memorable views of the Alhambra and the massive snow-covered backdrop of the Sierra Nevada.

The cathedral of Santa María de la Encarnación, designed by Diego de Siloe in 1528, is one of the finest Renaissance churches in Spain, impressive both in scale and in the harmony and proportion of its architecture. The interior, nearly 400ft long, contains a wealth of art treasures, including gilded statues of the apostles, beautiful stained-glass windows and numerous tapestries and paintings.

Close to the cathedral is the Alcaicería a reconstruction of the Arab silk exchange which was damaged by fire in the middle of the 19th century. It now houses a market of regional crafts. The remains of the 16th-century Monasterio de la Cartuja is also worth visiting with a cloister and refactory preserved as well as a sacristy with elaborate Baroque decoration. The 14th-century Casa del Carbón, a fascinating example of a Moorish inn, has a courtyard surrounded by three-storey arcades.

If you would like to explore some of the countryside between Granada and the coast an interesting day's round trip can be made into the Sierra de Almíjara. The N 323 leads south of the city through the Puerto del Suspiro del Moro, the pass of the Moor's sigh. It is here that, legend has it, the defeated Moorish King Boabdil wept as he looked back towards the city. A quiet country road strikes off to the south-west through a region of rolling, wheat-covered hills, and shortly afterwards, the road begins to climb into pine-covered mountains.

Quite suddenly you arrive at the summit of a mountain pass from where a vast panorama of mountain peaks is revealed with the road hugging and curving round the steep slopes as it descends. Lower, towards the valley floor, a small road climbs up to the village of Lentejil high on the mountainside surrounded by meadows and trees.

Beyond the small villages of Ortiva and Jete the valley and hillsides are covered by thick jungle-like vegetation. It is called the Tropical Valley because of enormous plantations of avocados, bananas and custard apples which spread through the valley like a wide green river. The road joins the main coast road, the N 340 at Almuñecar and the route now heads west to Nerja (see page 200). Beyond, at the resort of Torre del Mar, the C 335 leads north again to Vélez Málaga where there is a ruined castle. From here the road climbs along the side of a fertile valley, planted with market gardens of olive and almond groves, into the Sierra de Tejeda.

About 20km beyond Vélez Málaga a fork to the right leads to Alhama de Granada, an attractive old town overlooking a steep rocky gorge created by the Río Alhama. Near the town is a thermal spring and there

are both Moorish and Roman baths. The route continues through peaceful olive- and almond-covered hillsides and fields of wheat through Cacín, Ventas de
Huelma and Mala to rejoin the N 323 a few kms south
of Granada.

SIERRA NEVADA

THE FINAL STAGE OF THE TOUR is to the Parador Nacional
de Sierra Nevada, high on the slopes of the Pico Veleta

above the ski resort of Sol y Nieve. It is only 25km from
Granada but the unique location, nearly 8,000ft above
sea level, makes it a fascinating place to stay for at least
one night.

The road to the Parador runs, first, along a broad
fertile valley which gradually narrows. It then begins
to climb in a series of gentle sweeping curves. Soon the
tree line is passed and the landscape takes on a grey,
bleak appearance. The road continues to climb higher
with landscape resembling an aerial-survey photo-

graph. Wayside signs are passed, 1,000m above sea level, 1,500m, 2,000m – soon the road passes above the ski village of Sol y Nieve and the Parador comes into view.

The building is in the style of a mountain lodge with pine floors and ceilings and comfortable leather armchairs. A huge free-standing fireplace dominates the large galleried lounge which overlooks the first-floor restaurant. In front is a large terrace with awesome views of the valley and the massive stark grey peaks surrounding it.

There is usually a dish on the menu which features the famous mountain ham of Trevelez, a village on the other side of the mountains. I had it in the form of Habas con Jamón, casseroled with fresh young broad beans and flavoured with garlic. Gazpacho de Aguacates con Salmón Ahumado is a delicious chilled soup made from avocados and flavoured with pieces of smoked salmon; Salteado de Hongos con Mollejas is wild mountain mushrooms sauteéd with sweetbreads; and Chotos de Guijar en Salsa de Ajos, cutlets of young kid cooked in a garlic sauce.

An excursion from here not to be missed is to the Pico de Veleta. The road continues even higher beyond the Parador to the very summit – the highest road in Europe where the thin air makes itself felt. The twin peaks of Veleta and Mulhacén are the highest in Spain,

rising to over 3,400m. The panorama from the summit is memorable, receding ridges fade into distant haze like cardboard cutouts.

An exciting day's round trip can be made from the Parador. A small road crosses the Sierra Nevada just below the summit of the Mulhacén and descends into the beautiful mountain region of Las Alpujarras. I would hesitate to suggest this route however to a driver – or passenger – who felt anxious about mountain driving. Although not at all dangerous the first section of the road is rather daunting since it is unsurfaced, with an unguarded edge, and you can see the slender ribbon of road snaking round the steep mountainside for miles ahead. It is however a remarkable experience which you will not forget for a long while.

An alternative is to take the N 323 south of Granada and then the C 333 east to the attractive spa town of Lanjarón, known for its mineral water. The road continues to Orjiva where there is a 17th-century church and a castle which belonged to the Counts of Sastago.

The GR 411 leads north to Bubión and Capileira. It is to these towns which the mountain road descends from the summit. Capileira is set on the steep moun-

The mountain village of Juviles in the Alpujarras.

La Calahorra.

tainside and overlooks an immensely deep valley. The small flat-roofed houses, typical of the region, look almost like sugar cubes from a distance, dwarfed as they are by their enormous surroundings. The tiny village of Bubion is also pretty with several craft shops selling the distinctive cotton rugs of the Alpujarras which are woven on huge looms into fine ribbons of colour. From here the road skirts the mountain to the strikingly situated village of Busquístar overlooking a deep rocky valley.

The road now climbs along the side of another valley which leads high into the mountain. It is thickly wooded here, magnificent chestnut trees line the roadside and green meadows cover the slopes. The town of Trevelez soon comes into view. From a distance the cluster of brilliantly white houses look almost like an isolated snowdrift on the mountainside. It is the highest village in Spain, famed for its snow-cured hams and its legend of witches. The road returns along the other side of the valley to the picturesque village of Juviles and continues through Mecina Bombarón and Yegén, once the home of Gerald Brenan, towards the town of Ugíjar. The scenery all along this route is exceptional.

Just before reaching Ugíjar a road leads north to Laroles from where it begins to climb high alongside a huge valley with far-reaching views. It continues to the

Puerto de la Ragua from where a gradual descent through pine woods leads to Lacalahorra. There is a dramatic view from the road of the small white town far below and its solid fortress set on a brown rocky hill. A vast bleached plain reaches away to the far horizon which is rimmed by hazy blue ridges.

Beyond Lacalahorra the road joins the N 324, where the route continues westwards to Guadix. It is a historic town, once an Iberian settlement and a Roman military camp, whose magnificent cathedral of sepia stone has a monumental Baroque façade. There is also a 15th-century Moorish Alcazaba and a *plaza mayor* which has been restored after being damaged during the Civil War. There are many troglodyte dwellings in the low rocky hills which border this region. The road continues to Purullena and through the Puerto de la Mora back to Granada. As the road descends to the city there is a superb viewpoint called the Mirador of San Cristóbal, where the classic view of Alhambra is seen with the distant Sierra Nevadas rising up in the background.

The nearest alternative Paradors to those of Granada and the Sierra Nevada are at Nerja (page 200) and Málaga (page 176).

AFTERWORD

*E*ach of the tours has been planned to include the main places of interest in the environs of each parador. The suggested routes between each parador are also intended to ensure that you miss nothing of outstanding interest in the region.

However, such a guide is necessarily selective, and if you have a special interest, for example Romanesque churches, there may well be some additional buildings or locations worthy of a visit which have not been included.

I have used a number of reference books in my research and two have been particularly helpful. Blue Guide: Spain, *published by Ernest Benn Ltd and* Spain: A Phaidon Cultural Guide, *published by Phaidon Press Ltd. Both contain a wealth of detailed information on places of historical interest.*

The Spanish National Tourist Office produce a number of excellent booklets for each of the provinces and many of the cities. In most cases these are available from the relevant parador, so too are locally published guides and maps. For those wishing to book their holiday in advance, the tour operator, Mundi Color, can provide excellent advice and assistance on any tour included in this book.

As the weather plays an important role in any holiday, here are a few points to remember when deciding on the best times to visit Spain. Needless to say the summer months tend to be very hot in most of the country and are more suited to lazing on beaches than touring. At this time too the paradors are at their busiest and advance booking is advizable for many of them.

However, the season for visiting Spain is considerably longer than many other European countries, and visits throughout the year can be most enjoyable. Andalucía, for example, enjoys a mild winter climate with plenty of sunshine, most of the rain in this region tends to fall in April and early May.

Spring arrives early in many parts of Spain. I travelled through the Maestrazgo in February and the valleys were filled with almond blossom, the first wild flowers were stippling the grass and hedgerows, and it was warm and sunny enough to wear summer clothes.

Summer can also end much later. I drove from Madrid through the Sierra de Gredos to Extramadura and Andalucía returning through La Mancha in November. The weather was wonderful and second crops of wheat and sunflowers, with wild flowers still freshly blooming, made the countryside look like spring again.

Northern Spain however, has a less favourable climate and rain, low cloud and mist are a potential hazard even in summer. I found the best times to visit regions like Galicia, Cantabria and Asturias are in the late spring, early summer and the autumn.

I hope you enjoy Spain as much as I have and, like me, want to visit it again and again.

ACKNOWLEDGEMENTS

I would like to thank Alan Walmsley of Mundi Color for his kind and efficient help with my travel arrangements, Anne Mapson of Fujimex for keeping me supplied with film and Julien Busselle for his help with sorting, mounting and printing the photographs.

Mundi Color: O.T.A. Travel Ltd., 276 Vauxhall Bridge Road, London SW1V 1BE. Tel no: 01-834 3492.

INDEX TO THE PARADORS

NORTHERN SPAIN

TOUR ONE

GIL BLAS

A graceful manor house once the home of the local Barreda-Bracho family.
ADDRESS: *Plaza de Ramón Pelayo, Santillana del Mar, Cantabria.*
TELEPHONE: *(942) 81 80 00.*
CAPACITY: *52 beds. 24 double and 2 single rooms.*
CATEGORY: *Three stars.*
AMENITIES: *A bar, central heating, garage, garden and telephone.*
AUTHOR'S POINTS: *4.*
THE NEAREST PARADORS: *Fuente Dé (101 km), Gijón (166 km), Argómaniz (209 km), Santo Domingo de la Calzada (218 km), Tordesillas (262 km), and Fuenterrabia (273 km).*

MOLINO VIEJO

A modern building in the centre of the town beside a peaceful wooded park.
ADDRESS: *Parque de Isabel la Católica, Gijón, Asturias.*
TELEPHONE: *(985) 37 05 11.*
CAPACITY: *79 beds. 39 double rooms and 1 single room.*
CATEGORY: *Four stars.*
AMENITIES: *A bar, garage, garden, cider bar and telephone.*
AUTHOR'S POINTS: *1.*
THE NEAREST PARADORS: *León (145 km), Santillana del Mar (166 km), Ribadeo (170 km), Fuente Dé (186 km), Benavente (215 km) and Cervera de Pisuerga (220 km).*

RIBADEO

A modern parador built on a ledge overlooking the estuary.
ADDRESS: *Amador Fernández, Ribadeo, Lugo.*
TELEPHONE: *(982) 11 08 25.*
CAPACITY: *88 beds. 41 double and 6 single rooms.*
CATEGORY: *Three stars.*
AMENITIES: *A bar, central heating, garage, garden and telephone.*
AUTHOR'S POINTS: *1.*
THE NEAREST PARADORS: *Villalba (74 km), El Ferrol (142 km), Gijón (170 km), Santiago de Compostela (194 km), Cambados (248 km) and Pontevedra (253 km).*

EL FERROL

A parador with a sea-faring atmosphere of dark wood panelling, polished brass, and maps and charts on the walls.
ADDRESS: *Almirante Vierna, El Ferrol, La Coruña.*
TELEPHONE: *(981) 35 67 20.*
CAPACITY: *67 beds. 28 double and 11 single rooms.*

*T*he Paradors appear in order of the tours and are situated in the town-centre unless otherwise stated. In addition to the five-star hotel ratings system, I have added my own points system based on a combination of the ambience of a particular Parador, its setting, its outlook and the interest of the building or its immediate surroundings. The point system is as follows:

1. A comfortable and convenient place to stay.
2. Staying there is recommended.
3. Worth a detour to stay there.
4. Exceptional – a real experience – worth planning a trip around.

Parador Gil Blas

Parador Los Reyes Católicos

Parador Conde de Gondomar

CATEGORY: *Three stars.*
AUTHOR'S POINTS: *1.*
AMENITIES: *Air-conditioning, bar, garage, garden, Convention hall and telephone.*
THE NEAREST PARADORS: *Villalba (68 km), Santiago de Compostela (95 km), Ribadeo (142 km), Cambados (149 km), Pontevedra (154 km), Bayona (180 km) and Tuy (180 km).*

TOUR TWO

LOS REYES CATÓLICOS

A unique and historical building, once a hospital founded in 1499 by Fernando and Isabel.
ADDRESS: *Plaza de España 1, Santiago de Compostela, La Coruña.*
TELEPHONE: *(981) 58 22 00.*
CAPACITY: *308 beds. 148 double and 6 single rooms and 3 suites.*
CATEGORY: *Five stars.*
AMENITIES: *Air-conditioning, bar, individual safes, central heating, garage, garden, shops, concert and exhibition hall, night-club, convention hall and telephone.*
AUTHOR'S POINTS: *4*
THE NEAREST PARADORS: *Cambados (54 km), Pontevedra (59 km), El Ferrol (95 km), Tuy (108 km), Bayona (114 km) and Villalba (120 km).*

EL ALBARIÑO

A granite building in pazo style with a central courtyard and fountain.
ADDRESS: *Paseo de Cervantes, Cambados, Pontevedra.*
TELEPHONE: *(986) 54 22 50.*
CAPACITY: *114 beds. 51 double and 12 single rooms.*
CATEGORY: *Three stars.*
AMENITIES: *A bar, central heating, garden, Convention hall and telephone.*
AUTHOR'S POINTS: *2.*
THE NEAREST PARADORS: *Pontevedra (25 km), Santiago de Compostela (54 km), Bayona (69 km), Tuy (74 km), El Ferrol (149 km), Villalba (174 km) and Ribadeo (248 km).*

CASA DEL BARÓN

An 18th-century palace with a Baroque stone staircase.
ADDRESS: *Calle Maceda, Pontevedra.*
TELEPHONE: *(986) 85 58 00.*
CAPACITY: *91 beds. 44 double and 3 single rooms.*
CATEGORY: *Three stars.*
AMENITIES: *A bar, library, central heating, garden, Convention hall and telephone.*
AUTHOR'S POINTS: *3.*
THE NEAREST PARADORS: *Cambados (25 km), Tuy (49 km), Bayona*

Parador Condes de Villalba

(54 km), Santiago de Compostela
(59 km), El Ferrol (154 km) and
Verín (175 km).

CONDE DE GONDOMAR

Situated on a promontory
surrounded by ancient fortifications.
ADDRESS: *Carretera de Bayona,
Bayona, Pontevedra.*
TELEPHONE: *(986) 35 50 00.*
CAPACITY: *236 beds. 108 double and
20 single rooms.*
CATEGORY: *Four stars.*
AMENITIES: *A bar, central heating,
yachting club, garage, seafood
restaurant and tavern, swimming
pool, beach, Convention halls, social
halls, sauna, telephone and tennis.*
AUTHOR'S POINTS: *4.*
THE NEAREST PARADORS: *Tuy
(51 km), Pontevedra (54 km),
Cambados (69 km) and Santiago de
Compostela (113 km).*

SAN TELMO

A modern building decorated in
traditional pazo style.
ADDRESS: *Tuy, Pontevedra.*
TELEPHONE: *(986) 60 03 09.*
CAPACITY: *31 beds. 15 double and
1 single rooms.*
CATEGORY: *Three stars.*

AMENITIES: *A bar, central heating,
garden, swimming pool and
telephone.*
AUTHOR'S POINTS: *1.*
THE NEAREST PARADORS:
*Pontevedra (49 km), Bayona
(51 km), Cambados (74 km) and
Verín (178 km).*

TOUR THREE

CONDES DE VILLALBA

An unusual octagonal tower with
only six bedrooms.
ADDRESS: *Valeriano Valdesuso,
Villalba, Lugo.*
TELEPHONES: *(982) 51 00 11 and 51
00 90.*
CAPACITY: *12 beds. 6 double rooms.*
CATEGORY: *Three stars.*
AMENITIES: *An elevator, bar, central
heating, garden and telephone.*
AUTHOR'S POINTS: *2.*
THE NEAREST PARADORS: *El Ferrol
(68 km), Ribadeo (74 km), Santiago
de Compostela (95 km), Villafranca
del Bierzo (137 km), Pontevedra
(170 km) and Cambados (174 km).*

VILLAFRANCA DEL BIERZO

A modern two-storey building with
spacious bedrooms.

ADDRESS: *Avda. Calvo Sotelo,
Villafranca del Bierzo, León.*
TELEPHONE: *(987) 54 01 75.*
CAPACITY: *70 beds. 30 double and
10 single rooms.*
CATEGORY: *Three stars.*
AMENITIES: *Bar, central heating,
garage, garden and telephone.*
AUTHOR'S POINTS: *1.*
THE NEAREST PARADORS: *León
(131 km), Villalba (137 km),
Benavente (147 km), Ribadeo
(189 km), El Ferrol (213 km), and
Tordesillas (229 km).*

HOTEL DE SAN MARCOS

This ancient convent has a
magnificent hall with 16th-century
coffered ceiling.
ADDRESS: *Plaza de San Marcos, 7.,
León.*
TELEPHONE: *(987) 23 73 00.*
CAPACITY: *520 beds. 246 double
rooms, 10 doubles with sitting room
and 2 suites.*
CATEGORY: *Five stars.*
AMENITIES: *Air-conditioning,
central heating, private dining
rooms, children's day-care centre,
garden, hairdressers, banquet hall,
night club, beauty parlour,
Convention hall and telephone.*
AUTHOR'S POINTS: *4.*

THE NEAREST PARADORS:
*Benavente (70 km), Villafranca del
Bierzo (131 km), Cervera de Pisuerga
(133 km), Gijón (145 km) and
Puebla de Sanabria (120 km).*

FUENTES CARRIONAS

A large modern five-storey building
with large balconies overlooking
spectacular mountain scenery.
ADDRESS: *Cervera de Pisuerga,
Palencia.*
TELEPHONE: *(988) 87 00 75.*
CAPACITY: *160 beds. 80 double
rooms.*
CATEGORY: *Three stars.*
AMENITIES: *Air-conditioning,
elevator, bar, central heating, garage,
garden, Convention hall and
telephone.*
AUTHOR'S POINTS: *2.*
THE NEAREST PARADORS: *Fuente
Dé (80 km), Santillana del Mar
(112 km), Santo Domingo de la
Calzada (179 km), Tordesillas
(190 km), Benavente (203 km) and
Gijón (220 km).*

RIO DEVA

A low modern building, peaceful &
remote, standing at the head of the
valley.

Two views of the Parador de San Marcos

Parador Río Deva

Parador Santo Domingo de la Calzada

ADDRESS: *Parador Rio Deva, Fuente Dé, Cantabria.*
TELEPHONE: *(942) 73 00 01.*
CAPACITY: *150 beds. 72 double and 6 single rooms.*
CATEGORY: *Three stars.*
AMENITIES: *A bar, central heating, garage, Convention hall and telephone.*
AUTHOR'S POINTS: *4.*
THE NEAREST PARADORS: *Cervera de Pisuerga (80 km), Santillana del Mar (101 km), León (175 km) and Gijón (186 km).*

TOUR FOUR

EL EMPERADOR

Once the palace of Carlos V, this is one of the most evocative paradors.
ADDRESS: *Plaza de Armas del Castillo, Fuenterrabia, Guipúzcoa.*
TELEPHONE: *(943) 64 21 40.*
CAPACITY: *30 beds. 14 double and 2 single rooms.*
CATEGORY: *Three stars.*
AMENITIES: *A bar, central heating, garden and telephone.*
AUTHOR'S POINTS: *4.*
THE NEAREST PARADORS: *Argomaniz (129 km), Olite*
(156 km), Sos del Rey Católico (173 km), and Santillana del Mar (273 km).*

ARGÓMANIZ

A solid stone building, two modern wings each side of a 17th-century palace.
ADDRESS: *Argómaniz, Alava.*
TELEPHONE: *(945) 28 22 00.*
CAPACITY: *108 beds. 54 double rooms.*
CATEGORY: *Three stars.*
AMENITIES: *A bar, central heating, Convention hall and telephone.*
AUTHOR'S POINTS: *2.*
THE NEAREST PARADORS: *Santo Domingo de la Calzada (75 km), Olite (122 km), Fuenterrabia (129 km) and Calahorra (147 km).*

SANTO DOMINGO DE LA CALZADA

An old hospice, with huge stone arches and beautiful antique furniture.
ADDRESS: *Plaza del Santo, 3, Santo Domingo de la Calzada, La Rioja.*
TELEPHONE: *(941) 34 03 00.*
CAPACITY: *52 beds. 25 double and 2 single rooms.*

AMENITIES: *A bar, central heating, Convention hall and telephone.*
AUTHOR'S POINTS: *4*
THE NEAREST PARADORS: *Argómaniz (75 km), Calahorra (95 km) and Soria (151 km).*

TOUR FIVE

MARCO FABIO QUINTILIANO

A contemporary building with a traditional ambience.
ADDRESS: *Era Alta, Calahorra, La Rioja.*
TELEPHONES: *(941) 13 03 58 and 13 03 62.*
CAPACITY: *120 beds. 57 double and 6 single rooms.*
CATEGORY: *Three stars.*
AMENITIES *Air-conditioning, elevator, bar, central heating, garage, Convention hall and telephone.*
AUTHOR'S POINTS: *1.*
THE NEAREST PARADORS: *Olite (70 km), Santo Domingo de la Calzada (95 km), Soria (116 km) and Sos del Rey Católico (121 km).*

PRÍNCIPE DE VIANA

This parador forms part of a magnificent 15th-century castle with a complex of turrets, towers and battlements.
ADDRESS: *Plaza de San Francisco, Olite, Navarra.*
TELEPHONES: *(948) 74 00 00, 74 00 01, 74 01 50 and 74 02 01.*
CAPACITY: *77 beds. 38 double and 1 single rooms.*
CATEGORY: *Three stars.*
AMENITIES: *A bar, central heating, Convention hall and telephone.*
AUTHOR'S POINTS: *4*
THE NEAREST PARADORS: *Sos del Rey Católico (51 km), Calahorra (70 km), Argómaniz (122 km), Santo Domingo de la Calzada (136 km), Soria (142 km) and Fuenterrabia (156 km).*

FERNANDO DE ARAGÓN

Built with local wood and stone this modern building blends in well with the older parts of the town.
ADDRESS: *Sos del Rey Católico, Zaragoza.*
TELEPHONE: *(948) 88 80 11.*
CAPACITY: *126 beds. 60 double and 6 single rooms.*
CATEGORY: *Three stars.*
AMENITIES: *Air-conditioning, elevator, bar, central heating, garage, garden, Convention hall and telephone.*
AUTHOR'S POINTS: *3.*
THE NEAREST PARADORS: *Olite (51 km), Calahorra (121 km), Argómaniz (139 km), Fuenterrabia (173 km), Santo Domingo de la Calzada (192 km), Soria (193 km) and Vielsa (304 km).*

TOUR SIX

FERNANDO II DE LEON

A restored castle, with original 18th-century keep.
ADDRESS: *Benavente, Zamora.*
TELEPHONES: *(988) 63 03 00 and 63 03 04.*
CAPACITY: *83 beds. 39 double and 5 single rooms.*
CATEGORY: *Four stars.*
AMENITIES: *Air-conditioning, bar, garage, garden, Convention hall and telephone.*
AUTHOR'S POINTS: *2.*
THE NEAREST PARADORS: *Zamora (65 km), León (70 km), Tordesillas (82 km), Puebla de Sanabria (84 km) and Villafranca del Bierzo (147 km).*

PUEBLA DE SANABRIA

A modern building simply decorated with marble floors and wooden panelling.
ADDRESS: *Puebla de Sanabria, Zamora.*
TELEPHONE: *(988) 62 00 01.*

Parador Príncipe de Viana